ABOUT THE AUTHOR

Dorothy West was born in 1912, the daughter of Isaac Christopher West, a prominent black businessman in early twentieth-century Boston, and his wife, Rachel. A thoroughly-bred Bostonian, she attended Girls' Latin School and Boston University before moving to New York to participate in the cultural ferment of the Harlem Renaissance. She studied at Columbia's School of Journalism and founded *Challenge,* a literary magazine that published the prose and poetry of the "newer Negroes." For the past thirty-five years Dorothy West has lived on Martha's Vineyard, where she wrote *The Living Is Easy* in 1948. She contributes a regular column to the *Vineyard Gazette.*

Adelaide M. Cromwell is Professor of Sociology and Director of Afro-American Studies at Boston University.

TO IKE

The Living Is Easy

Dorothy West

With an afterword by Adelaide Cromwell Gulliver

THE FEMINIST
PRESS
Old Westbury, New York

Cover: Richmond Barthe, *Portrait of a Woman/* (A'Leila Walker), 1931.
Schomburg Center for Research in Black Culture, The New York Public Library, Astor, Lenox and Tilden Foundations.

PART ONE

CHAPTER 1

"W ALK UP," hissed Cleo, somewhat fiercely.

Judy was five, and her legs were fat, but she got up steam and propelled her small stout body along like a tired scow straining in the wake of a racing sloop. She peeped at her mother from under the expansive brim of her leghorn straw. She knew what Cleo would look like. Cleo looked mad.

Cleo swished down the spit-spattered street with her head in the air and her sailor aslant her pompadour. Her French heels rapped the sidewalk smartly, and her starched skirt swayed briskly from her slender buttocks. Through the thin stuff of her shirtwaist her golden shoulders gleamed, and were tied to the rest of her torso with the immaculate straps of her camisole, chemise, and summer shirt, which were banded together with tiny gold-plated safety pins. One gloved hand gave ballast to Judy, the other gripped her pocketbook.

This large patent-leather pouch held her secret life with her sisters. In it were their letters of obligation, acknowledging her latest distribution of money and clothing and prodigal advice. The instruments of the concrete side of her charity, which instruments never left the inviolate privacy of her purse, were her credit books, show-

3

ing various aliases and unfinished payments, and her pawnshop tickets, the expiration dates of which had mostly come and gone, constraining her to tell her husband, with no intent of irony, that another of her diamonds had gone down the drain.

The lesser items in Cleo's pocketbook were a piece of chamois, lightly sprinkled with talcum powder, and only to be used in extreme necessity if there was no eye to observe this public immodesty, a lollipop for Judy in case she got tiresome, an Irish-linen handkerchief for elegance, a cotton square if Judy stuck up her mouth, and a change purse with silver, half of which Cleo, clandestinely and without conscience, had shaken out of Judy's pig bank.

Snug in the bill compartment of the bag were forty-five dollars, which she had come by more or less legitimately after a minor skirmish with her husband on the matter of renting a ten-room house.

She had begun her attack in the basement kitchen of their landlady's house, a brownstone dwelling in the South End section of Boston. Judy had been sent upstairs to play until bedtime, and Bart had been basking in the afterglow of a good dinner. Ten years before, he had brought his bride to this address, where they had three furnished rooms and the use of the kitchen and the clothesline at a rent which had never increased from its first modest figure. Here, where someone else was responsible for the upkeep, Bart intended to stay and save his money until he was rich enough to spend it.

Cleo had bided her time impatiently. Now Judy was nearing school age. She had no intention of sending her to school in the South End. Whenever she passed these schools at recess time, she would hustle Judy out of sight and sound. "Little knotty-head niggers," she would mutter unkindly, while Judy looked shocked because "nigger" was a bad-word.

These midget comedians made Cleo feel that she was back in the Deep South. Their accents prickled her scalp. Their raucous laughter soured the sweet New England air. Their games were reminiscent of all the whooping and hollering she had indulged in before her emancipation. These r'aring-tearing young ones had brought the folkways of the South to the classrooms of the North. Their numerical strength gave them the brass to mock their timid teachers and resist attempts to make them conform to the Massachusetts pattern. Those among them who were born in Boston fell into the customs of their southern-bred kin before they were old enough to know that a Bostonian, black or white, should consider himself a special species of fish.

The nicer colored people, preceded by a similar class of whites, were moving out of the South End, so prophetically named with this influx of black cotton-belters. For years these northern Negroes had lived next door to white neighbors and taken pride in proximity. They viewed their southern brothers with alarm, and scattered all over the city and its suburbs to escape this plague of their own locusts.

Miss Althea Binney, Judy's private teacher, who for the past three years had been coming four mornings weekly to give Judy the benefit of her accent and genteel breeding, and to get a substantial lunch that would serve as her principal meal of the day, had told Cleo of a house for rent to colored on a street abutting the Riverway, a boulevard which touched the storied Fens and the arteries of sacred Brookline.

On the previous night, Thea's brother, Simeon, the impoverished owner and editor of the Negro weekly, *The Clarion*, had received a telephone call from a Mr. Van Ryper, who succinctly advised him that he would let his ten-room house for thirty-five dollars monthly to a respectable colored family. Notice to this effect was to be inserted in the proper column of the paper.

Thea, *The Clarion's* chronicler of social events, had urged Simeon to hold the notice until Cleo had had first chance to see the house. Cleo had been so grateful that she had promised Thea an extravagant present, though Thea could better have used her overdue pay that Cleo had spent in an irresistible moment in a department store.

The prospect of Judy entering school in Brookline filled her with awe. There she would rub shoulders with children whose parents took pride in sending them to public school to learn how a democracy functions. This moral obligation discharged, they were then sent to private school to fulfill their social obligation to themselves.

"It's like having a house drop in our laps," said Cleo dramatically. "We'd be fools, Mr. Judson, to let this opportunity pass."

"What in the name of common sense," Bart demanded, "do we want with a ten-room house? We'd rattle around like three pills in a box, paying good money for unused space. What's this Jack the Ripper want for rent?"

"Fifty dollars," Cleo said easily, because the sum was believable and she saw a chance to pocket something for herself.

"That's highway robbery," said Bart, in an aggrieved voice. It hurt him to think that Cleo would want him to pay that extravagant rent month after month and year after year until they all landed in the poorhouse.

"Hold on to your hat," Cleo said coolly. "I never knew a man who got so hurt in his pocketbook. Don't think I want the care of a three-story house. I wasn't born to work myself to the bone. It's Judy I'm thinking of. I won't have her starting school with hoodlums. Where's the common sense in paying good money to Thea if you want your daughter to forget everything she's learned?"

Bart had never seen the sense in paying Thea Binney to teach his daughter to be a Bostonian when two expensive doctors of Cleo's uncompromising choosing could bear witness to her tranquil Boston birth. But he did not want Cleo to think that he was less concerned with his child's upbringing than she.

Slowly an idea took shape in his mind. "I'll tell you how I figure we can swing the rent without strain. We can live on one floor and let the other two. If we got fifteen dollars a floor, our part would be plain sailing."

"Uh huh," said Cleo agreeably.

He studied her pleasant expression with suspicion. It wasn't like her to consent to anything without an argument.

"You better say what you want to say now," he advised her.

"Why, I like a house full of people," she said dreamily. "I've missed it ever since I left the South. Mama and Pa and my three sisters made a good-size family. As long as I'm the boss of the house, I don't care how many people are in it."

"Well, of course," he said cautiously, "strangers won't be like your own flesh. Matter of fact, you don't want to get too friendly with tenants. It encourages them to fall behind with the rent."

"I tell you what," she said brilliantly, "we can rent furnished rooms instead of flats. Then there won't be any headaches with poor payers. It's easier to ask a roomer to pack his bag and go than it is to tell a family to pack their furniture."

He saw the logic of that and nodded sagely. "Ten to one a roomer's out all day at work. You don't get to see too much of them. But when you let flats to families, there's bound to be children. No matter how they fell behind, I couldn't put people with children on the sidewalk. It wouldn't set right on my conscience."

Cleo said quietly, "I'd have banked my life on your saying that." For a moment tenderness flooded her. But the emotion embarrassed her. She said briskly: "You remind me of Pa. One of us had a sore tooth, Mama would tell us to go to sleep and forget it. But Pa would nurse us half the night, keeping us awake with kindness."

He accepted the dubious compliment with a modest smile. Then the smile froze into a grimace of pain. He had been hurt in his pocketbook.

"It'll take a pretty penny to furnish all those extra bedrooms. We don't want to bite off more than we can chew. Don't know but what unfurnished flats would be better, after all. We could pick settled people without any children to make me chicken-hearted."

She stared at him like an animal at bay. Little specks of green began to glow in her gray eyes, and her lips pulled away from her even teeth. Bart started back in bewilderment.

"You call yourself a businessman," she said passionately. "You run a big store. You take in a lot of money. But whenever I corner you for a dime, it's like pulling teeth to get it out of you. You always have the same excuse. You need every dollar to buy bananas. And when I say, What's the sense of being in business if you can't enjoy your cash, you always say, In business you have to spend money to make money. Now when I try to advise you to buy a few measly sticks of bedroom furniture, a man who spends thousands of dollars on fruit, you balk like a mule at a racetrack."

He rubbed his mustache with his forefinger. "I see what you mean," he conceded. "I try to keep my store filled with fruit. I can't bear to see an empty storeroom. I guess you got a right to feel the same way about a house. In the long run it's better to be able to call every stick your own than have half your rooms dependent on some outsider's furniture."

She expelled a long breath. "That's settled then."

He thought it prudent to warn her. "We'll have to economize to the bone while we're furnishing that house."

She rolled her eyes upward. "We'll even eat bones if you say so."

He answered quietly: "You and the child will never eat less than the best as long as I live. And all my planning is to see to it that you'll never know want when I'm gone. No one on earth will ever say that I wasn't a good provider. That's my pride, Cleo. Don't hurt it when you don't have to."

"Well, I guess you're not the worst husband in the world," she acknowledged softly, and added slowly, "And I guess I'm the kind of wife God made me." But she did not like the echo of that in her ears. She said quickly, "And you can like it or lump it."

Bart took out an impressive roll of bills, peeled off a few of the lesser ones, and laid them on the table. The sight of the bank roll made Cleo sick with envy. There were so many things she could do with it. All Mr. Judson would do with it was buy more bananas.

She sighed and counted her modest pile. There were only forty-five dollars.

"It's five dollars short," she said frigidly.

"Yep," he said complacently. "I figure if this Jack the Ripper wants fifty dollars he'll take forty-five if he knows he'll get it every month on the dot. And if he ever goes up five dollars on the rent, we still won't be paying him any more than he asked for in the first place. In business, Cleo, I've learned to stay on my toes. You've got to get up with the early birds to get ahead of me."

CHAPTER 2

HER EYES FLEW OPEN. The birds were waking in the Carolina woods. Cleo always got up with them. There were never enough hours in a summer day to extract the full joy of being alive. She tumbled out of the big old-fashioned bed. Small Serena stirred, then lay still again on her share of the pillow. At the foot of the bed, Lily and Charity nestled together.

She stared at her three younger sisters, seeing the defenselessness of their innocent sleep. The bubbling mischief in her made her take one of Lily's long braids and double knot it with one of Charity's. She looked back at Serena, who tried so hard to be a big girl and never let anyone help her dress. She picked up Serena's little drawers and turned one leg inside out.

She was almost sorry she would be far away when the fun began. She could picture Lily and Charity leaping to the floor from opposite sides of the bed, and their heads snapping back, and banging together. As for Serena, surprise would spread all over her solemn face when she stepped into one leg of her drawers and found the other leg closed to her. She would start all over again, trying her other foot this time, only to find she had stepped into the same kettle of hot water. She would wrassle for fif-

teen minutes, getting madder and madder. Cleo had to
clap her hand to her mouth to hush her giggles.

She would get a whipping for it. Mama would never
see the joke. Mama would say it was mean to tease your
sisters. You had to walk a chalkline to please her.

Sometimes Cleo tried to walk a chalkline, but after a
little while, keeping to the strait and narrow made her
too nervous. At home, there was nothing to do except
stay around. Away from home, there were trees to climb,
and boys to fight, and hell to raise with Josie Beauchamp.

She climbed out of the open window and dropped to
the ground at the moment that Josie Beauchamp was
quietly creeping down the stairs of her magnificent house.
Some day Cleo was going to live in a fine house, too. And
maybe some day Josie was going to be as poor as church
mice.

They met by their tree, at the foot of which they had
buried their symbols of friendship. Josie had buried her
gold ring because she loved it best of everything, and
Cleo best of everybody. Cleo had buried Lily's doll,
mostly because it tickled her to tell her timid sister that
she had seen a big rat dragging it under the house. Lily
had taken a long stick and poked around. But every time
it touched something, Lily had jumped a mile.

Cleo and Josie wandered over the Beauchamp place,
their bare feet drinking in the dew, their faces lifted to
feel the morning. Only the birds were abroad, their vivid
splashes of color, the brilliant outpouring of their waking
songs filling the eye and ear with summer's intoxication.

They did not talk. They had no words to express their
aliveness. They wanted none. Their bodies were their
eloquence. Clasping hands, they began to skip, too im-

patient of meeting the morning to walk toward it any longer. Suddenly Cleo pulled her hand away and tapped Josie on the shoulder. They should have chosen who was to be "It." But Cleo had no time for counting out. The wildness was in her, the unrestrained joy, the desire to run to the edge of the world and fling her arms around the sun, and rise with it, through time and space, to the center of everywhere.

She was swift as a deer, as mercury, with Josie running after her, falling back, and back, until Josie broke the magic of the morning with her exhausted cry, "Cleo, I can't catch you."

"Nobody can't never catch me," Cleo exulted. But she spun around to wait for Josie. The little sob in Josie's throat touched the tenderness she always felt toward those who had let her show herself the stronger.

They wandered back toward Josie's house, for now the busyness of the birds had quieted to let the human toilers take over the morning. Muted against the white folks' sleeping, the Negro voices made velvet sounds. The field hands and the house servants diverged toward their separate spheres, the house servants settling their masks in place, the field hands waiting for the overseer's eye before they stooped to servility.

Cleo and Josie dawdled before the stables. The riding horses whinnied softly, thrusting their noses to the day. Josie's pony nuzzled her hand, wanting to hear his name dripping in honey. And Cleo moved away. Anybody could ride an old pony. She wanted to ride General Beauchamp's roan stallion, who shied at any touch but his master's.

She marched back to Josie. "Dare me to ride the red

horse," she challenged. Her eyes were green as they bored into Josie's, the gray gone under in her passion.

"No," said Josie, desperately trying not to flounder in the green sea. "He'd throw you and trample you. He'd kill you dead."

"He can't tromp me! I ain't ascairt of nothing alive. I dare you to dare me. I double dare you!"

"I won't, I won't! I'm bad, but I'm not wicked."

"I'm not wicked neither! I just ain't a coward."

She streaked to the stall and flung open the barrier. The wild horse smelled her wildness. Her green eyes locked with his red-flecked glare. Their wills met, clashed, and would not yield. The roan made a savage sound in his throat, his nostrils flared, his great sides rippled. He lowered his head to lunge. But Cleo was quicker than he was. She grasped his mane, leaped on his broad neck, slid down his back, and dug her heels in his flanks.

"Giddap, red horse!" she cried.

He flung back his head, reared, and crashed out of the stall, with Josie screeching and sobbing and sidestepping just in time.

Cleo hung on for ten minutes, ten minutes of dazzling flight to the sun. She felt no fear, feeling only the power beneath her and the power inside her, and the rush of wind on which she and the roan were riding. When she was finally thrown, she landed unhurt in a clover field. It never occurred to her to feel for broken bones. She never doubted that she had a charmed life. Her sole mishap was a minor one. She had split the seat of her drawers.

She got up and brushed off her pinafore, in a fever now to get home and brag to her sisters. She knew that she ought to let Josie see that she was still alive. The riderless horse would return, and Josie would never tell who had ridden him off. But she would be tormented by fear for as long as Cleo stayed away.

Josie would not want to eat, no matter what fancy things the white folks had for breakfast. She would not want to ride in her pony cart, no matter how pretty a picture she made. She would not want to go calling with her stylish mother, not even if she was let to wear the dress that came all the way from Paris. On this bright day the sun had darkened for Josie, and nobody but Cleo could make it shine again.

The four sisters sat around the kitchen table, eating their salt pork and biscuit and hominy, slupping down their buttermilk. Charity was nine, two years younger than Cleo, Lily was eight, Serena four. Their faces were tear-streaked. Cleo's was not, though she was the one who had got the whipping. Mama couldn't keep track of the times she had tanned Cleo's hide, trying to bring her up a Christian. But the Devil was trying just as hard in the other direction.

There Cleo was this morning, looking square in Mama's eye, telling her she must have been sleepwalking again. Couldn't remember getting dressed or tying her sisters' braids together. Just remembered coming awake in a clover field. Mama had tried to beat the truth out of her, but Cleo wouldn't budge from her lie. Worst of all, she wouldn't cry and show remorse. Finally Mama had to put away the strap because her other children looked as if they would die if she didn't.

They couldn't bear to see Cleo beaten. She was their oldest sister, their protector. She wasn't afraid of the biggest boy or the fiercest dog, or the meanest teacher. She could sass back. She could do anything. They accepted her teasing and tormenting as they accepted the terrors of night. Night was always followed by day, and made day seem more wonderful.

Mama stood by the hearth, feeling helpless in her mind. Cleo was getting too big to beat, but she wasn't a child that would listen to reason. Whatever she didn't want to hear went in one ear and out the other. She was old enough to be setting an example for her sisters. And all they saw her do was devilment.

With a long blackened fireplace stick Mama carefully tilted the lid of the three-legged skillet to see if her corn bread was done. The rest of Pa's noon dinner — the greens, the rice, the hunk of fresh pork — was waiting in his bucket. Gently she let the lid drop, and began to work the skillet out of its covering of coals that had been charred down from the oak wood. As the skillet moved forward, the top coals dislodged. Their little plunking sounds were like the tears plopping in Mama's heart.

Sulkily Cleo spooned the hominy she hated because she mustn't make Mama madder by leaving it. Mama bleached her corn in lye water made from fireplace ashes. Pa spit tobacco juice in those ashes. He spit to the side, and Mama took her ashes from the center, but that didn't make them seem any cleaner. Mama thought everything about Pa was wonderful, even his spit.

Cleo made a face at Mama's back, and then her face had to smile a little bit as she watched the dimples going in and out of Mama's round arms. You could almost touch their softness with your eyes. A flush lay just under the surface, giving them a look of tender warmth. For all the

loving in Mama's arms, she had no time for it all day.
Only at night, when her work was done, and her children
in bed, you knew by Mama's silver laughter that she was
finding time for Pa.

Mama loved Pa better than anyone. And what was left
over from loving him was divided among her daughters.
Divided even, Mama said whenever Cleo asked her.
Never once would Mama say she loved one child the
most.

On their straggling way to the mill with Pa's dinner,
Cleo told her sisters about her wild ride. They were bewitched by her fanciful telling. Timid Lily forgot to
watch where she was walking. Her toes uncurled. She
snatched up a stick and got astride it.

Serena clung to Charity's hand to keep herself from
flying. Cleo was carrying her away, and she wanted to
feel the ground again. She wanted to take Pa his dinner,
and go back home and play house.

Charity saw a shining prince on a snow-white charger.
The prince rode toward her, dazzling her eyes with light,
coming nearer and nearer, leaning to swoop her up in his
arms. And Cleo, looking at Charity's parted lips and the
glowing eyes, thought that Charity was seeing her riding
the red horse into the sun.

Her triumphant tale, in which she did not fall, but
grandly dismounted to General Beauchamp's applause,
came to its thrilling conclusion. She turned and looked at
Lily scornfully, because a stick was not a horse. Lily felt
foolish, and let the stick fall, and stepped squish on an
old fat worm. Serena freed her hand. Released from
Cleo's spell, she felt independent again. Charity's shining

prince vanished, and there was only Cleo, walking ahead
as usual, forgetting to take back the bucket she had
passed to Charity.

Pa was waiting in the shade, letting the toil pour off
him in perspiration. His tired face lightened with love
when they reached him. He opened his dinner bucket
and gave them each a taste. Nothing ever melted so good
in their mouths as a bite of Pa's victuals.

He gave them each a copper, too, though he could
hardly spare it, what with four of them to feed and
Mama wanting yard goods and buttons and ribbons to
keep herself feeling proud of the way she kept her children. Time was, he gave them kisses for toting his bucket.
But the day Cleo brazenly said, I don't want a kiss,
I want a copper, the rest of them shamefacedly said it
after her. Most times Pa had a struggle to dig down so
deep. Four coppers a day, six days a week, was half a
day's pay gone up in smoke for candy.

Pa couldn't bring himself to tell Mama. She would
have wrung out of him that Cleo had been the one started
it. And Cleo was his eldest. A man who loved his wife
couldn't help loving his first-born best, the child of his
fiercest passion. When that first-born was a girl, she could
trample on his heart, and he would swear on a stack of
Bibles that it didn't hurt.

The sisters put their coppers in their pinafore pockets
and skipped back through the woods.

Midway Cleo stopped and pointed to a towering oak.
"You all want to bet me a copper I can't swing by my feet
from up in that tree?"

Lily clapped her hands to her eyes. "I doesn't want to
bet you," she implored. "I ain't fixing to see you fall."

Serena said severely, "You bust your neck, you see if Mama don't bust it again."

Charity said tremulously, "Cleo, what would us do if our sister was dead?"

Cleo saw herself dressed up fine as Josie Beauchamp, stretched out in a coffin with her sisters sobbing beside it, and Pa with his Sunday handkerchief holding his tears, and Mama crying, I loved you best, Cleo. I never said it when you were alive. And I'm sorry, sorry, I waited to say it after you were gone.

"You hold my copper, Charity. And if I die, you can have it."

Lily opened two of her fingers and peeped through the crack. "Cleo, I'll give you mine if you don't make me see you hanging upside down." It was one thing to hear Cleo tell about herself. It was another thing to see her fixing to kill herself.

"Me, too," said Serena, with a little sob, more for the copper than for Cleo, whom she briefly hated for compelling unnecessary sacrifice.

"You can have mine," said Charity harshly. Her sweet tooth ached for a peppermint stick, and she almost wished that Cleo was dead.

Cleo flashed them all an exultant smile. She had won their money without trying. She had been willing to risk her neck to buy rich Josie Beauchamp some penny candy. Now that it was too late to retrieve Josie Beauchamp's lost hours of anxiety, Cleo wanted to carry her a bag of candy, so that when Josie got through with being glad, and got mad, she wouldn't stay mad too long.

She held out her hand. Each tight fist poised over her palm, desperately clung aloft, then slowly opened to release the bright coin that was to have added a special sweetness to the summer day.

Cleo couldn't bear to see their woe-begone faces. She felt frightened, trapped by their wounded eyes. She had to do something to change their expressions.

"I'll do a stunt for you," she said feverishly. "I'll swing by my hands. It ain't nothing to be ascairt to see. You watch."

Quickly, agilely she climbed the tree and hung by her hands. Wildly, wildly she swung, to make them forget she had taken their money, to let them see how wonderful she was.

Then a boy came by, just an ordinary knotted-headed, knobby-kneed boy. He looked at her and laughed, because to him a girl carrying on so crazy cut a funny figure. She wanted to kill him. He made her feel silly. She climbed down, and she knew he was watching her, watching the split in her drawers.

When she reached the ground, she whirled to face him, and found his feet waving in front of her. He was walking on his hands. And her sisters were squealing with delight. They had seen her walk on her hands a thousand times. What was there so wonderful about watching a boy?

She flung herself upon him, and they fought like dogs, the coppers lost irrecoverably. Her sisters circled them, crying and wringing their hands. She had to win, no matter how. She bent her head and butted him in the groin, where the weakness of boys was — the contradictory delicacy.

The fight was knocked out of him. He lay very still, his hands shielding his innocent maleness from further assault, and the blood on his lips where his anguished teeth had sunk in.

Her sisters fluttered around him. They felt no pride for her victory. Instead they pitied him. She watched them with wonder. What was there to being a boy? What was there to being a man? Men just worked. That was easier than what women did. It was women who did the lying awake, the planning, the sorrowing, the scheming to stretch a dollar. That was the hard part, the head part. A woman had to think all the time. A woman had to be smart.

Her sisters weren't smart. They thought Pa was the head of the house. They didn't know the house was run by the beat of Mama's heart. There was an awful lonesomeness in Cleo when Mama went across the river to Grandma's. She did not want to be bad then. She wanted to be good so God would send Mama back safe. But she was wildly bad again the moment Mama returned. She could not bear the way she felt inside, like laughing and crying and kissing Mama's face.

She never kissed Mama. Kisses were silly. Pa kissed Mama when he came home from work. There was sweat on him from his labor, but Mama lifted her mouth to his. His mustache prickled against her lips, but Mama did not pull away.

Looking at her sisters, standing above the suffering boy, she saw in each some likeness of Mama — in Charity the softness and roundness, the flush just under the thin skin, the silver laughter; in Lily the doe eyes, liquid and vulnerable, the plaited hair that kept escaping in curls; in small Serena the cherry-red mouth, the dimpled cheeks. She knew that she looked like Pa. Everyone said so.

Everyone said she was a beauty. What was wrong with their seeing? How could looking like Pa, with his sweat and his stained mustache, make anybody a beauty? Sometimes she would stare at herself in Mama's mirror and stick out her tongue.

Now, seeing her sisters, with their tender faces turned toward the boy, a terrible sorrow assailed her. Some day they would all grow up. They would all get married and go away. They would never live together again, nor share the long bright busy days. Mama, too, would go. Mama would die. Didn't she always say that her side of the family were not long livers? They were dead before they were fifty. Dead with their loveliness alive in their still, smooth faces. When Mama was gone in a last luminous moment, there would be the look of her and the silver laughter in the children she had blessed with her resemblance.

So long as her sisters were within sight and sound, they were the mirrors in which she would see Mama. They would be her remembering of her happy, happy childhood.

She flung herself down on the ground, and her torture was worse than the boy's. For hers was spiritual suffering and immeasurable frustration. All her terror of the future, all her despair at knowing that nothing lasts — that sisters turn into wives, that men take their women and ride away, that childhood is no longer than a summer day — were in her great dry sobs.

The boy staggered to his feet in complete alarm. He thought he had hurt her in some dreadful way mysterious to girls, her breast, her belly where the babies grew. Her father would skin him alive. He made a limping dash across the road and the trees closed in.

Then her sisters knelt beside her, letting their soothing fingers caress her face. Her sobbing quieted. She jumped up and began to turn cartwheels. A wildness was in her. She was going to turn cartwheels all the way home, heretofore an impossible feat.

Mama was in the doorway, watching her hurtle down a dusty road, seeing a girl eleven years old turning upside down, showing her drawers. Mama got the strap again and laid it on hard and heavy. Cleo just grinned, and wouldn't wipe the grin off, even with the whole of her on fire and hurting. Mama couldn't bear such impudence from her own flesh and blood. She let the strap fall and sat down and cried.

Mama didn't know what made Cleo so wild. Cleo got more of her attention than all of her other children put together. God help her when she grew up. God help the man who married her. God help her sisters not to follow in her footsteps. Better for her sisters if Cleo had never been born.

Somewhere in Springfield, Massachusetts, at that moment, Bart Judson, a grown man, a businessman, too interested in the Almighty Dollar to give any thought to a wife, was certainly giving no thought to an eleven-year-old hell-raiser way down South. But for Bart, whose inescapable destiny this unknown hoyden was to be, it might have been better if her sisters had never been born.

CHAPTER 3

CLEO ARRIVED in Springfield three years later. She and
Josie reached their teens within a month of each other.
Cleo became the Kennedy kitchen help and caught her
hair up in a bright bandana to keep it out of the cooking.
Josie caught her hair up, too, but with pins and combs in
the fashion. She put on a long dress and learned to pour
tea in the parlor. Cleo learned to call her Miss Josephine,
and never said anything that was harder.

Providence appeared as an elderly spinster, a northern
lady seeking sun for her sciatica. Cleo's way home lay past
her boarding place. She was entranced by Cleo's beauty
as she returned from work, her hair flying free, the color
still staining her cheeks from the heat of the cookstove
and the fire in her heart, and her eyes sea-green from her
sullen anger at working in the white folks' kitchen.

Miss Peterson, hating to see this sultry loveliness ripen
in the amoral atmosphere of the South, urged Mama to
let her take Cleo North. Mama considered it an answer
to prayer. With Cleo getting so grown, Mama's heart
stayed in her mouth. She didn't know what minute Cleo
might disgrace herself. The wildness in the child might
turn to wantonness in the girl. And that would kill Pa.
Better for him if she sent Cleo North with this strict-
looking spinster.

24

Cleo considered going North an adventure. Miss Josephine, who had never been outside of Carolina, would turn green with envy. In her secret sessions with her heartsick sisters, Cleo promised to send for them as soon as she got rich. She did not know how she was going to do it, but this boastful promise was more important than the performance.

She had thought she was going to night school when she reached the North. But her conscientious custodian, seeing that Cleo looked just as vividly alive in Springfield as she had looked in South Carolina, decided against permitting her to walk down darkened streets alone. There were too many temptations along the way in the guise of coachmen and butlers and porters.

Cleo's time, between her easy chores, was spent in training her tongue to a northern twist, in learning to laugh with a minimum show of teeth, and in memorizing a new word in the dictionary every day.

The things that Cleo never had to be taught were how to hold her head high, how to scorn sin with men, and how to keep her left hand from knowing what her right hand was doing.

She saw Bart Judson six months after her arrival, on one of the few occasions that she was let out of her cloister. This brief encounter, with a plate-glass window between them, made no impression on either participant. The wheels of their inseparable destiny were revolving slowly. For shortly thereafter Bart was to be on his way to Boston. And not for five years more was Cleo to follow, and then with no knowledge that Bart Judson had preceded her.

As they stared disinterestedly at each other, he seeing only a pretty, half-grown, countrified girl, she seeing only a shirt-sleeved man with a mustache, and neither recognizing Fate, the disappointed goddess had half a mind to change their charted course. Then with habitual perversity thought better of it.

Cleo had come to a halt before a store front, where an exquisite pile of polished fruit was arrayed on a silver tray, the sole and eye-compelling window display. Two men were busy inside the store, one, a fair-skinned man whom Cleo mistook for white and the proprietor, was waiting on the customer, the other man, obviously the colored help, was restocking the counters. The colored man stared briefly, as did Cleo. Then her eyes moved to a wide arch which made convenient access to an ice-cream parlor next door.

Two retail stores on busy State Street was the distance Virginia-born Bart had come in his lucky boots on his way to the banana docks of the Boston Market. Cleo, with ten cents burning a hole in her pocket and her throat parched for a fancy dish of ice cream, slowly walked away, because she wasn't certain that the owner wanted colored customers. And, as a matter of fact, Bart didn't.

When he and Cleo met five years later, again it was pure chance. But this time Fate flung them headlong at each other, and for Bart, at least, there was no mistaking that he had met the woman he wanted for his wife.

Cleo was sent to Boston by the relatives of her Springfield benefactress when the old lady's lingering illness was inevitably leading her to the grave. The relatives rallied around her, for there were always cases of elderly people deciding to leave their estates to faithful servants. They arrived *en masse,* for there were cases, too, of elderly people deciding that one devoted relative was more deserving than the rest.

They overflowed the small house. There was no room for Cleo, and also no need, for the women industriously cooked and cleaned, went errands, and wrote letters. One of the letters was to a Boston friend of Miss Peterson, who knew Cleo slightly from her occasional visits to Springfield. She was importuned to give shelter to this young Negro girl. With Christian charity, she promptly did so.

She shared her home with a nephew, whom she had raised and educated. The young man, coming of age, was not grateful. He wanted to get married. He intended to leave home. He was so obdurate about these matters that his aunt, Miss Boorum, was nearly resigned to spending her declining years alone, regretting the sacrifice that had caused her spinsterhood.

Cleo seemed a light in the gathering gloom. She was southern, she was colored. From what Miss Boorum had read of southern colored people they were devoted to what they quaintly called "my white folks," and quite disdainful of their own kind, often referring to them as "niggers." They liked to think of themselves as an integral part of the family, and preferred to die in its bosom rather than any place else. It was to be hoped that Cleo would show the same sterling loyalty.

In Boston Cleo settled into the same routine that she had endured in Springfield. She was indifferent to the change. One old white woman looked just like any other old white woman to her. Only difference was Miss Boorum wore false teeth that slipped up and down when she talked. She paid the same five dollars a month, the sum that Cleo had been receiving, obliquely, since she was sixteen. It was not considered wages. The amount was not the thing that mattered so much as the spirit

that prompted it. Though Cleo's duties were similar to a
servant's, she was considered a ward. She was fed and
clothed, and given a place at table and a chair in the
parlor, except when there was company. At such times
she put on an apron, held her proud head above the level
of everybody's eyes, and wished they would all drop dead.

Both her Springfield and Boston protectresses felt that
Cleo was better off without money. Each month Miss
Boorum, as had her predecessor, sent five dollars to Mama
affixed to a little note in an aging hand full of fancy flour-
ishes that Mama spent a day deciphering. These cus-
todians of Cleo's character had no wish to teach her to
save. Nothing, they knew, is a greater inducement to independent action than knowing where you can put your
hand on a bit of cash.

Their little notes reported to Mama on Cleo's exemplary
behavior. But Cleo was neither good nor bad. She was
in a state of suspension. She knew she was paying pen-
ance for all the joyous wildness of her childhood. She
had been exiled to learn the discipline that Mama's punishments had not taught her. She did not mind these
years of submission any more than she had minded Mama
strapping her. If you were bad, you got punished. But
you had had your fun. And that was what counted. These
meek years would not last forever. The follies of childhood were sweet sins that did not merit eternal damna-
tion. This was the period of instruction that was preparing
her for adulthood. Yet she knew she was not changing.
She was merely learning guile.

She was going to run away the minute she got her
bearings in Boston, leaving a sassy note saying, Thank
you for nothing. Good-bye and good riddance. If I never
see you again, that will be too soon.

Then she was going on the stage. She was going to
sing and dance. That would be wickeder than anything
she had ever done, but almost as much fun as there had
been in the Carolina woods. Pa would disown her, and
Mama would pray for her soul. But she would fix up the
house for Mama with furniture and running water, and
buy her some store clothes and a horse to hitch the buggy
to in place of Pa's old mule.

She sat in Miss Boorum's parlor, reading *Little Women*
aloud, looking demure and gray-eyed, hearing the richness of her own voice, being thrilled by its velvet sound,
and seeing herself singing and kicking her heels on a
stage in a swirl of lace petticoats. The only thing was
she wasn't going to have any partner. She wasn't going to
sing an old love-song with any greasy-haired coon. She
wasn't going to dance any cakewalk with him either, and
let his sweaty hand ruin her fancy costumes.

Miss Boorum's nephew, looking at Cleo across the
table, was profoundly disturbed by his emotions. He, too,
had heard about Negroes. He had heard mostly about
Negro women, and the information was correct. Desire
was growing in his loins and there was nothing he could
do to stop it. All he could do was try to keep it from
spreading to his heart.

He talked no more of marriage now, nor of moving
away. He rarely went out in the evening. He gloomed
about the house, staring moodily at Cleo. Miss Boorum
supposed he was beset by the jealous fear that her ward
would supplant him in her affections. To punish him for
the pain he had caused her, she made his ears ring with
Cleo's praises. Cleo supposed he was jealous, too, as the
Springfield relatives had been, and took a wicked delight

in tormenting him by being her most appealing in his presence.

Mama died. The letter came. Nobody down home had sense enough to send a telegram. Mama was buried by the time the letter reached Boston. She died bearing a dead child. Pa had just as good as killed her.

Cleo hadn't seen Mama since she was fourteen. Mama standing in the station saying, "God watch between me and thee, while we are absent one from another." Mama with the flush in her face from her fast-beating heart, and the tears held tight in her searching doe eyes, her coral lip trembling between her white teeth, and her arms reaching out, the rounded arms with dimples. Mama was dead, and the lid was shut down. Now Mama could never say, Cleo, I loved you best of all my children.

Cleo's grief was an inward thing that gave her a look of such purity that Miss Boorum's nephew was even further enmeshed. The enchantment of knowing that she was no one's was monstrous. He was seduced by her chastity. He would never be free as long as he knew he could be her first lover. Until he could see the face of her purity replaced by the face of surrender, her image would lie on his lids to torment him.

He grew thin and wan. Cleo looked at him and thought indifferently that he was coming down with something, and hoped it wouldn't be catching.

Miss Boorum's nephew began his campaign. He bought Cleo a bicycle. Ostensibly it was to solace her sorrow. Actually it was because he could not afford to deck her in diamonds.

He did not ride with her, nor would he instruct her in the intricacies of balance. Subconsciously he had the bloody hope that she would break every bone in her body and destroy her beauty, if not herself.

She pedaled away as easily as if she had been cycling all her life, for she still did not know there was anything she was incapable of doing. In Norumbega Park she sped around a curve and rode unromantically into Mr. Judson's stomach.

The impact sent them sprawling on either side of the path, with the shiny new bicycle rearing like a bucking horse, flinging itself against a boulder, and smashing itself to pieces.

Because she had not long lost Mama, and now she had lost her new bicycle, Cleo burst into heartbroken howls. Her heretofore unshed tears flowed in a torrent. Mr. Judson sat and rubbed his upset stomach and felt himself drowning helplessly in her welling eyes and tumbled hair.

When she could speak, she sobbed accusations. Why didn't he look where he was going? Why hadn't he jumped out of her way? Look at her brand-new bicycle. Who did he think was going to get her another one?

He was, Mr. Judson assured her gallantly. He helped her to her feet, though she fought him all the way, jerking and twisting out of his unexploring hands. He asked her for her name and address, and she gave them to him defiantly. She knew this poor darky didn't have one thin dime to lay against another, but if he wanted to talk big, let him back up his promise. He told her his name, and she forgot it immediately. What did she want to know his name for? She wasn't going to give him a bicycle.

He offered to see her home. She refused so vehemently that he pictured her parents as martinets, and supposed that the courtship, on which he had decided the minute he got back his breath, would be long and hazardous.

She took the poor wreck of her bicycle and pushed off unaided. It was a painful journey, and she was often admonished to get a horse. She reached home footsore and furious. Miss Boorum's nephew flew to the door, for Cleo rang the bell so sharply that the unhappy young man had the rather pleasurable foreboding that a policeman had brought bad tidings.

It was Cleo. He had never seen her in a wild moment, and he was further undone. For now he saw her with all her aliveness, her dark hair streaming, her eyes sparking green stars, the blood in her cheeks with the tear streaks and dust streaks, and her apple breasts betraying the pulse of her angry heart. He knew God was punishing him for his desire to see her dead by sending her back more alive than ever.

That night Miss Boorum's nephew and Mr. Judson tossed and turned in their restless sleep, while Cleo slept like a rock from all the air she had imbibed on the long ride and the long walk.

Mr. Judson was ardently in love. Why it had come upon him like this, he could not have explained, except that he had reached the age for it. He had distrusted women until now. He thought all they saw in a man was his pocketbook. When they asked him flattering questions, he imagined they were prying into his affairs, trying to find out how much he had that they would have if they married him. Artfully he had sidestepped them all, spending his days in such hard work that sleep came easily, and there were no wakeful hours of aching loins. On Sunday afternoons he strolled in the city's parks.

His excursions into society were infrequent and unsuccessful. He did not look like a rich man, for he wore a disguise of ancient suits to confuse the predatory. He did not resemble a Bostonian. His tongue was soft and liquid. He was dark. He was unimpressed by backgrounds. He made it plain that if you were a State House attendant, you were only a porter to him, no matter how many of your forebears had been freeborn.

The men with whom he had daily contact were unpretentious rich men, the bankers, the brokers, the shipowners, the heads of wholesale houses. When he moved among colored men, he was slightly contemptuous, though he thought he was merely bored. He had been in business for himself since he was ten, and was never wholly able to understand anyone who was content to let someone else be the boss man.

Bart bought the finest bicycle he could find in Boston and dispatched it next day, with a crate of oranges and two handsome hands of bananas that he hoped would impress Cleo's parents.

He called the following Sunday, and was surprised to find that Cleo worked in service, but rather pleased. She ought to consider herself a lucky girl to be courted by a man of substance. Miss Boorum, herself, showed him into the parlor, and sat down with a colored man for the first time in her life. Though she had not seen through her nephew, she saw through Bart immediately. He was in love with Cleo. This did not surprise her. It was typical of colored men.

Her nephew, hearing a male voice below with a Negro flavor, came down from his study in acute anxiety. Here was the stranger his common sense had commanded to come. Here was the man who would set him free. And his eyes were hot with hatred. Bart saw the young man's anguish. He saw that Cleo did not see it. Nor Miss Boorum. He had to get Cleo out of this house before the fever in the young man's eyes spread to his loins. He could not let her be lost in one wanton night. Or her image would lie on his eyelids for the rest of his life.

All the next day he worried like a hen with one helpless chick. When his picture-making grew too intolerable, he washed off his surface sweat and went to Miss Boorum's. He approached the house by way of the alley, hoping to find Cleo in the kitchen, where he could talk unheard. He had better luck than he bargained for. She was in the clothes yard. She had clothespins in her mouth, and was too surprised to take them out.

He began to whisper fiercely, and she only heard half of what he said, for he kept jerking his head around to see who might be coming. He told her hurriedly and harriedly that she was in great danger, a wolf was abroad in Miss Boorum's nephew's clothing. She was not safe, and never would be safe, so long as she stayed within reach of his clutches. She was too young to be alone in Boston. She had no mother to guide her. She needed a good man's protection. She needed a husband. He would marry her today if she would have him. If she would have him, he would apply for a license today and marry her at City Hall at nine o'clock on Thursday morning.

If he had proposed to her any other way, if he had courted her for a longer time, she might have refused him, out of sheer contrariness. He had not frightened her with his fears. She felt that she could subdue any man with her scorn. But she wanted to get away. She couldn't stand seeing Miss Boorum's nephew moping around like a half-sick dog if woman hankering was what ailed him.

If he ever came hankering after her, she'd stab him dead with an ice-pick. And no man on earth, let alone a white man, was worth going to hell for.

She was still so wrapped up in murderous thoughts and daring Miss Boorum's demoralized nephew to come within a foot of her that she married Bart without thinking about it. When she found herself in her marriage bed, she let him know straightaway that she had no intention of renouncing her maidenhood for one man if she had married to preserve it from another.

Bart had expected that he would have to lead her to love with patience. He was a man of vigor and could wait without wasting for Cleo's awakening. Some part of him was soothed and satisfied by the fact of his right to cherish her. It did not torment him to lie beside her and know that he could not possess her. He threw his energy into buying and selling. For he loved his fruit almost as much as he loved his wife. There was rich satisfaction in seeing it ripen, seeing the downiness on it, the blush on it, feeling the firmness of its flesh.

When Cleo was twenty, their sex battle began. It was not a savage fight. She did not struggle against his superior strength. She found a weapon that would cut him down quickly and cleanly. She was ice. Neither her mouth nor her body moved to meet his. The open eyes were wide with mocking at the busyness below. There was no moment when everything in her was wrenched and she was one with the man who could submerge her in himself.

Five years later, she conceived a child on a night when her body's hunger broke down her controlled resistance. For there was no real abhorrence of sex in her. Her need of love was as urgent as her aliveness indicated. But her perversity would not permit her to weaken. She would not face the knowledge that she was incomplete in herself.

Yet now, as she walked toward the trolley stop, she was determined not to live another year without her sisters.

CHAPTER 4

Cleo sailed up Northampton Street with Judy in tow. Dark, unshaven faces split in wide grins, and low, lewd whistles issued from between thick lips. This was her daily cross to bear in this rapidly deteriorating section of Boston. The once fine houses of the rich were fast emptying of middle-class whites and filling up with lower-class blacks. The street was becoming another big road, with rough-looking loungers leaning in the doorways of decaying houses and dingy stores. Coarse conversations balanced like balls in mouths stretched wide to catch the dirty pellets and toss them to other agile word jugglers all along the way.

They kept on the lookout for Cleo because she walked proud with her eyes on a point above their bullet heads. They had sworn to a man to make her smile.

"Look away, look away," moaned an ogling admirer. "The yeller sun has took up walking like a natchal woman."

Roars of appreciative guffaws greeted this attempt at wit. As the laughter subsided, a falsetto voice implored, "Lawd, take me to heaven while I'm happy. You done open my eyes and I done see a host of angels coming at me. She look like fire, and she ack like ice. I'm hot, I'm cold. Oh, Lawd, have mercy on my soul."

Twin spots glowed in Cleo's cheeks. A stream of white-hot words erupted inside her, but did not pass the thin line of her lips. She swallowed them down and felt the spleen spread to the pit of her stomach. Men were her enemies because they were male.

The trolley wires began to hum. "Here comes the trolley," said Cleo, with an expelled breath of profound relief. "Pick up your feet and don't you dare fall down. If you get yourself dirty before we get to Brookline, I'll give you to a Chinaman to eat."

The trolley halted, and she boosted Judy aboard. She dropped a single fare in the slot — Judy was small for going on six — asked for a transfer, guided Judy down the aisle of the swaying car, and shuttled her into a window seat. She sank down beside her and fanned herself elegantly with one gloved hand, stirring no air whatever.

She looked herself now, gay and earth-rooted and intensely alive. Her gray eyes sparkled at Judy, at the slyly staring passengers, at the streets that grew cleaner and wider as the trolley left the Negro neighborhood, at the growing preponderance of white faces.

Judy's nose was pressed against the glass. Cleo nudged her and whispered, "Judy," what do I tell you about making your nose flat?"

Judy sighed and straightened up. The exciting street scene was a whole inch farther away. She withdrew into an injured silence and studied her reflection in the glass. It was not very clear, but she knew what she looked like. She looked like Papa.

The people on the streetcar didn't know that. They regarded her in a way that she was quite used to. They were wondering where Cleo got her. They carefully scrutinized Cleo, then they carefully scrutinized her, and raised their eyebrows a little.

She was dark. She had Papa's cocoa-brown skin, his soft dark eyes, and his generous nose in miniature. Cleo worked hard on her nose. She had tried clothespins, but Judy had not known what to do about breathing. Now Cleo was teaching her to keep the bridge pinched, but Judy pinched too hard, and the rush of dark blood made her nose look larger than ever.

A little white dog with a lively face and a joyful tail trotted down the street. Judy grinned and screwed around to follow him with her eyes.

Cleo hissed in her ear: "Don't show your gums when you smile, and stop squirming. You've seen dogs before. Sit like a little Boston lady. Straighten your spine."

The trolley rattled across Huntington Avenue, past the fine granite face of Symphony Hall, and continued up Massachusetts Avenue, where a cross-street gave a fair and fleeting glimpse of the Back Bay Fens, and another cross-street showed the huge dome of the magnificent mother church of Christian Science. At the corner of Boylston Street, within sight of Harvard Bridge and the highway to Cambridge, Cleo and Judy alighted to wait for the Brookline Village trolley.

Cleo saw with satisfaction that she was already in another world, though a scant fifteen-minute ride away from the mean streets of the Negro neighborhood. There were white people everywhere with sallow-skinned, thin, austere Yankee faces. They had the look that Cleo coveted for her dimpled daughter. She was dismayed by Judy's tendency to be a happy-faced child, and hoped it was merely a phase of growth. A proper Bostonian never

showed any emotion but hauteur. Though Cleo herself
had no desire to resemble a fish, she wanted to be able
to point with the pride of ownership to someone who did.

The Village trolley came clanging up Boylston Street,
and Judy clambered up the steps, pushed by her mother
and pulled by the motorman. Cleo was pleased to see that
there were no other colored passengers aboard. The occu-
pants of the half-filled car were mostly matrons, whose
clothes were unmodish and expensive. All of them had
a look of distinction. They were neither Cabots nor
Lowells, but they were old stock, and their self-assurance
sat well on their angular shoulders.

They did not stare at Cleo and Judy, but they were dis-
creetly aware of the pair, and appreciative of their neat
appearance. Boston whites of the better classes were
never upset nor dismayed by the sight of one or two
Negroes exercising equal rights. They cheerfully stom-
ached three or four when they carried themselves incon-
spicuously. To them the minor phenomenon of a colored
face was a reminder of the proud rôle their forebears had
played in the freeing of the human spirit for aspirations
beyond the badge of house slave.

The motorman steered his rocking craft down a wide
avenue and settled back for the first straight stretch of
his roundabout run. Cleo looked at the street signs, and
her heart began to pound with excitement. This was
Brookline. There wasn't another colored family she knew
who had beaten her to it. She would be the first to say,
"You must come to see us at our new address. We've
taken a house in Brookline."

She began to peer hard at house numbers. A row of
red-brick houses began, and Cleo suddenly pulled the bell
cord.

"We get off here," she said to Judy, and shooed her down the aisle.

Cleo walked slowly toward the number she sought, taking in her surroundings. Shade trees stood in squares of earth along the brick-paved sidewalk. Each house had a trim plot of grass enclosed by a wrought-iron fence. The half-dozen houses in this short block were the only brick houses within immediate sight except for a trio of new apartment houses across the way, looking flat-faced and ugly as they squatted in their new cement sidewalk.

In the adjoining block was a row of four or five weathered frame houses with wide front porches, big bay windows, and great stone chimneys for the spiraling smoke of logs on blackened hearths. The area beyond was a fenced-in field, where the sleek and beautiful firehorses nibbled the purple clover and frisked among the wild flowers. Near-by was the firehouse with a few Irish heads in the open windows, and a spotted dog asleep in a splash of sun.

Directly opposite from where Cleo walked was a great gabled mansion on a velvet rise, with a carriage house at the end of a graveled drive. The house was occupied, but there was an air of suspended life about it, as if all movement inside it was slow. Its columned porch and long French windows and lovely eminence gave the house grandeur.

A stone's-throw away was the winding ribbon of the Riverway Drive, over which the hooves of carriage horses clip-clopped and shiny automobiles choked and chugged. Beyond were the wooded Fens, at the outset of their wild wanderings over the city to Charlesgate.

Cleo was completely satisfied with everything she saw.

There were no stoop-sitters anywhere, nor women idling
at windows, nor loose-lipped loiterers passing remarks.
Her friends who lived in Dorchester, or Cambridge, or
Everett had nice addresses, of course. But Brookline was
a private world.

She stopped and glanced down at her daughter to see
if her ribbed white stockings were still smooth over her
knees, and if the bright ribbons on the ends of her bobbing braids were as stiff and stand-out as they had been
when she tied them. She scanned the small upturned
face, and a rush of protective tenderness flooded her
heart. For a moment she thought she had never seen anything as lovely as the deep rich color that warmed Judy's
cheeks. She herself had hated being bright-skinned when
she was a child. Mama had made her wash her face all
day long, and in unfriendly moments her playmates had
called her yaller punkins. Now her northern friends had
taught her to feel defensive because Judy was the color
of her father.

"Don't speak unless you're spoken to," Cleo warned
Judy, and mounted the steps of the house before which
they stood.

In a moment or two a colored maid responded to her
ring. She looked at Cleo with open-mouthed surprise,
then her look became sly and secret. "Y'all come see
about the house?" she asked in a conspiratorial whisper.

"I beg your pardon," Cleo said coolly. "I've come to
see Mr. Van Ryper."

The maid's face froze. She knew these stuck-up northern niggers. Thought they were better than southern
niggers. Well, all of them looked alike to the white man.
Let this high-yaller woman go down South and she'd find
out.

"Step inside," she said surlily. "You're letting in flies."

"I'm sorry," Cleo said sweetly. "I see a big black fly got in already." With a dazzling smile she entered the house, and instantly drew a little breath at sight of the spacious hall with its beautiful winding stairway.

"What's the name?" the maid asked briefly. If this woman wanted to be treated like white folks, at least she wasn't going to be treated like quality white folks.

"The name is Mrs. Judson," Cleo said readily. She had been asked a proper question, however rudely, and she was perfectly willing to answer it. This peevish incivility was much less insulting than the earlier intimacy. If she had wanted to gossip with the servant before seeing the master, she would have used the back door.

"Wait here," the woman said, and began a snail-pace ascent of the stairs, with her rocking buttocks expressive of her scorn.

"Always remember," said Cleo loudly and sweetly to Judy, "that good manners put you in the parlor and poor manners keep you in the kitchen." The maid's broad back seemed to swell the seams of her uniform. "That's what I'm paying good money to your governess for," Cleo added impressively. "So you won't have to wear an apron."

Judy stared down at her shoes, feeling very uncomfortable because Cleo's voice was carrying to the woman on the stairs. Miss Binney always said that a lady must keep her voice low, and never boast, and never, never say anything that might hurt somebody's feelings.

"She heard you," said Judy in a stricken voice.

Cleo gave her a look of amiable impatience. "Well, I expected her to hear. Who did you think I was talking to? I certainly wasn't talking to you."

Her eyes grew lively with amusement as she studied
her daughter's distress. Sometimes she wondered where
she had got Judy. Judy had no funny bone. Thea was
probably responsible. She had no funny bone either.
Their diversions were so watery. What was the sense in
Judy's taking delight in a dog's wagging tail if she was
going to miss the greater eloquence of that woman's wagging rear, and then look shocked when her mother talked
back at it? You really had to love Bostonians to like them.
And the part of Cleo that did love them was continually
at war with the part of her that preferred the salt flavor
of lusty laughter.

Her eyes clouded with wistfulness. The more the
years increased between the now and the long ago, the
more the broad A's hemmed her in, the more her child
grew alien to all that had made her own childhood an
enchanted summer, so in like degree did her secret heart
yearn for her sisters. She longed for the eager audience
they would have provided, the boisterous mirth she would
have evoked when she flatfooted up an imaginary flight of
stairs, agitating her bottom. Who did she know in the
length and breadth of Boston who wouldn't have cleared
an embarrassed throat before she got going good on her
imitation?

Sometimes you felt like cutting the fool for the hell
of it. Sometimes you hankered to pick a bone and talk
with your mouth full. To Cleo culture was a garment that
she had learned to get into quickly and out of just as fast.

She put on her parlor airs now, for Mr. Van Ryper was
descending the stairs. Her eyebrows arched delicately,
her luscious mouth pursed primly, and a faint stage smile
ruffled her smooth cheeks. These artifices had no effect
on Mr. Van Ryper, who was elderly.

He reached the bottom step and peered at her. "Carrie should have shown you in here," he said fussily, piloting Cleo and Judy into the parlor.

He waved at a chair. "Sit down, Mrs. — uh — Jenkins, and you, young lady. What's your name, Bright Eyes or Candy Kid? Let's see if it's Candy Kid. Look in that box on the table, and mind you don't stick up yourself or the furniture."

Judy murmured her thanks and retired. She had learned to dissolve when grown-ups were talking. They forgot you and said very interesting things.

"Now, then, Mrs. — uh — Jordan," said Mr. Van Ryper. "I expect you've come about the house."

Cleo looked about the gracious room. The lacquered floors were of fine hardwood, the marble above the great hearth was massive and beautiful. The magnificent sliding doors leading into the dining room were rich mahogany, the wallpaper was exquisitely patterned. From the center of the high ceiling the gas chandelier spun its crystal tears.

"It's a beautiful house," said Cleo with awe.

"Best house on the block. Sorry to leave it, but I'm too old to temper my prejudices."

Cleo looked startled and felt humiliated. Were there colored people next door? Was that why Mr. Van Ryper was moving away? Should her pride make her rise and exit with dignity, or should she take the insult in exchange for this lovely house? Who were the people next door? If they were anybody, Miss Binney would have known them. They must be old second-class niggers from way down South, whom she wouldn't want to live next door to herself.

"Do you happen to know what part of the South the family came from?" she asked delicately.

Mr. Van Ryper looked startled now. "What family?" he asked testily, peering hard at Cleo with the intent of reading her foolish feminine mind.

"The colored family you're prejudiced at," Cleo said belligerently.

Mr. Van Ryper rose to his feet. His face purpled with anger. "Madam, my father was a leader in the Underground Movement. I was brought up in an Abolitionist household. Your accusation of color prejudice is grossly impertinent. I believe in man's inalienable right to liberty. Let me lecture you a bit for the enlightenment of your long-eared child, who is probably being brought up in cotton batting because she's a little colored Bostonian who must never give a backward look at her beginnings.

"We who are white enslaved you who are — to use a broad term, madam — black. We reduced your forebears to the status of cattle. It must be our solemn task to return their descendants to man's estate. I have been instrumental in placing a good many southern Negroes in the service of my friends. My maid Carrie is lately arrived from the South. She is saving her wages to send for her family. They will learn here. They will go to night school. Their children will go to day school. Their grandchildren will go to high school, and some of them will go to college.

"Negroes are swarming out of the South. The wheat and the chaff are mixed. But time is a sifting agent. True, the chaff will forever be our cross to bear, but one fine day the wheat will no longer be part of the Negro problem."

Cleo looked unimpressed. She had lent an unwilling

ear to this long speech, and had stubbornly closed her mind every time Mr. Van Ryper used the word Negro, because colored Bostonians were supposed to feel scandalized whenever they heard this indecent appellation. This fancy talk was just to cover up his saying he didn't like niggers.

"Well, it's nice when people aren't prejudiced," Cleo said politely.

"Madam, I am distinctly prejudiced against the Irish," Mr. Van Ryper said wearily, thinking that colored women, for all they had to endure, were as addlepated as their fairer-skinned sisters. "The Irish present a threat to us entrenched Bostonians. They did not come here in chains or by special invitation. So I disclaim any responsibility for them, and reserve the right to reject them. I do reject them, and refuse to live in a neighborhood they are rapidly overrunning. I have decided to rent my house to colored. Do you or don't you want it?"

"I do," said Cleo faintly, thinking this was the oddest white man she had ever met. It would take an educated person like Miss Binney to understand how his mind worked.

"And is the rent within your means? Thirty-five dollars, but it struck me as a fair sum. There are ten rooms. I hope you won't mind if I don't show them to you now. The parish priest is waiting upstairs in the sitting room. Seems some neighbors have complained about my attitude. He's a man of taste and intelligence. Pity he has to be Irish, but I understand that some of his blood is English."

Cleo rose, with a little nod at Judy, who came as obediently as a puppy trained to heel. There was a ring of

chocolate around her mouth that made her look comical,
and a smudge of it on one of her gloves. Cleo sighed a
little. Children made a mess with chocolate candy. Any
fool ought to know that. What did this old man think
lollipops were invented for?

"About the rent, Mr. Van Ryper," she said, wiping
Judy's mouth with the cotton handkerchief and taking
this opportunity to glare in her eye, "thirty dollars would
suit me better. And you wouldn't have to wait for it.
You'd have it every month on the dot. My husband told
me to tell you that."

Mr. Van Ryper gestured toward the dining-room doors.
His voice was patient and instructive. "Madam, each one
of those doors cost two hundred dollars. The staircase
cost a small fortune. There is a marble bowl in the master
bedroom. The bathtub is porcelain, and so is the — ah —
box. But if thirty dollars is all you can afford, I hope you
will make up the difference in appreciation."

"Indeed I will," Cleo promised fervently. "It's been my
dream to live in Brookline."

"This isn't Brookline," Mr. Van Ryper said crossly.
"The other side of the street is Brookline. This side is
Roxbury, which that thundering herd of Irish immigrants
have overrun. They have finally pushed their boundary
to here. Time was when Roxbury was the meeting place
of great men. Now its fine houses are being cut up into
flats for insurrectionists. I'm moving to Brookline within
a few days. Brookline is the last stronghold of my generation."

Cleo swallowed her disappointment. Several colored
families were already living in Roxbury. They didn't talk
about the Irish the way Mr. Van Ryper did. They called

them nice white people. They said they lived next door to such nice white people, and made you feel out of fashion because your neighbors were colored.

She opened her purse, taking great care that its contents were not wholly revealed to Mr. Van Ryper.

"Just one other thing first," he said. "Your reference. That is to say, your husband's employer."

"My husband's in business," Cleo explained. "He has a wholesale place in the Market. All kinds of fruit, but mostly bananas."

Mr. Van Ryper's eyes filled with interest. "Bart Judson? The Black Banana King? Never met him, but I hear he's pretty amazing. Well, well. I'm happy to rent my house to him. I like to do business with a businessman. Tell you what. We'll settle on a rental of twenty-five dollars. Ah, that pleases you, doesn't it? But there's a condition to it. I'd want your husband to take care of minor repairs. You see, I'm a tired old man, quite unused to being a landlord. I'd hate to be called out of bed in the middle of the night to see about a frozen water pipe."

The matter was settled at once and Cleo handed over the money. Mr. Van Ryper found a scrap of paper and a stub of pencil in his pockets, and paused in the writing of the receipt to make an inquiry. Did Mrs. Judson want it in ink? Cleo answered hastily and heartily that pencil was fine.

CHAPTER 5

Wнен тне door closed behind her, Cleo drew a long contented breath. Then she walked briskly to the trolley stop, with Judy bobbing alongside again.

"Are we going home now?" asked Judy, who had been hurried through a scant breakfast and was hopeful of an early lunch.

"We're going to your father's store," said Cleo abstractedly. "Now don't ask any more questions. Try saying your table of twos. Bet you can't finish before the trolley comes."

Judy opened her mouth with alacrity, because it was rare that her mother took time to admire her accomplishments. But Cleo said briskly, "Try saying them silently. I'm thinking."

Her mind was revolving around her sisters, plotting the most direct route between the two points of wish and fulfillment. All of her sisters were as blind as bats when it came to their husbands. They loved them. What could they find in them to love? Not a man among them was a decent provider. Serena and Charity worked in service whenever times were harder than usual. Lily would have gone to work, too, if she could have taken her child on her job as her sisters did in the South.

50

What kind of way was that for her sisters to live, from hand to mouth, from payday to payday, from what she could scrape up to send them? Yet they still believed they belonged to their husbands, for richer or poorer, in sickness and health. If they demanded no more of life than a man in the house, it was time someone else demanded more for their children.

Serena and Charity were still down home. But Lily had left the South when Pa in his lonesomeness married Miss Hattie. Lily was scared of mild Miss Hattie, who had never raised her voice in her life. But Lily was scared of everything, including her shadow. When she was little, she had to be put to bed before the lamps were lighted. If she saw her shadow, she screamed like a banshee, and ran like something was after her.

The old folks said Mama had birthmarked Lily the time old Spot went mad in the yard and came near chewing a hunk out of three-year-old Cleo, who had been teasing the poor old dog to play all the long hot day. Mama had never held a gun in her life. But she ran and grabbed Pa's hunting piece and aimed true, though she was shaking with fright. She was white as death when she fired. Her color didn't dreen back for two days, and Lily was born before it did. Lily came into the world so white she wouldn't have browned in an oven, and she was always the scariest thing on two feet. The old folks said she was marked.

Cleo's letters home, after Pa's second marriage, didn't include one kind word about Miss Hattie. She couldn't bear the thought of the woman who had taken Mama's place, and she tried to turn her sisters against her. She succeeded in turning Lily, who had always believed any-

thing Cleo told her. Lily let herself believe that Miss
Hattie didn't want Mama's children anywhere near her,
reminding her, whenever she looked at them, of Pa's
greater love for another woman. She grew so nervous
around Miss Hattie that Pa decided to send her up North
to her married sister.

She got as far as New York. But she might as well be
at the North Pole. For Cleo had never been able to visit
her. She had talked too freely to Mr. Judson about her
fears for her timid sister in such a wicked city. He had
acquired the same fears for her and refused to let her set
foot in Sodom.

Lily had never been to Boston. When she got off the
train in New York, she promised God she would never
get on another one as long as she lived. It was weeks
before she recovered from the animality of Jim Crow, and
the additional horrors of sweating through hot waves of
nausea, of swooshing through tunnels of terrible black-
ness, of riding high above swirling water, of fighting off
sleep to watch her belongings, of feeling her eyes and her
unrelaxed limbs ache with weariness each morning.

In Washington, Victor Bates, a Pullman porter, had
taken her under his wing. All the way to New York he
ran back and forth between his duties and her coach. She
was eighteen, and her youth and helplessness made him
accept her as his charge. She clung to the comfort and
masculine strength his kind brown face and big broad
frame personified to her grateful heart.

When they reached New York, she refused to be put on
the Boston train. She said she would die if she rode another mile. In one of her rare seizures of stubbornness,
when fear gave her the courage to hold fast, she stood

firm as a rock in the middle of the station, with muttering people pushing past her.

Victor took her to a married friend's house. He thought if she rested a day, she would feel differently in the morning. But after an evening in her company, with her liquid eyes never leaving his face, he knew he did not want her to go to Boston either.

Victor Bates was no worse than the average second-rate husband, Cleo conceded. But he was a road man. Lily spent half of her nights alone, with only a sleeping child to look to for protection. Victoria was going on seven. It wasn't doing her any good to have a jack rabbit for a mother. She and Lily would be better off in Boston, where Cleo could look after them both, than in New York with one little man who spent most of his time bowing and scraping to white folks.

Yet all of this was rationalization. Though Cleo did not know the word, and would not have admitted that its meaning was applicable, her yearning for her sisters was greater than her concern for them. All of her backward looks were toward the spellbinding South. The rich remembering threw a veil of lovely illusion over her childhood. Her sisters, with their look of Mama, would help her keep that illusion alive. She could no longer live without them. They were the veins and sinews of her heart.

"Here comes the trolley car," said Judy, who had finished her table of twos and was patiently reviewing her table of threes because she knew Cleo's shut-away face and the uselessness of intruding her image on the broad bright canvas that Cleo called "long before you were ever thought of."

The trolley halted and they boarded it. There were several vacant seats at this hour of the day. Cleo herded Judy into one that was farthest away from the other passengers, who were, as usual, mildly diverted by the pair. Judy stared slightly open-mouthed while Cleo opened her purse, extracted the rent receipt, and wondered exasperatedly why children seemed to have nothing to do but mind the business of grown-ups. She rummaged around in the bottom of her bag, finally gave up her useless search, and surreptitiously surveyed the passengers. She settled on a lone man and pointed him out to Judy.

"You see that man? Go ask him nicely to lend your mother a pencil. Tell him I want to write an address before I forget it."

Judy rose eagerly, feeling important, and started down the aisle.

"Judy!" Cleo called softly.

She turned and gaped at her mother.

"A pencil with an eraser."

Judy came back and hung over Cleo. Cleo held the pencil poised and looked at her coldly. Then her face cleared. "Now," she said sweetly, "go ask the conductor if this trolley goes to Scollay Square. My, but you're a big girl!"

Judy danced away, dizzy with happiness.

Carefully Cleo erased the figure that Mr. Van Ryper had written in and substituted forty-five. With that bit of deception she had twenty dollars in her possession that Mr. Judson didn't know she had. If she stayed on her toes, she would have twenty dollars every month until Mr. Judson caught up with her.

Cleo sighed. Some day she would run out of ways to

skin the cat. Then her head went up and her chin looked stubborn. But she'd give Mr. Judson a run for his money until she did.

Judy came back tripping over her tongue as she imparted her information. Looking at the eager innocent face, Cleo remembered the many times Mr. Judson had said to her, "We should pull in harness for the child's sake, Cleo. When you work against me, you work against her." Her sluggish conscience stirred. She said quickly, almost appealingly, "Judy, don't you ever get lonesome all by yourself? I had three sisters to play with when I was growing up. Wouldn't you like two little girls and a little boy to keep you company when we move into that big house?"

"Oh, I would, I would," said Judy ecstatically.

"I thought so," said Cleo contentedly, and her conscience bogged down again.

CHAPTER 6

$\mathbf{B}$ART JUDSON stared over the shimmering sea, his eyes screwed up against the sun and his sixth sense straining for some inner awareness of the merchant ship *Lucy Evelyn* sailing up from Jamaica under the English flag. Incoming craft bent their bows toward the busy harbor, their whistles blasting holes in the morning. Sea gulls dipped and screamed and soared. In their upward flight toward the sun, their breasts had the beauty of alabaster. Sparows twittered in the eaves of the wharves, and pigeons searched the gutters. Greek stevedores, with curls and classic faces, descended like dirty gods into the holds of ships at anchor. Jobbers darted about, shouting directions to shore workers. Over all was the ceaseless rumble of wagon wheels on the cobbled streets of the Boston Market.

Bart stood alone, responding absently to the hurried genial greetings of the market men, whose places of business, along with his, formed the sprawling city of warehouses, wholesale stores, and retail stalls that made up the old historic market, which was the terminal point for the produce that came by sea and rail to feed the city and her neighbors north to Canada.

All of Bart's living had led to this place, and even this

hour when he watched for a sea-scarred ship from
Jamaica, bringing a cargo of bananas, of which his con-
signment was more than a thousand bunches. The fancy
gold lettering over his store read: Bartholomew Judson,
Foreign and Domestic Choice Fruits and Vegetables,
Bananas a Specialty. There was no other man in the
market who knew better than Bart how to ripen the delicate and perishable banana. From the great hooks in his
ripening rooms hung the heavy fruit winter and summer.
Always there was the ripening smell. Always it hung
about Bart. His weekly bath could not wash away the
odor of tropic fruit.

He had seen his first banana when he was ten, somewhere along the middle seventies, and nine years after
Mary, his mother, had snatched him from his crib, and
tossed him in the air, and laughed, and cried, and told
him he was free.

He took his first step out of bondage that night, and
walked without faltering straight to the shining object his
mother held out to him. It was a piece of silver money
that she had found the year before. She closed his tiny
fist over it, and counseled him to treasure it, for money
was the measure of independence.

His year-old mind had not grasped that, but his mother
dinned it into him over the period of his formative years
until it was part of everything he thought. Mary knew
what she wanted for herself and for him. She had no
recollection of her own parents, and her man had been
sold away from her. She was determined that she and
her son would be the forerunners of a solid family.

She packed her few belongings in a bandana, put her

heavy baby on her hip, and walked off the ruined plantation into Richmond. She knew where she wanted to go
and what she wanted to do. She went to the Widow
Mears, who had sometimes hired slaves from the Judson
plantation and who was known to be a just mistress.
Widow Mears kept a rooming house for drummers and
farmers in town for a brief stay. Mary had been a field
hand all her life, but she talked herself up as the finest
cook on the Judson plantation, and Widow Mears was
persuaded to advertise meals.

Mary fixed up the back shed and moved into it. Then
she got a cigar box and cut a slit in it. She ripped the
stitches in Bart's pinafore pocket, where she had sewed
the silver piece for safety. She placed it in his hand again
and urged him to drop it down the hole. He yelled and
resisted. She tugged at his tightened fist and pried it open.
The coin fell through with a plunking sound that caught
Bart's ear. He picked up the box, shook it carefully, heard
the roll and rattle of his savings, swallowed his sobs, and
grinned.

Every penny Mary made went into that box. As soon
as her son was five years old and smart and strong enough
to do a few chores, Mary got Widow Mears to put him to
work shining shoes, filling pitchers, emptying slops. Each
morning he followed her to the open market with a basket
on his arm for rush things. Watching the dealers polish
and praise, and Widow Mears pick and choose and warily
watch the scales, Bart learned the elementary lessons of
trade.

As he grew older, there formed in his mind his dream of
buying and selling. He began to live close, denying himself the peppermint sticks and candy apples that his sweet

tooth hankered for, in order to swell the cigar box. When
he was grown enough, he was going into business, and
he would need capital.

When he was eight, he put himself in school, not because he had any interest in formal education, but because
he wanted to learn how to figure, and to write with a
flourish, so that men would see he had schooling and
would know in advance that he wasn't a poor ignorant
darky who would take a dime for a dollar.

When he was ten, he knew exactly the line his life
should follow. He borrowed a word from the Bible —
beget. He liked the sound of the saying, money begets
money. He and Mary counted their savings and rented
an eating house in the center of town. Bart did the buying, and doubled as barker, shouting the specials of the
day through the business section and taking orders
drawled at doorways and windows. At the noon hour he
trotted up and down office stairs in a long, immaculate
apron that missed tripping him by a miracle.

He saw his first banana on a cluttered desk in Lawyer
Smith's seedy office. He set down his tray and bugged
his eyes. Lawyer Smith and his visitor, a sea captain,
watched him indulgently. The captain's ship had touched
the Bay Islands, off Honduras, and he had come away
with two magnificent stems of the strange, exotic fruit as
souvenirs for his friends. Half of them had ripened and
rotted on the long sail to New Orleans. The rest the captain had separated into hands, and one now lay on the
desk of his old friend Smith, a dozen luminous yellow
fingers, faintly tinged with green and slowly beginning
to speckle.

"Excuse me, Massa Smith, Cap'n, suh, what all is that?"

Bart asked, bowing and scraping, and feeling no shame
at abasing himself, since the quest was knowledge of what
might be a marketable edible.

"Bananas, boy," said the captain expansively. His own
acquaintance with the fruit being recent, he had the
initiate's irrepressible desire to pass on information lately
come by as if it were old knowledge.

"You eats it, Cap'n, suh?" Bart asked ingenuously. "I
never see such on any stall."

"You know where Honduras is, boy?" asked the captain,
casting an amused look at Lawyer Smith.

"Nawsuh, Cap'n, suh."

"It's a heap of miles and a heap of ocean away. Bananas
grow there on trees. And the trees grow in the jungles.
And nigger natives climb them trees like monkeys."

"You reckon," Lawyer Smith interposed, his palate still
relishing the rich fruit, "there's money in bananas?"

"Hear tell of a Cap'n Baker, Boston way," said the
captain sententiously, "is starting to bring 'em in regular
from Jamaica. Began about six or seven years ago. He
was master of a schooner then, eighty-five tons or so. Used
to fish winters, carry freight summers. Started making
port at Jamaica and bringing bananas back to Boston.

"Wasn't much steady demand for 'em. Trip took sixteen, seventeen days. Most of his cargo rotted on the
way, and not many folks got to sample 'em. But this here
Baker sees a future in bananas. Built himself a bigger
ship more cargo space, more speed.

"Latest thing is he's got some kind of setup in Jamaica
and is loading other vessels along with his own to bring
bananas back to Boston. Commission house sells 'em
through a man name of Preston. Him and Baker are

talking about forming some kind of consolidation to make bananas a year-round trade, 'stead of splitting it up with fish in winter."

"They'd better stick to fishing," said Lawyer Smith judiciously. "Everybody eats fish, and I don't know another soul in this town but me a minute ago who ever put his teeth in a banana."

Bart let his eyes roll around in his head. His tongue darted out and made a persuasive circle of his lips. "Please, Massa Smith, and Cap'n, suh, I sure would like to be the onliest black boy in this town to taste one."

"Well, here you are," said Lawyer Smith largely, stripping a finger from the cupped hand and tossing it across his desk.

Bart caught it deftly. "Thank you kindly, Massa."

"Now be off with you," said Lawyer Smith, removing the snowy napkin and beginning to uncover the savory dishes.

"Yes, suh!" said Bart, and scooted out, his humility falling away from him as he clattered down the stairs.

He saved his banana all day. When the last late diner had been fed, he walked two miles to the one-room cabin of Mr. Alonzo White, a black man of good education, who had been schooled with his delicate young master to satisfy the white lad's whim. The lesson was geography at Bart's request that he might trace the course from Boston to Jamaica and from Richmond to Boston. The lesson concluded, Bart paid the twenty-five cents that was Mr. White's fee for an hour's education, and walked slowly home, his mind afire with dreams.

He looked up at the stars. He believed that he had been born under one of the lucky ones, and that everything he touched would turn to money. In the darkness he walked with his head held back and feet slapping proudly on the dirt road. Some day he was going North to Boston. It was a long way from the South. White folks there weren't apt to know too much about how black folks were used to being treated. Folks up North fought to make the South free. Stood to reason then that they wouldn't want to treat any man anywhere as if he were a humble dog. In the North they respected money, whether it was white or black. You could look a man level in the eye and keep your hat on your head if you had as much cash on the line as he did.

When Bart reached home, he got his banana out of the kitchen safe and carried it to the table, where Mary sat rocking and resting and humming a paean to Jesus. Carefully he peeled the fruit, watching the petals fall away, revealing the delicate filament of their undersides. Mary bent forward to stare at the slender, golden-white spear. It was small and uncultivated, but firm-fleshed, and its heavy exotic odor struck some dormant stream of atavistic longing for the breast of jungle earth.

"Take a big bite, Mam," Bart said generously, and held the fruit to her dreaming mouth.

She bit into it and chomped with delight. Bart's square white teeth cut out a cylinder, and the taste ran down his throat like milk and melted butter and honey.

"Mam," he said reverently, "I reckon this tastes like manna mus' taste in heaven."

All night he dreamed on his narrow bed of bananas and Boston and ships setting sail from Jamaica.

Now, staring out across Boston Harbor, he was troubled

by his dream of the night before. He had dreamed that the *Lucy Evelyn* had foundered, and her cargo of thirty thousand stems had washed out of the hold and plunged heavily to the bottom of the sea. He had waked in a cold sweat, with the cries of drowning men in his ears, and his eyes still seeing the helpless ship and her sunken cargo.

He believed in his dreams. To him they were visions, and were the Lord's way of making revelations. Still, the *Lucy Evelyn* was a stout ship, as were all the big banana boats that plied between the West Indies and Boston and Central America and New York and New Orleans under the charter of the Consolidated Fruit Company, bringing a prize crop of highly cultivated fruit from the banana plantations of the leveled jungles to the tables of North America all the seasons of the year.

The weather this morning was sunny and clear. There had been no reports of a storm sweeping up the Atlantic to force the *Lucy Evelyn* off her course. Her run was seven days or eight, and this was the morning of the eighth day. She had until sundown to keep within running time.

But on his way to the dock, Bart had detoured to the office of the Consolidated Fruit Company. He had barged in on their busy representatives, who had assured him that they had had no unfavorable word from the *Lucy Evelyn,* who would make port sometime that day as she had been doing, fair weather or foul, for ten years. Bart had not been reassured. The premonition was too strong in him. God was too surely signifying.

He believed in God. He believed in himself and he believed in God. There was constant communion between them, and he never doubted for a moment that God spent a lot of His time looking out for his interests. His conversion had come when he was seventeen, and his faith had deepened with the years of his prosperity. He rarely went to the South End church of his faith because Cleo would never go with him. The congregation was largely composed of transplanted Southerners, hard-working simple worshipers, who broadly hinted, to Bart's embarrassment, that his wife considered herself too good for them. He was a shouting Baptist, and Cleo thoroughly disapproved. She had never felt the spirit, and he supposed she never would. Her Episcopalian friends were persuading her to their wishy-washy way of worship. They really believed you could get to heaven without any shouting.

He remembered how his mother had worried until he wrestled with the Devil. Their blessings had increased beyond her greatest expectations. They owned a home and a horse and buggy. Their restaurant employed five in help. Fried chicken was their specialty, and they catered to supper parties. Mary's mattress was lined with money. She spent most of her free time on her knees, thanking God for His generosity.

She did not think Bart gave God enough credit. Bart couldn't see where God figured in. Their success was their own doing. But Mary was afraid that Bart might be tempted by the Devil to throw his money away in riotous living if he did not walk with God by his side. They went to church, and the spirit did not move him. He sat in sinners' row with the other unsaved souls, and none of the singing and shouting sent him to his knees.

One Sabbath dawn Mary shook him awake. He opened his eyes and stared sleepily at her transfigured face.

"Bart," she commanded, "kneel and pray."

He blinked in bewilderment and burrowed deeper into his pillow.

She went on in a breathless singsong, "De Lawd, He come in a vision, and I see His eyes running over with tears of blood, and I hear His voice like a mournful pleading, 'Mary, Mary, wake your child and teach him to pray.'"

He peeped at her over the edge of the sheet. She began to moan, strangely and beautifully. Her small spare body rocked back and forth. Her tears were streaming.

He was frightened and stirred. He reached for her hand. "Mam, Mam, I can't find Jesus. I search' in the Bible. He warn't there! I search' one night in the lonesome graveyard, and I heard the ha'nts wail. But I couldn't find Jesus. He warn't there!"

Mary beat upon her breasts. "Search your heart, my son!"

His face was tortured. It was screwed up in a desperate agony of straining toward God. An icy chill rushed over him.

Mary persisted inexorably: "Can't you hear de rush of wings? Can't you hear de los' lambs bleating on de hills? Can't you hear de Marster's voice, 'Come up higher. Sinner, rise! Come up higher. Sinner rise!'? Ain't you feel de monstrous light what strike and blind? Ain't you heart rise up in your mouth, and your conscience stab like a sword? Can't you see de little Jesus holding out His bleeding hands, and de water and blood gushing out of His side? Rise, my son, rise!"

He was swept out on the tide of her passion. She began again her strange sweet moaning. He found himself swaying. Music surged through him. He flung back the covers and stood erect. His face became radiant.

Mary stared at him, still now and watchful.

The music grew. Suddenly there emanated from his heart a voice of matchless purity singing over and over, "Kind Jesus, kind Jesus, thy servant waits on the Lord."

He stretched out his hands and groped toward the open window. Mary did not touch him. She would rather have seen him fling himself out than disturb the mysterious ways of God.

In the half-light, with the little bird calling, Bart saw the vision. He saw the heavens split asunder, and God with a crown on His long white hair, and His face too powerful for the eyes of man. God in a chariot with golden wheels and golden spokes that shone like a thousand glittering suns.

And Bart saw the Devil wrestling with a boy, and the boy was Bart. All around them the red flames leaped like horrible licking tongues. The Devil had gained the uppermost hand, for what with the fire and the face of God the boy could not see.

The Lord said, "Satan, let my servant go!" The sound of that voice was a peal of thunder. The Devil clapped his hands to his ringing ears. His proud tail shriveled between his legs. He fell into outermost darkness without a mumbling word.

The boy began to plead toward that blinding light for mercy on his soul. God in His chariot barred the way to the gates of gold. The boy pleaded, "Lord God, have mercy!" But God was stern.

Then the boy saw Jesus standing in the gates with the crown of thorns on His head, the mark of the nails in His bleeding hands and His bleeding feet, and the water and blood in a sad stream down His side. The face of Jesus was the face of a little child. Bart stretched out a humble hand, and Jesus smiled. Jesus spoke in a voice like a rippling brook. Jesus said, "Father, forgive this poor sinner. For him I done suffer and die. Forgive him as I have forgive him. Bid him enter into Thy kingdom."

God was soothed. God said gently, "Come, my son." The boy ran along beside that chariot into the kingdom of heaven.

Bart cried out in a loud voice, "Hallelujah! I been redeemed! The Lord is my savior! I been redeemed!"

The great tears sluiced down Mary's smiling face.

That was the hour that Bart got religion. From that day on, God walked beside him like a natural man.

A mournful wail cut across Bart's thinking. *Who-ee, Who-ee!* and the sound was a soul in torment. It was the *Lucy Evelyn* giving up the ghost and going to meet the mermaids of the sea. For a moment Bart brooded over this poignant fancy, then he struck his fist in the palm of his hand and muttered softly, "Great Scott! I see now, Lord."

His suppliant attitude changed to furious energy. The *Lucy Evelyn* had sunk. He had no doubt of that at all now, nor any more time or pity to waste on her. The *who-ee, who-ee,* was the whistle of a train pulling into South Station. It was also a sign from God.

He streaked through the crowded market. The cobbled streets and narrow sidewalks struck crashing cymbals of fierce activity against his seasoned ear. The rumble of wagon wheels was continuous, and drivers cursed each other as they tried to thread their huge loads and huge horses through the nearly impassable lanes. Pushcart

peddlers were everywhere, balancing their beautiful pyra-
mids of showy fruit and making a precarious way out of
the market center to the street corners of Boston. Wagon-
ers, bound for the alleyways of suburbs and housewives at
kitchen windows, beat against the incoming traffic, and
here and there a horse reared in protest.

Curb salesmen shouted their wares, their piled-up
produce blocking the sidewalks along with retail buyers
inspecting the open crates. Wholesalers stood in their
doorways watching the truckers unload their freight.
Faneuil Hall was a droning hive in and out of which
darted agile jobbers to inform the busy sellers, at their
rented stalls, of merchandise en route by train or boat
from every corner of the country and the farthest reaches
of the earth.

The scent of fruit and vegetables struck the morning
freshness from the air and substituted the headiness of
summer produce. Color overwhelmed the eye, glowing
apples, golden apricots, oranges, lemons, green avocados,
cream-yellow cantaloupes, purple plums, buttery pears,
prickletop pineapples, wine-red cherries, blush peaches,
sweet Georgia melons, dust-brown figs, the dark oblong
of dates, and the last of the season's strawberries.

Out of crates and barrels and bags and boxes poured
summer squash, asparagus, broccoli, beets, artichokes,
onions, lettuce, peas, cucumbers, peppers, potatoes, corn,
string beans, spinach, tomatoes, and limas in the more
modest livery of vegetables.

Italian faces, Greek faces, Jewish faces, and Yankee
faces swirled past Bart as he ducked a box of apples and
slid around a side of beef. He was in frantic search of
his broker. He was going to tell Pennywell to wire every

jobber in New York and Philadelphia until he got enough favorable answers for two carlots of bananas. There would be a banana shortage in Boston. He believed this with everything in him. He would corner the market and make a killing while his competitors were feverishly canvassing the concerns that had already sent him their limit.

CHAPTER 7

Cleo and Judy came out of the subway at Scollay Square and turned toward the market center. Cleo felt a sharp distaste at the surge and clangor around her that made her pause at every store front where a man might come charging out of a doorway to brush aside any women or children who stood in the path of commerce.

Here in the market was all the maleness of men. This was their world in which they moved without the command of women. The air hung heavy with their male smell and the pungent odor of their sweat. Their rolled-up sleeves showed the ripple of their hard muscles. Their thin, wet shirts outlined their iron backs. Curses ran lightly over their lips, wonderful expressive words that Cleo stored in the back of her head. As she neared them, their eyes approved and dismissed her, because they were too busy for long appraisal of anything that could not be bought and sold in the Boston Market.

Cleo, walking carefully over the cobblestones that tortured her toes in her stylish shoes, was jealous of all the free-striding life around her. She had nothing with which to match it but her wits. Her despotic nature found Mr. Judson a rival. He ruled a store and all the people in it. Her sphere was one untroublesome child, who gave insufficient scope for her tremendous vitality. She would show Mr. Judson that she could take a house and be its heart. She would show him that she could bend a houseful of human souls to her will. It had never occurred to her in the ten years of her marriage that she might be his help-mate. She thought that was the same thing as being a man's slave.

She had told Mr. Judson on the night of their marriage that she wasn't born to lick the boots of anybody living. It was dawn before she got through telling him what she would and wouldn't do, and by then it was time for him to get up and go downtown to regulate the heat in his banana rooms.

It was not a long walk to Scollay Square down Cornhill to Market Street, through an area which at some point or other touched the tortuous streets and squares which had rung to the heels of disembarked British soldiers, and had heard John Hancock read aloud to a listening world the articles of independence.

Bart's basement store was on the south side of Market Street, directly across from Faneuil Hall, in the busiest trading section of the district. Cleo looked exasperatedly at the flight of unswept stairs down which she must descend, seeing the slippery trail of peels and pulps of the morning's fast and furious unloading. She remembered the elegance of the ice-cream parlor in Springfield and the polished fruit behind plate glass. She saw herself sweeping through the high arch with a reverent friend at heel, whom she had favored with a ribbon-tied basket of beautiful fruit, and whom she now led to a center table, as a black boy dashed forward to pull out their chairs and fashionable white folks whispered across their silver dishes that the best-dressed one was the owner's wife.

As she gathered up her skirts to show her disdain of the dirty steps and guided Judy down them with exaggerated care, Cleo felt distinctly peevish. There wasn't a decent chair to sit on in the sunless rooms below, and all that fruit piled everywhere you looked made you sick of the sight of it.

The bookkeeper's small, gaslit office was just to the left of the entrance. Through the narrow glass window with its small slot for the intake of money, Cleo saw Bart talking excitedly to Miss Muldoon and Christian Christianson, his manager. They were looking rapt while he told a long-winded tale. Cleo could not bear to see him being indulged by their undivided attention.

"Mr. Judson," she called imperiously.

He jerked around, then his whole face splintered into smiles. He opened the office door and rushed forward, holding out his arms to Judy.

She flung herself into them, and he swung her up. His mustache tickled as he planted a large wet kiss on her cheek. She hugged him hard and uttered little sighs of adoration.

"Put her down," said Cleo jealously.

He set her down quickly and stretched out his hand to smooth her mussed frock. He saw his grimy palm. Judy seized his hand before he could conceal it and cuddled her cheek against his arm. He looked at Cleo guiltily, then he said gently to Judy, "Let go papa's hand. Papa's not clean enough to touch you. If I'd known my best girl was coming, I'd have washed up."

She did not release him. "You're my papa," she said loyally. "I don't care if you're dirty. I like the way you smell."

Bart squeezed his armpits against his side, and his eyes appealed to Cleo. She saw how alike he and Judy were, and this likeness, which might denote a similarity in their souls, irritated her so much that she jerked Judy to her and smoothed her so hard that it was like spanking.

"A little Boston lady doesn't discuss the way people smell," she scolded, and she glared at Mr. Judson, thinking angrily that he stank like a ram.

"Come speak to Miss Muldoon and Chris," Bart said quickly. "They see you so seldom." He lowered his voice and said urgently to Cleo, "Act nice."

He led the way into the office. Chris shooed Jinks, the rat-catcher, off a rickety chair. Bart took a fruit-stained handkerchief out of his pocket and dusted it. Presently Cleo was gingerly seated on its edge, with Judy leaning hard against her knee because Jinks was a large and formidable cat.

"It's nice to see you again, Mrs. Judson," Chris said delightedly. He was Swedish, and he felt no embarrassment in the presence of a beautiful Negro woman. He did not know that she was not his equal, and he was charmed to see a striking face so early in the day.

"It's nice to see you," said Cleo, giving him a brilliant smile. She thought his blond good looks were wasted on anything as lowly as a man. But she could not resist feeling flattered by his obvious pleasure at seeing her.

"How are you, Mrs. Judson?" Miss Muldoon said warily from her perch beside the money till. She had been Bart's bookkeeper for fifteen years. She had been middle-aged when she met him and now she was nearly old. It had never occurred to her in her wildest dreams to want to be the wife of a colored man, but she had had a vague resent-

ment when Bart married Cleo Jericho. She had felt that
any woman so young and pretty was hardly the right sort
of wife for a hard-working, sober-minded man. She preferred to picture Negro women as fat, black, and plain-
faced. It upset her when Mrs. Judson condescended to
put in her brief and radiant appearances. At such times
she felt unhappy that she helped to gild the lily.

"I'm very well, thank you," Cleo said sweetly. "I've
thought about you all summer, and hoped you were standing the heat."

She thought about Miss Muldoon summer and winter,
and never with concern about her constitution. She was
certain that Miss Muldoon was stealing Mr. Judson's
money. She could not imagine that Miss Muldoon might
not be tempted. Often it preyed on Cleo's mind that Miss
Muldoon had access to that money till, and she had not.

"Hasn't my little girl grown, Miss Muldoon?" Bart
asked proudly.

"She's a walking doll," said Miss Muldoon warmly, for
it always pleased her to see that Judy was not a beauty
like her mother.

"She's you all over, Bart," Chris said happily. Bart was
the first black man he had known in his life. After five
years he was still enchanted with him.

"We're going to live in a great big house," said Judy,
excited by all the eyes upon her, and eager to say something important.

"You got it all right?" Bart asked Cleo. "No trouble
about the rent?"

Cleo thought a moment. "It was sort of a compromise. He took the forty-five dollars, but I owe him five
dollars more. He wanted fifty the first month, and if

we're satisfactory tenants, he'll take forty-five thereafter."

Bart considered that. "Seems fair enough. No reason we shouldn't be satisfactory tenants. I guess he was thinking about children being destructive. But Judy's good as gold. Isn't as if we had a boy," he added rather regretfully.

"Cleo promised me a little boy to play with," Judy piped.

Miss Muldoon coughed agitatedly and stole a look at Cleo's figure. Chris's smile widened, for he knew how much Bart wanted a son to follow him in business.

But Bart knew better. At least he thought he did. Or did he? A wild hope began to pound in his heart. It was foolish, of course. He could count on one hand, and have fingers to spare, the number of times that Cleo had let him approach her. But perhaps that last time — though he certainly didn't see how it was possible, with Cleo's rigidity turning his blood to ice. Still, God worked in a mysterious way His wonders to perform. And out of the mouths of babes — Judy was God's messenger, bearing good tidings.

"I didn't exactly promise," Cleo corrected Judy. "I just said maybe." She looked a little flustered. She didn't want Judy to give the show away. She intended to lead Mr. Judson by degrees and duplicity.

Bart saw the betraying look of confusion. "Don't bother your mother, Judy," he said. "And don't lean against her. You're heavy." He regarded Cleo with awe and tenderness.

She was aware that Miss Muldoon and Mr. Christianson were looking at her in a special way, too. Mr. Christianson's eyes were full of gentle concern, and Miss Muldoon was staring disapprovingly at her stomach.

She gave a little gasp of horror, then her whole Rabe-laisian soul shook with silent laughter. These three poor gaping fools thought she was pregnant. Where in the world did Mr. Judson think babies came from? And what were Miss Muldoon and Mr. Christianson sticking their noses in her business for? Mr. Judson was going to have more babies than he'd bargained for, but none of them would bear him the slightest resemblance.

Suddenly Bart said, "Oh, Great Scott!" and slapped his hands together. Worry lines wrinkled his forehead. What now, thought Cleo in exasperation, wondering if he'd been doing some figuring and was going to air the disap-pointments of his private life in public.

Bart was disturbed by quite another matter. "I'm sorry now you rented that place. It'll be too much care. I wouldn't be easy here all day with you in a big house breaking your back. I got a good mind to call that man and tell him we've changed our minds."

Cleo thought of the pickings in her purse, and of her sisters, who were waiting, unknowingly, to be sent for.

"No," she said violently. "You can't bear to let money go, can you, Mr. Judson? You'd use any excuse to get forty-five miserable dollars back."

Chris flagged Bart an urgent eyebrow that asked, Oughtn't you to humor them when they're expecting? Miss Muldoon was appalled and intrigued at the prospect of a scene, and made little sounds of disaster in her throat.

"Take it easy, Cleo," Bart said soothingly. "No need to fly off the handle. You got your heart set on that house. It suits me you're satisfied. I just don't want you over-working. Tell you what." He paused. Slowly he scratched his bald spot. A great upheaval was going on inside him. "Tell you what," he repeated as if it were wrung out of him, "you could hire a girl to help you. It'd kill two birds with one stone. She could take full charge of the roomers' rooms, and help in our part of the house. If you get a young girl, you could pay her next to nothing. Or maybe a lonesome widow lady would work for room and board."

"I know the very woman," Cleo said quickly. Bart had played into her hand, and she was ready with her trump card. "She might as well be a lonesome widow. Her husband's never home. Leaves her alone night after night. She'd do the work of a dozen to be free of him for good. She's got a little girl, and I hate to think of that poor child with a father who'll never be worth any more than he is right now. She's around Judy's age. And poor little Judy told me not an hour ago how she wished she had someone to play with. That mother would go down on her knees if you gave her child shelter. You'd be snatching them both from the jaws of despair."

"Such a shame, such a shame," Miss Muldoon murmured sympathetically. She felt very sorry for colored women, and it annoyed her that she could never feel sorry for Mrs. Judson.

"Does the brute beat her?" Chris wanted to know. In the American movies that he had seen, Negro men were brutish creatures. He was glad that Mrs. Judson gave every evidence of good treatment, because he did not want to think of Bart as one of the animal Negroes.

All that was sentimental in Bart's nature responded to the unhappy woman's plight. That a man could abuse the tender beings that God had given him to cherish struck him as monstrous, and such a man deserved no better than having them torn from his bosom.

"Who is this poor woman?" he asked belligerently.

"My sister Lily," said Cleo.

Bart was astounded, and both Miss Muldoon and Chris were dismayed and embarrassed that Bart's brother-in-law was a worthless scoundrel.

"Your sister Lily!" Bart repeated in disbelief. "First I ever heard tell that her husband was mean to her."

"There are some things," said Cleo stoutly, "that I try to keep from you, so you won't worry about my family's troubles."

"Well, this'll never do," said Bart distractedly, remembering the bridal picture of Lily, looking young and small and scared beside a big man with what he now thought of as a mean expression. "I'll give you some money before you leave here, and you write that poor girl our home is hers as long as she has need of it."

"And since she's my sister, will you pay her a little something for helping me?" Cleo asked gently. "It would keep her from feeling like a poor relation. You wouldn't have to give it to her yourself. She might be bashful about taking it. It could come from me."

"Well, it won't be much, but I won't see her ragged. Just don't you worry about your sister. I don't want you worrying about anything."

"You've taken a load off my mind," Cleo said thankfully. She added, almost ashamedly, "You're a good man, Mr. Judson."

"Well, I feel good," Bart said expansively. "God's walking by my side. I was telling Miss Muldoon and Chris when you came in. My luck's running high. And that isn't a guess. I got that straight from heaven. And that isn't all I got. I got two cars of bananas coming here

bright and early tomorrow from New York and Philadelphia. I had Pennywell wiring and telephoning all
morning. I want you all to witness what I say. The *Lucy
Evelyn* has foundered. Tomorrow won't be a soul in the
Market but me got a single stem of bananas."

"I believe you, Bart," Chris said quietly. "You have a
way of knowing. God knows where you get it." He
smiled. "Unless you do get it from God." He crossed to
Bart quickly and put his arm around his shoulder. "I wish
I had your faith instead of my unbelief. You expect the
best. I expect the worst."

"I try to live right," Bart said simply. "I had my faith
tried once by God. When He destroyed my Springfield
stores. No need for Him to test me again. He knows my
faith is rock-ribbed. He's been showering blessings on me
ever since. What you think you see ahead?"

Chris leaned against the wall. He made a futile gesture
with his hands. He looked Old World and weary. "There
is a war in Europe. It is a little war. But I am a European. I know how war spreads. We have many entangling alliances. Germany will be involved and may
be at this minute. Then England will get into it. And if
America should aid her English cousin, the seas will be
unsafe for merchant shipping."

Bart thrust his hands in his pockets and rocked on his
heels. "This is July in the year of our Lord nineteen-
fourteen. I'm willing to lay you a bet that England will
never go to war. Wasn't nothing happened in those two
little queer-named countries to put her back up. And
should it happen — though I say it won't — that England
does decide to fight, it'd take a long time before America
could get worked up enough to follow suit. We're for

peace in this country. We got a peace-minded President. And no war between two little old dots on a map would last long enough in a civilized world to bring America into it."

"I won't take your bet because I want to believe you," Chris said wryly.

"And you can believe me, doubting Thomas," Bart said, with a smile. "Because I'm not claiming I got this from God. I'm just talking plain common sense."

Judy tugged at Cleo and whispered in her ear. Bart saw her and grinned. "Come on, girls. I want to show you the stock."

Cleo, returning from her hurried trip with Judy, found Bart waiting at the rear of the store. His face lighted up at sight of them. She could see that he was bursting with pride to show them the world he had made for them out of his talent for buying the best and bringing it to perfection. She had seen the store too often to be moved in any way. He had seen sixteen years in these rooms, but when he turned his key in the lock at dawn of every morning, he felt a great joy that all of this was his.

"Let's go," he said eagerly, clapping and rubbing his hands as he did when excited. In a way he was going to show his store to his son.

Cleo looked bored and bit her lip. "Judy hasn't had lunch."

He said quickly, apologetically: "I won't keep you long. And I'll give you the money to take Judy to lunch in the best restaurant in Boston." He heard the expensive echo of that in his ears. "Though there's some nice clean places right here in the Market, and she won't have to go far before she eats. I'd take you myself, but I'm due at an auction. Big shipment of grapes and onions from Spain. Be a crowd at inspection. I want to get there with the early bird."

"Don't you bid too high," she said fretfully, seeing the milling men throwing money away with the flick of a hand.

"You worry your head about woman affairs. I'll do the rest of the worrying," he said paternally.

"In other words, don't meddle with your money," she snapped.

"It's the child's money," he answered soberly, "and should God bless us with another, it's for them both. Everything I do is to secure the future. No one of mine will ever want when I'm not here to take care of them."

"Let's get going," she said impatiently, for he was talking about saving again, and she was sick of the subject.

Suddenly he swept Judy up in one arm and caught Cleo close to him with the other. His devotion to his wife and child was like an aura around them. Cleo felt her throat contract with a strange compassion, and she could not bear the emotion that made her see his singleness of heart. She tore herself away from him lest she reveal her understanding and return his tenderness.

"You show Judy the store," she said shakily. "I'll go ask Miss Muldoon for a piece of paper to write to Lily. The quicker she gets word from me, the quicker she'll take heart."

She turned and fled from his love.

The horn of plenty had poured its harvest into every available foot of space in the store. Three of the four big rooms ran over with produce, and the fourth would be filled with Jamaican bananas when the freight cars rolled

into the yards the next morning. From the ceiling in the
banana room depended a thousand hooks from which
swung the knotted ropes that held the heavy stems. The
long middle section of the store, off which these storage
and ripening rooms opened, was piled high with crates
and barrels and boxes ready for shipment to various cities
in New England and Canada.

The murmurs and movements of the six Greek helpers
were continuous. Three of them were year-round helpers,
the three others were hired when the earth's yield was
richest and the daily turnover was tremendous. They
respected the black man who was their exacting boss because he could do any one of their tasks, from making a
crate to sizing fruit for the count, with more speed and
efficiency than any one of them. As Bart and Judy walked
past them, they lifted their peasant faces. They had the
same look of earth and toil as Bart.

In the office Cleo wrote busily, while Chris checked
accounts with Miss Muldoon in a low voice so that he
would not disturb her. Every once in a while Cleo raised
her head to peep at them suspiciously, but she never
caught either one of them toying with the till.

She signed her scrawl to Lily and read it.

Dear Lily,
I will not write a long letter. There is nothing to say
but to beg you to come as soon as you can get yourself
and Victoria together. I am enclosing your fare, so there
won't be any holdup while Victor hems and haws. I know
how you hate to travel, so you know I would not send
for you if I could straighten things out without your help.
I am moving to a new address. Things will be brighter
there. It will seem like a different life. Mr. Judson didn't
want me to go, but I couldn't stand it any longer. Write

at once to my old address what day to expect you, and
I will meet your train.

Hastily,
CLEO

She smiled with satisfaction. Lily would think she was
leaving Mr. Judson. Since Lily, along with poor mis-
guided Serena and Charity, was such a firm believer in
the bonds of matrimony, she would brave the iron mon-
ster to shepherd her sister back into the marriage fold.

This speculation produced a natural sequel in Cleo's
wily mind. She released a quiet chuckle, then touched
the tip of her pencil with her tongue and began to
scribble furiously on a second sheet of paper. Things got
done if you did them without thinking. If you thought,
your scruples stopped you. It was always better to do
today what your conscience might not let you do tomorrow.

Dear Charity [her pencil scratched hurriedly]
Lily is coming to see me. I guess she's written you
time and again how she hates to travel. So it must be a
serious matter to get her on a train. It is my guess she's
planning to stay. She's been eight years making up her
mind to make the trip to Boston. It will take a power of
persuasion to get her back to New York. That is where
you come in. We sisters don't turn our backs on each
other in time of trouble. I'm enclosing fare for you and
Penny. As soon as I get my hands on more money, I'm
sending for Serena. Don't try to write Lily. Victor might
get hold of the letter and make it hard for her. Tell Ben
not to expect you until we've straightened Lily out and
sent her back to her husband. Write me by return mail
what day you can come, and I will meet your train.

Hastily,
CLEO

She inserted her composition in one of Bart's envelopes, leaving it unsealed until she could include a money order. If Mr. Judson was giving her Lily's train fare, she had the means for Charity's.

She heard Bart and Judy approaching and thrust the second letter in her purse. As they entered, she held up her letter to Lily.

"It's finished. I left it open so I could put in the money."

Bart nodded approval, then turned to Miss Muldoon. "How much cash can we spare?"

She opened the till. "How much do you want?"

He calculated rapidly. "Five dollars for that landlord, about fifty dollars to send my wife's sister. Don't want her and the child coming here naked. And five dollars for Cleo to fritter away." He turned to her. "Does that fit the bill?"

"Yes," she said faintly. She was piling up a surplus at such a rapid rate that even she could not ask for more.

"And we'll see about furniture whatever day you feel like shopping for it. And, oh, Miss Muldoon, better add another five dollars. And, Cleo, I want you to go by the doctor's before you go home."

Miss Muldoon counted out sixty-five dollars, with Cleo watching carefully to see if she palmed a bill.

"You'd better send Lily a money order," Bart advised. "I wouldn't put too much cash in a letter."

"Neither would I," said Cleo.

She rose to go. Bart walked with her and Judy to the sidewalk.

He suddenly remembered something. "Was there anything special you came for? Anything you want?"

"I came to ask you for some money," she said truthfully. The bank roll that Bart had had last night had worried her all morning. It had been her plan to shame him into parting with some more of it to avert a family spat before Miss Muldoon and Chris. "I sort of wanted to go to a sale," she explained, with a show of diffidence. "But after all you're doing for Lily, I wouldn't be telling you if you hadn't asked me."

"Never mind about what I'm doing for Lily. You know I don't want you or the child to go without as long as I'm able to see that you don't. You know it's my pride to be a good provider." He dug in his pocket and produced some crumpled bills. "I paid a big bill this morning, but I'll give you all I've got. This ought to buy some sensible thing you see."

She stuffed the money in her plump purse and smiled up at the bright blue sky. "It's one beautiful day," she said peacefully.

She caught Judy's hand and walked away, and it seemed to her that behind her walked all the Jerichos, following her lead.

CHAPTER 8

A<small>T TWO O'CLOCK</small>, Cleo climbed the stairs of a fine old brownstone dwelling. Judy wearily plodded after her, taking the steep steps one at a time and wanting sympathy for her bruised shank. A ribbon had come untied and dangled dismally down her back. A brown begrimed knee emerged from a hole in her stocking. The patent-leather toes of her buttoned shoes were badly scuffed, and a button had wrenched off one cloth upper in the disgraceful fall that followed her race with Cleo to a closing elevator door.

Cleo stood on the top stair and eyed her daughter with disapproval. She hoped that Judy was not going to be a careless dresser when she grew up. Judy returned her frosty stare with a look of such solemn reproach that Cleo blushed a little and gave her a guilty smile. There were times when she was thoroughly disconcerted by the fact that her child was a separate being with independent emotions. To her a child was a projection of its mother, like an arm which functioned in unison with other component parts and had no will that was not controlled by the head of the woman who owned it.

Judy took advantage of Cleo's small shame and let her lower lip quiver. Her midday meal had been a gulped

glass of milk and a ham sandwich swallowed in half-
chewed lumps, with Cleo urging her to haste and talking
her out of her soft request for ice cream.

"I'll telephone your father to bring home a pint of
vanilla for you to eat all by yourself," Cleo promised,
though she knew that was not the same thing as spooning
a vanilla sundae from a silver dish at a downtown drugstore.

Judy gave a delicate sniff which was meant to convey
that she was receptive to this suggestion but not reconciled. She stood quietly while Cleo shifted her packages
and dug for her doorkey. In Cleo's packages were evening slippers and an evening dress for Thea, who was more
in need of a daytime dress and street shoes. And most in
need of her overdue wages. Cleo had meant to reserve
some money for Serena, but the saleslady had influenced
her choices, and she could not resist her flattering assumption that money was no object. As usual, she had had to
count her pennies to pay her trolley fare.

As she opened the door and butted Judy inside, she
heard her landlady's "Psst!" from the parlor. Miss Johnson came toward her, feeling her way among the Victorian
furniture that she had inherited, along with the house, at
the death of the mistress she had served so faithfully.

It was this bizarre bequest, made in consideration of
Miss Johnson's failing sight and her forty-year familiarity
with every inch of the house, that had started the exodus
of well-to-do whites from this particular street. At the
time of this mass removal, there was a scattering of Negro
householders on neighboring streets. But they were
moneyed people whose progeny went to white Sunday
schools and played decorously in next-door yards while

they were still young enough to come under the general heading of children. Miss Johnson was a lady's maid, and therefore an undistinguished Negro who deserved no more special consideration than a white servant who happened to be left a house. As the tone of a street is considerably lowered when mistress and maid live side by side, the high visibility of a Negro maid, added to this, plunged its desirability to zero.

"You want to see me, Miss Johnson?" asked Cleo, meeting her midway the room. She stared with pity and revulsion at the wrinkled monkey face, the dim eyes behind the gold-rimmed spectacles, and the mottled hands that were like burnt matchsticks. Her own hand tightened on Judy's for the young feel of it. She was frightened in the presence of old people. She did not like to face the fact that some day she must surrender the reins of power to someone whose strength was as hers was now.

"I wanted to see you on a matter of my discretion," Miss Johnson said, in the careful manner of speaking that had been part of her since she had come by Underground to Boston with an untutored tongue which had acquired the accent and intonation of her mistress.

"Oh?" said Cleo politely, wondering what on earth this poor old sinner was talking about.

"It's Miss Binney," explained Miss Johnson. "She came while you were out, and seemed very anxious to wait until you returned. I thought you wouldn't mind if I let her go up to your rooms."

"That was all right," said Cleo hurriedly, for now she was reminded that she had rented a house and was leaving on short notice. She might as well break the news to Miss Johnson while she had the chance to escape to a waiting visitor.

"Oh, by the way, Miss Johnson," she began, "my husband surprised me to death last night by telling me we're moving. He heard about a house yesterday and rushed right out to rent it before anyone else. I went to look at it this morning. It's in Brookline, and, of course, we're very fortunate. But I've spent some very pleasant years in this house, and I'm leaving reluctantly. The thing is, day before yesterday I got a letter from a sister of mine, saying she was coming to Boston to put her child in a Boston school. I told my husband, and I guess he thought it would be nice for us to be together, since she's a widow. So yesterday he got this house. I'm sure you're not sorry. One child walking over your head is enough."

"I love children," Miss Johnson said quietly. "I like the noise their little feet make. When you lose your eyes, you lean on your ears."

Judy wriggled her hand free and went to stand before Miss Johnson, lifting her small serious face. "I'll miss you," she said gently, and laced the gnarled fingers in her own.

Cleo wanted to snatch her child away from this childless woman who stood among the Victorian relics of her meaningless life, and had no hope of anything but heaven. "Judy, Miss Binney's waiting," she said coldly. Then she was sharply aware that in all her years in this house she had never sat down in Miss Johnson's parlor. It had never occurred to her to do so. Miss Johnson knew no one that she knew. In consequence she had never thought that Miss Johnson herself was anyone to know.

"Life moves so fast nowadays," Cleo murmured, "it hardly gives you time to call your soul your own. When I do get a minute to myself, I'm a real bookworm."

"That's when Judy comes to see me," Miss Johnson said, with a soft sly smile. "We sit together by the window, and we talk about everything that enters our minds. Children have time for old folks, and old folks have time for children."

"When I'm big enough to ride on the trolley by myself, I'll come back and visit you," Judy promised fervently.

"But, of course, I'll bring her back long before that," Cleo said, with charming insincerity. She fixed her child with a meaningful eye. "Come, Judy."

All the way upstairs Cleo felt surprised that Judy met on common ground with Old Lady Johnson. She could not imagine what a five-year-old could have to say that would be interesting for more than five minutes. And certainly nothing ever happened in Miss Johnson's monotonous life that could entertain even a drooling infant. She gave a little start of horror. Surely Miss Johnson wouldn't be fool enough to tell a little Yankee girl a lot of foolishness about way back in slavery time. Slavery was too hard a thing to tell a child.

There was time enough for Judy to know that the North and the South were not indivisible, with liberty and justice for all. Let her learn to hold her head up first. Let her learn to walk proud like the Jericho women who had died before her. Like Great-aunt Fanny who hung herself in the hay loft where her master left her running blood after he gave her her first whipping for stepping on the tail of his valuable hunting hound. She was her master's whelp, too, but she wouldn't take a whipping just because she was a mongrel. And Great-grandmother Patsy — the time Old Missus scolded her for burning biscuits, the only time she ever burned an old pan of bread in forty years of baking, Great-grandmother Patsy walked out of that kitchen and down to the river. When they fished her out by her long black hair, her soul had got free and she didn't have to listen to anybody's lip forever after.

The old-time Jericho women lived proud as long as they could. When they couldn't live proud, they preferred to die. Not one of them was born to take anybody's lip or anybody's lash. When Judy was ready to know about slavery, these were the tales to tell her.

CHAPTER 9

Miss Althea Binney sat in Cleo's small parlor, biting her lower lip. She was doing this to keep her control. She was very close to crying. And she was unaccustomed to showing her emotions, even when there was no one to see.

Thea was Cleo's model of perfection. She had been a day pupil at private school, and later a boarding student at a select academy, an institution which had taken her natural airs and graces and cast them in the same impeccable mold that produced the young ladies who were to take their inherited places behind the tea-tables of Boston. These young ladies were now the young wives of wealthy businessmen with old if not illustrious names. They lived on fashionable streets and were served by butlers who were, as often as not, old friends of Thea's father.

Sometimes Thea was asked to tea on a quiet day. She generally accepted, because she did not want her hostess to feel that she was in the least offended at her exclusion from a larger function. Nor was she, knowing that she would not invite her white friends to a large affair of her own, although her reasons for not doing so would have been entirely different from theirs.

There was never any problem when Thea was passed

a plate of cake by a silver-haired butler who had known her from babyhood. She saw only the servant's garb and knew that the man inside it would resent being spoken to with the same familiarity with which she would have spoken in his house or hers.

Thea's father had been the awe-inspiring owner of a tailoring establishment in a downtown shopping center. His rent had been several thousand dollars a year, and his income had been triple that figure. His daughter and his son at Harvard had had the best of everything. Then the readymade suit grew in favor, and a well-dressed man was not ashamed of his appearance when he wore one. Where Mr. Binney's store had once stood, a great department store soared seven stories and sold readymades at a price that would have sent Mr. Binney spinning into bankruptcy sooner than he did.

Mr. Binney, forced to vacate his premises, had moved across the street to continue his business, against the advice of his lawyer, who was of the opinion that he should sell out while his chances of breaking even were good. But Mr. Binney couldn't believe that a man above a laborer's station would wear a readymade suit on Sunday. When his business failed and his creditors were appeased, his assets were a splendid servantless house in Cambridge with magnificent furnishings, a neglected property in the South End, his insurance, and his late wife's jewels. His liabilities were a lovely daughter who was betrothed to a poor man, and a son engaged in the highly unprofitable venture of publishing a newspaper for Boston Negroes, who disliked being singled out for special attention.

All day Mr. Binney smoked Havana cigars and drank

Scotch whiskey like a disillusioned gentleman in the disordered library of his Cambridge house which his helpless daughter could not keep clean. He sat sunk deep in his upholstered chair with his chin gently rubbing his diamond stickpin and plotted ways to beat the roulette wheel and regain his fortune. At night he tried out his systems with a spectacular lack of success.

Thea gave Judy lessons because it was a genteel way to keep herself in gloves and shoes while she waited for her fiancé to complete his interneship and establish a practice. Her young man was not handsome, but he did not have to be. Thea's complexion was peaches and cream, and her chestnut hair was soft as silk. She could have married any man short of a Zulu, and still have had children who passed the test of hair and color.

"Thea!" cried Cleo, rushing into the parlor and dropping her packages into a chair. "What a nice surprise! Or did you forget you don't come to Judy today? Let me fix you a bite. I got the house!"

"Good afternoon, Miss Binney," said Judy.

"Good afternoon, Judith," Thea said. "You've hurt your knee. I'm so sorry."

"I'll fix her up as soon as I catch my breath," Cleo said quickly. "Judy, don't you want to run and play by yourself? Why don't you go and tell your dolls what you did this afternoon?"

"I don't talk to dolls," said Judy with dignity. "I'm big."

"Are you big enough to take your own bath?" asked Cleo sweetly.

"Of course," said Judy, with a wonderful vision of herself splashing water as much as she liked.

"Then run and take it, and put on the blue dress your father likes, and I'll tell him to take you to the drugstore after dinner. Scrub everything good. Don't splash. And pin up your braids."

The child trotted out. Cleo shut the door quietly and carefully, then turned to Thea. She was radiant. "I've got something to show you," she said happily.

Thea gave her a tremulous smile. "Can it wait, Cleo? I must talk to you. I need your help. You're the only friend I have who won't be too shocked to advise me." She drew a long, shuddering breath. "Father's dying."

Quickly Cleo crossed to her and took her hand. "The doctor may be wrong," she said urgently.

Thea shook her head. "Father's been drinking heavily for five years. Ever since his failure. He had a stroke this morning. He's in a coma, and the doctor doesn't expect him to rouse. It's only a matter of hours. I'm glad. I don't want him to talk to Simeon. He talked to me just before he collapsed. I came to you as soon as Simeon could leave the office and take my place at Father's bedside." Her voice shook with horror. "Father's dying, Cleo, and everything he has, his property deeds, his insurance, and mother's jewels, are all in the hands of a West End woman."

Cleo drew a chair close to Thea's. "His mistress?" she asked quietly.

"I don't know," said Thea wearily. "That doesn't matter. Last night she asked Father to marry her. He told her he wouldn't disgrace his name. She gave him until today to change his mind. And I think it was knowing he must that caused his stroke. His mouth began to twist while he was telling me."

"Who is this devil of a woman?" asked Cleo impatiently.

"All of the old Bostonians know her," said Thea, with no awareness of her small snub, "but her name is never mentioned. The men who go to her gambling place call her The Duchess."

"Oh," said Cleo, for the pieces were beginning to fall into place. "I see now. Your father lost everything at her place, and she told him she'd give it back on condition. And your father thought he was too good for her, and preferred to die. Go to her now and tell her your father's life depends on her. If she loves him, she'll return everything, if that will keep him alive."

"She hates him," said Thea stilly.

Cleo wanted to shake her. "Thea, talk sense. How could she hate him and want to marry him?"

"To settle a very old score. And now it cannot be settled through Father. And she will take the lesser revenge of depriving Simeon and me of our inheritance. I don't care for myself. I care for Simeon. The paper means everything to him. I don't understand why it's so important. I'm not sure I even approve." She paused, and her candor forced her to add: "You must keep it out of Judith's way. She is learning to read very well. But I believe in Simeon. And he believes in his paper. I cannot bear to see him fail." She could not control her tears any longer.

Cleo got up and walked restlessly around the room. She looked at Thea and felt pity and impatience that Thea looked so confoundedly helpless. It would be like sending a lamb to slaughter to expect her to hold her own with a vulgar creature in a gambling dive. She didn't care a fig about Simeon's paper. Let him go get a job.

But Thea should have her mother's jewels. The thought of that West End woman with Thea's jewels on her thick ugly neck filled Cleo with loathing.

She stopped her tramp around the room. "Thea," she said sharply, "have you got any change?"

Thea said dully, "I suppose so."

Cleo picked up the shabby purse and took out a quarter. "Where does this Duchess live?"

"On Dover Street. I don't know the number."

"I'll find it," Cleo said briefly.

Thea lifted her wet eyes. "What are you going to do?"

"Go there," said Cleo calmly, "and scare the bejesus out of her. I'll threaten to call the police and expose her. I'll make her wish she'd never been born. I've got a tongue that can cut like a knife when I'm mad. I won't come away empty-handed. I'll have her heart or your inheritance." Her face softened. "You go home. I'll telephone you as soon as I leave there."

Thea rose and said brokenly, "Oh, Cleo, she has to listen for Simeon's sake. I'll be praying until I hear from you."

The devil with Simeon, Cleo thought briskly. "Just don't worry about anything," she said gently. "And while you're praying, pray for yourself."

Thea left, and Cleo hid her packages so that Mr. Judson wouldn't start asking a lot of prying questions. It hadn't seemed quite the occasion to give Thea dancing slippers. Then she went down the hall and into the bathroom where Judy was standing on the bath mat, vigorously drying herself.

"Aren't you a big smart girl," Cleo said admiringly.

Judy flashed her a sidelong glance. She had had her quota of fulsome praise.

"I have to run out for a while," Cleo said companionably. "Don't go down and bother Miss Johnson. You can amuse yourself until I get back. If you take a nice nap, I'll take you to the pictures tomorrow. And if your father comes, tell him I went on an errand of mercy. Let me hear you say it."

"Cleo went on an errand of mercy," Judy repeated dutifully.

"That's right. And don't tell him anything else. Just tell him I had to leave you to go on an errand of mercy."

"What's an errand of mercy?" Judy asked shyly.

"It's none of your business," said Cleo.

CHAPTER 10

Cleo read the guiding sign above a tippler's head and
turned down the street she sought. Here were no amiable
loafers. Here were the sullen and shifty-eyed, the deni-
zens of the dark. These were the dregs, the men without
women, the women without men. These were the haters
who thought they were beaten because they were black.
There were no children here. Sometimes a wizened, rat-
faced gnome in the shape of a child hugged the shadows
of a stoop, from which he would never emerge to walk
in the sun. Here were the hunted, the thieves and killers,
the nameless, the faceless. These were the blood brothers
of all men everywhere who are born without race pride.

The men and women looked at Cleo with hate. They
did not want her to walk with her head erect. For a black
is a black, their thoughts ran, and as no-account as the
next.

They stood silent. They stood motionless, and the sick
smoldering went on inside them because here was one of
their own who would disown them. The minds of the men
shouted whore as she passed, because they knew she was
not. The women's thoughts hurled Miss White Lady at
her because they could not bear to admit she could walk
with dignity and still be colored.

Cleo knew she had better not ask anybody anything. The thing to do was to keep on going down this ruined street of rotting frame houses until she found one with some distinguishing mark, a clean curtain or a swept walk, that would set it apart from the others.

In the middle of the block she saw it. A two-storied, flat-roofed, snow-white house, with open green shutters and sparkling windows. She pulled at the doorbell and heard its muted tinkle. In a moment or so the door opened. A round-faced, gray-haired colored maid stared at her without expression.

Cleo felt a quick resentment that this sporting woman could flaunt a maid. Like enough the maid had had to teach the mistress manners.

She said coldly, "Will you tell your madam that a lady" — the word was underlined — "wishes to see her? It's a very urgent matter."

The woman hesitated, then stepped aside to let her enter. "Will you wait here, please?" She left Cleo in the long reception hall and started up the stairs.

Again Cleo had a moment of wonder that this West End Duchess had found a colored woman willing to work for her. Cleo's friends who could afford maids had never been able to get colored help. The experienced domestics from the South could not be induced to work for people of color, feeling a natural embarrassment at the scorn to be found in their own stratum that they would use the back doors of a social group who could not use the front doors of their former employers.

In the employ of this upper colored class were the "green girls," the young, untutored immigrant girls who held their jobs until their more sophisticated countrymen explained the insurmountable distinction between a man who looked white and a man who was white.

There were only twenty-odd colored families who counted themselves the élite. Since most of that number could not afford maids, there was not really a servant problem.

While she waited impatiently, Cleo became aware of the graceful Chippendale pieces in the hall and the darkly glowing mahogany in the long parlor and dining room beyond. A magnificent grand piano engulfed a corner of the parlor. Cleo yearned to own it. She had been working on Bart a year to buy Judy an upright. All nice children started piano lessons at five. She sighed. For a moment she pictured this beautiful furniture in the high-ceilinged rooms of her new house. She knew that their cost was far beyond anything Bart would consider paying for tables and chairs to eat at and sit in, which depreciated in value the more you ate and sat.

The maid returned. "Will you follow me, please."

They reached the upper hall. The maid murmured, "The lady." Cleo crossed the threshold of a charming morning room.

A woman rose from behind a tea-table set with exquisitely patterned china and surveyed Cleo quietly, with a still, unrevealing smile. She was ash-blond. Her imperial eyes were blue. Cleo was thoroughly disconcerted, for she was unprepared for the dignity of the West End Duchess. She had come for a fishwives' brawl, and the woman before her was patrician. There was breeding in every fragile bone.

"Won't you sit down?" the Duchess said.

Cleo sat down dumbly, though she had meant to stand,

as befitting her position as a man's wife when faced with
a sporting woman. But despite herself, she was impressed
by this woman's superior status.

The Duchess appraised her. "I don't think we've ever
met."

Cleo braced herself for the next observation, the common knowledge of Negroes forewarning her that the
Duchess would make some casual mention of her servants,
with the subtle intention of reminding Cleo that all
colored people were in the same category.

Cleo said lightly, "You are not entirely a stranger to
me. My cook has mentioned you often, but, of course,
she may know you only by reputation."

The imperial eyes were veiled. The delicate chin lifted
a little. "I cannot believe that you have come to exchange
backstairs gossip. May I ask you who you are and why
you are here?"

Cleo could feel herself getting mad. Did this outcast
from her own kind consider herself too good to waste her
expensive time on a colored woman? Still she could not
unleash the hot words that would reduce her to a level
beneath the dignity of this Duchess.

"I'm Mrs. Bart Judson. I've come on behalf of Miss
Althea Binney. Her father is dying."

The Duchess said quietly, almost reprovingly, "You
cannot mean that. I am seeing him tonight."

"Not after the stroke he had this morning. He'll never
live to see daybreak. You might as well make up your
mind you've seen him for the last time."

The Duchess said witheringly: "Since Althea could not
face me with such a grisly fabrication, I am sure she must
admire the boldness which enables you to do so. You may

tell Carter Binney that I would have more respect for him if he had chosen a less unscrupulous way to send word that he is dead to me."

"It was God's way," said Cleo furiously. "God's way of punishing that old fool for getting mixed up with your kind of trash. I never told a lie in my life, and I wouldn't perjure myself for you. When they put Carter Binney in the ground, you go tell the police he was buried alive, and see how long it takes them to cart you off to the booby hatch."

There was a pause, and Cleo's angry breathing filled it. Her green eyes blazed. After a little the Duchess said painfully, "I believe you now. It is God's way of punishing me for wanting Carter Binney."

Cleo lost complete control of her temper. She jumped to her feet and flung herself into that bitter, unending, secret war between white and colored women.

"Don't fool yourself!" she shouted. "God's forgotten you're on earth. It's the Devil who's licking his lips over you. And you've been a good disciple. I know why you hated Carter Binney. You couldn't stay out of bed with him, and you hated him instead of yourself. Well, you've got him lying at death's door with not a penny to bury him, and not a penny to leave behind. There's no more damage you can do. Get out of my race and stay out."

The Duchess said, out of her suffering, "It is my race, too."

Cleo's mouth fell open. She said, in a soft, incredulous voice, "God have mercy, you're not all white?"

"My mother was colored."

Cleo sank back on her chair, and wished for her fan. "It wasn't your skin and hair that fooled me. We come

every color under the sun. But the way you carry yourself, I thought you were born on Beacon Hill."

The Duchess said, without expression, "My father was."

Cleo thought of Thea, who had come to her for help,
Thea with the tear stains on her pretty face. And Thea's
image paled a little. Nothing tremendous had ever happened to Thea except her father's taking a fit because a
born lady wanted to marry him. All of Cleo's zest for life,
her insatiable love of conspiracy were roused to search
behind the imperial eyes.

"If I had known you were colored, I wouldn't have hit
you from so many sides. If I had known you were such
a lady, I wouldn't have come for a fight at all. I never
heard of you until an hour ago, and all I heard was one
side of the story. There has to be another side. And you
have a right to tell me yours."

Her eyes were gray again, and very gentle. Her voice
was tender and persuasive. The Duchess felt her warm
sympathy, and was drawn to it. And Cleo's sympathy was
real. In this moment she wanted nothing more than to
know about this lovely woman. Her whole intensity was
directed to that end. The power of her personality was
like a tongue of fire that ignored locked doors and penetrated whatever reticences might stand in the way of her
passion to probe the lives of other women and tell them
how to live them.

"May I give you tea?" the Duchess asked.

Cleo smiled radiantly. "I'd love a cup of tea while we
talk."

The Duchess poured. This was her first tea party. She
found a thin amusement in the fact that she was pouring
for Mrs. Bart Judson. She knew of Bart Judson and his

wholesale business. She had never invited him to her gaming tables because he had nothing she wanted. She did not want money. The men who lost at her roulette wheel were the husbands of the women she wanted around her tea-table.

They were the women whose impregnable positions had been established by Boston birth and genteel breeding. They acknowledged no more than a hundred best families in Boston, New York, Philadelphia, and Washington. Their lives were narrowly confined to a daily desperate effort to ignore their racial heritage. They did not consider themselves a minority group. The Irish were a minority group, the Jews, the Italians, the Greeks, who were barred from belonging by old country memories, accents, and mores. These gentlewomen felt that they had nothing in common except a facial resemblance. Though they scorned the Jew, they were secretly pleased when they could pass for one. Though they were contemptuous of the Latins, they were proud when they looked European. They were not too dismayed by a darkish skin if it was counterbalanced by a straight nose and straight hair that established an Indian origin. There was nothing that disturbed them more than knowing that no one would take them for anything but colored.

It was a bitter truth, to be discussed only in special groups, that a sporting woman in the West End was, by these standards, the most beautiful colored woman in Boston.

The Duchess passed Cleo a cup of tea. Cleo sipped it with her little finger crooked carefully. She wondered what Mr. Judson would say if he could see her sipping tea with the Duchess. It wouldn't make a bit of difference to him that she carried herself like a lady. She had passed money across a green table. She had entertained married men. Mr. Judson believed there were good women and bad women and no in-between. That was what made it so easy to pull the wool over his eyes.

Cleo put her cup down and assumed an attentive expression. It was getting on to four. In an hour Mr. Judson would be starting home for supper. Men were nothing but stomach and the other thing. It would be a happy day for women if both could be cut out.

"Tell me about yourself," said Cleo richly.

The imperial eyes widened and darkened. The Spode cups cooled. The Duchess gave a little sigh and began her story.

"Althea Binney's mother and mine were foster sisters. My grandfather married her grandmother. Their marriage gave back their children the parents they had lost. Grandfather was butler for a Beacon Hill bachelor, who had never married because the only women to whom he would have given his name bored him in every way.

"Grandfather died in his employ. And this man, Thad Tewksbury, came to the funeral and saw my mother for the first time. To him she looked exotic. Her mother had been Irish."

Cleo remembered a tintype that she had seen in Thea's album, a regal brown man, an austere-faced woman stiffly corseted, and two little girls with their arms entwined, one as lovely as dawn. That lovely child had had a white mother, an Irish maid who had married a colored butler. And she, this immigrant Irisher, had obligingly died at her daughter's birth, thus removing herself from the circle of the colored élite, in which her peasant background would have been embarrassing. No one Cleo knew in the

North admitted to having a white relation of the lower classes. When such a bride was chosen, it was considered very poor taste to discuss her humble origins. Her marriage had elevated her to her husband's higher station. White antecedence was only exploited when the daughter of bluebloods eloped with her coachman.

The Duchess said: "Thad made my mother his mistress. He defiled her the day he sent his carriage to fetch her to his house. The coachman said it was some matter concerning her continuing in Normal School. With her father dead, her stepmother could not support her while she finished her teacher's training. Her stepmother helped her dress in her best to go to see Thad Tewksbury. They thought it was important that she impress him with her neat appearance.

"My mother never reached the house on Beacon Hill. She was driven here. Thad was waiting. He showed her this house, and said he had bought it with the intention of giving it to her father, whom he had planned to retire because of his failing health. My mother was too ignorant of the world to know that no one would furnish a house in such style for a servant. She supposed that Thad knew no better than to buy the best. He gave my mother the deed to this house. He gave her a bank book. And she wept with gratitude. For one hour of her life she loved him: the hour they sat and talked during dinner. For a caterer came, and they celebrated his investment in her teaching career. My mother had never touched wine in her life, but she did not want to offend Thad by refusing the champagne he had ordered especially for her. And after the first glass, she never knew how many times it was refilled.

"When she waked, it was morning. The clothes she had

worn were nowhere. She opened a closet door and found
a dozen expensive costumes. But she knew she could not
go home in them. She could not go home at all. Her stepmother would never believe that she had been innocent
of Thad's intentions. She was a fallen woman. She looked
at herself in the mirror, and saw her sin in her face, and
did not know it was mostly the after-effect of champagne.
She was too ashamed to walk out of this house, and sat
and waited in a fine gown for Thad to come and tell her
what to do."

Through the first years of Thad's fantastic indulgence,
and forever after, Corinne never stopped regretting her
acquiescence, or feeling self-pity. To the listening child
in the fine French frocks her mother's nostalgic stories of
the stern simplicity of her prim upbringing became the
pattern of all her thinking.

At six the silver-haired child began to pray God to turn
her a color that would make her unmistakably a member
of her mother's race. The servants were her only contact
with her kind. They were resentful that she and Corinne,
without lifting a finger, lived in a luxury they could never
hope to attain, no matter how long they labored in God's
vineyard. They showed their resentment in their manner,
which was just a shade under scorn, and were deliberately
indifferent to the child, never stopping to listen to her
prattle, never permitting her to play around them, speaking sharply whenever she strayed across the threshold of
their privacy.

Her nurse was a pious old Frenchwoman, who loved
her because she was a small innocent, and had forgotten
that a child of sin should be treated as if that child had
committed it. It was a natural thing for the child to love
her in return. Seeing this, Corinne, her pride in her past

increasing as the years made her return to it more remote
than the moon, taught her daughter to dismiss the servants' churlishness as envy of her class superiority. The
child dreamed of her mother's world of remembering as a
paradise which some day she might enter.

Corinne's New England conscience deplored the life
that she had grown too indolent to leave. She did not
want her daughter to grow up with the belief that a
wealthy white protector was worth a colored woman's
loss of caste. For there was no city to which a notorious
woman of color could escape where her reputation would
not follow her. The special Negro groups were too small
and too interlocked by marriage and old friendships for
an aspirant to seek to disclaim her past.

As the years advanced, and passion slaked in Thad, the
habit of Corinne's hearth grew stronger in him. He
wanted to be with her, for she was his wife, in the way
that a woman's complete dependency makes a man
cherish her in spite of himself. She was not amusing. She
sat too quietly with her interminable tatting, and her
little sad smile, and her velvet eyes with their veiled reproach. He could not stay away. Yet the dull evenings
were unendurable, with Corinne occasionally consenting
to a game of checkers, which she played with an exas-
perating lack of skill.

So it was that Thad got in the way of bringing in a
friend or two to while away the night with cards. Other
friends pressed him for invitations. To them it seemed
an enormous adventure to see the inside of a colored con-
cubine's house, and watch her walk among them with her
sadness and disdain and her little gold box, in which she
deposited her share of this new sin with imperceptible
cleansing of the fingertips.

CHAPTER 11

T HE DUCHESS'S EYES MET CLEO'S. She gave a little wavering smile and said: "I was sent to a convent in Canada when I was eight. This house was virtually a gambling house, and my mother wanted me out of it. I lived under the simplest and strictest régime in the convent. The prim little girls in their plain dark frocks, the gentle Sisters, the beauty and mystery of the Mass, and never any men except the priests in their covering cassocks. I could not bear the thought of leaving. I began to prepare myself to take the vows."

For a moment Cleo felt a shock along her spine. In this dishonored setting, so far removed from a celibate's cell, sat a woman of the world, whose pale gold hair was unshorn and unhidden, whose Paris gown was hardly suggestive of sackcloth, whose hands nightly counted paper money that had neither the feel nor the yield of told beads. Yet Cleo, who had not been able to see the Duchess as anything less, was incapable of belittling her piety, too. Her earnestness outreached derision. Her spirit disavowed her flesh. Cleo, who felt that she understood women, could not find the niche in which to fit her, or could not reach high enough above her comprehension.

"I wrote my mother of my intention," the Duchess was

saying. "She had not been raised a Catholic because her
stepmother had considered the Pope a foreigner. My
letter was never answered. Instead, the Mother Superior
received a telegram instructing her to send me home at
once. I thought my mother wanted to plead with me to
remain in the world. And all the way home I went over in
my mind how I would plead with her to be reconciled
to my leaving it.

"But I had not been sent for because of my letter. I'm
sure my mother dismissed it as a young girl's daydream.
She was dying, and the one thing she wanted had become
an obsession that made everything else seem frivolous.
She wanted to die in the world in which her father's name
had been a proud one. My marriage to someone securely
inside it would sanction her reacceptance. Thad Tewksbury had been dead six months. He had left her considerable money. But this house was still open to his
friends. That was one of the things that aggravated her
illness. Her doctor had ordered a complete rest in bed.
But my mother believed that the more she could add to
my dowry, the easier it would be to buy Cole Hartnett
for me."

Cleo gave a little gasp. Cole was Thea's fiancé. He
was poor, but as a Hartnett he belonged to a family even
older than the Binneys. The Hartnetts had been freemen
for five generations, and no one of them in those hundred years had been born or schooled outside of Boston.

The first Hartnett had been a coachman, the second
had had his own hack for hire, the third had owned two
and money enough to pay a man to drive one of them,
and the fourth, Cole's father, had operated a livery stable
covering half a city block. There the rich had rented

sleek riding horses, and boarded their splendid thorough-
breds, and kept their magnificent carriages, and lounged
in the perfectly appointed waiting room with ebony un-
derlings to jump to orders. There was even an unhallowed
place for some of the city's workhorses, though these lum-
bering beasts used a back door and never nosed their
betters.

The senior Hartnetts and son were able to live like
lords. They did not save. For were not horses the delight
of kings, and what could supplant them in the hearts of
civilized men? The automobile, the dirty sputtering automobile. The rich, who should have had more taste, began
to buy them. Mr. Hartnett failed in business, and blew
his brains out just like a white man. Everybody was a
little proud of his suicide.

"Cole Hartnett was just entering Harvard Medical. He
was a brilliant student. He had a brilliant future. And
then his father's death made his career uncertain. It was
my mother's plan to finance his education, close this
house, and go abroad until after my marriage. She intended to ask Carter Binney to act as my guardian. She
hoped that Althea and I would be like sisters to compen-
sate for her lost relationship with Althea's dead mother,
whom she had never been able to face after Thad. Carter
Binney's social position was secure. As was Cole's. If I
became the ward of one and the wife of the other, no one
would question my right to belong to society. Nor my
mother's right to be received by my friends."

Cleo felt a surge of helpless anger. What was this business of belonging? What was it worth? A tailor and a
stable-owner were the leaders of society. And the Duchess was saying this seriously. This woman, who could

have crossed the color line and bought her way into any
worldly circle, preferred to yearn for a counterfeit of the
Brahmin cult.

"And Cole refused?" she asked, rather irritably.

The Duchess misunderstood her irritation. "I've never
thought ill of Cole. I doubt that he's ever known what my
mother's letter to Carter Binney contained. Carter went
straight to Mrs. Hartnett. They decided that Cole and
Althea should quietly enter into a long engagement.
Carter didn't believe he would never rebuild his business.
He thought he could afford to promise his daughter to a
poor student and help him establish a practice when it
was time. He answered my mother's letter in person. He
did not address her by name. He would not sit down. He
would not remove his gloves, nor let her servant take his
hat or cane. None of the millionaires my mother had
known had shown her such contempt. That was the day
her death became certain. She had her severest heart
attack. It was heartbreak. She kept alive until I could
come. God rest her soul, my mother died the next day.
But not before she had my promise to marry into her
circle."

The low voice shook. She rose. Her eyes were remembering the look of her mother, the look of shriveled pride.

"I didn't want Cole Hartnett then. I wanted Carter
Binney."

The little French clock on the mantel was quietly ticking away the moments that remained to a gentleman in
Cambridge, who was dying of his disgrace, as a tawny-
eyed woman in this West End house had died of hers.
They had been born into a world which took no real
notice of their existence. Their leave-takings were as un-

ceremonious. Yet there is no life that does not contribute
to history. One added to one is the eternal abundance,
the greatness and baseness of man, the mortification of his
flesh, the purification of his spirit. The death of those
done with living opens the door for the new life. And in
that tender, terrible moment of birth there is a renewal
of belief. As long as there is a child alive, man can look
upward toward the stars.

The Duchess heard the time ticking away. The hour
she had set for her wedding had almost run out. She was
twenty-four. She felt tired and old. She was virginal,
and she wanted the nun's way. The world outside the
cloister walls was too violent. But how could she enter
God's house until she was shriven of hate? How could
she be God's bride if she was thought unworthy to be
sinful man's? What could she do with a Catholic heart
among uncaring people? Better to bury that heart. Better
to turn apostate.

It was six years now since she had made confession.
She could not seek absolution for an unfinished sin. She
had stayed on the fringe of her class, neither in it nor
quite out of it. She had attended Mass, and she had entertained gentlemen at roulette. But she had not been a
communicant at the sacred functions of either.

"There is little left to tell," she said tonelessly. "After
my mother's death, this house was closed to white men.
I sent her houseboy to South Station to talk to the redcaps. So many young men were working their way
through Harvard by red-capping. Cole was one of them.
I knew that he would pass on the news to Carter. His
creditors had closed his doors, and he needed money.

"Cole and Carter and their friends won hundreds here

that first night. They felt that they had won fortunes in this house where my mother had seen millionaires win and lose thousands. They came again, and won again, and for a long time I let them win." She paused, then said proudly, "And the young men have never lost, the young men putting themselves through college." Her face closed. "But the married men began to lose. I wanted to keep them coming back to try their luck again. These were the men who would make their wives receive me in return for my silence concerning their activities here. For it is the nature of women to imagine more than is true." The imperial eyes emptied of expression. "And now it is finished."

She turned away and crossed the Brussels carpet to the Hepplewhite desk. Cleo sighed and saw herself crossing a Brussels carpet to a Hepplewhite desk in her fine new house where such appointments would match its magnificence more than the Mission sets Mr. Judson was bound to buy. She would give her soul to sit behind this exquisite tea-table and pass these fragile cups to the admiring ladies of her acquaintance.

The Duchess turned back to her. In her hand she held a small packet.

"These are Carter Binney's deeds and legalized documents transferring his properties to me. And every penny of the money from his cashed-in insurance and his wife's jewels. Give them to him or to his son."

This was what Cleo had come for. The Duchess had put in her hand Thea's inheritance, Thea's happiness. There would be money to marry Cole, to outfit his office, to live without hunger while he was building up a practice. And the Cambridge house would be sold to stran-

gers. Simeon had no need for it. His shabby rooms above
The Clarion's offices better suited his bachelor inclina-
tions. With his looks, his education, his name, Simeon
should have been the catch of Boston, but he had no pros-
pects. His time and talents and every penny went into
his unpopular paper. Only a woman with the Duchess's
wealth could afford to trust her future to a man who
couldn't half-feed himself, let alone a wife.

She gave a little start. Simeon had no respect for any
woman's intelligence. He had never wanted anything a
woman had to offer. Well, he might as well get ready to
climb off his high horse and let the Duchess sit in the
saddle.

"Would you have Simeon?" asked Cleo softly.

The Duchess looked bewildered. "I am asking for
nothing in return. I have no hate for Simeon Binney. I
read his paper. I know his humanity."

"His paper needs money," said Cleo encouragingly.
"You've helped so many young men through college. You
could help Simeon save *The Clarion.*"

"Would he accept my money?" asked the Duchess
earnestly. "It's the money of white men, and he despises
them."

"Why, that's all the better," said Cleo quickly. "It's
using their money against them. He takes their money
and tells them off. That's really hitting where it hurts."

"I will write him a check for whatever amount he needs.
Please see him soon and telephone me."

Cleo gave her a look of sheer exasperation. Here was a
woman who wanted respectability, and didn't have the
horse sense to take it off the platter.

"He won't accept your money as a gift," she explained

patiently. "That would cause talk. People would say you were keeping him. They would boycott his paper. But as his wife, you would have their respect. You could help Simeon become a great man."

"If he will have me, I will be honored to share his beliefs," the Duchess said, with humility.

"Leave it to me," said Cleo briefly.

"Is there some way I can thank you?" the Duchess implored.

"If I've given you hope, that's thanks enough," Cleo said prettily, and waited to be urged.

"Please," the Duchess pressed her. "I have heard that your husband is rich, but isn't there some small service that I am able to do for you?"

"You've received a somewhat false impression of my husband," Cleo corrected gently. "Mr. Judson is not exactly rich. Men in business spend as much as they make. And my husband spends more. He's helping my sisters. It isn't them I'm concerned about as much as it is their children. I suffer for children. I lie awake nights wondering if those poor little things have enough to eat, or proper clothes to wear, or a decent place to lay their heads. I persuaded my husband to let me send for them, and their mothers, too. I won't know peace until we're all under the same roof, where I can tend my flock to the best of my ability."

"The saints preserve you," the Duchess said tenderly. "Your hand is held out wherever there is need of help."

Cleo made a modest little sound in her throat. "I searched and searched, and today I found a house." She was going to beg, but she had to brag first. "A lovely place in Brookline. Ridiculous rent, sixty dollars a month,"

she exaggerated with a weary little shake of the head.
"But what can you do when there are children to consider? Whatever the cost, you owe them a good address.
We're having to furnish ten rooms to fit us all into. I hope
I don't sound shameless. But I haven't taken my eyes off
your furniture since I've been here. Everything is perfectly beautiful. If there's an odd piece or two tucked in
your attic, don't think you would offend me by letting
me use it."

"Everything in this house," said the Duchess tightly,
"was bought by Thad Tewksbury. You are welcome to
any or all of it. I only ask you not to think of it as payment for what you have given me."

The little mantel clock whose ticking had been the toll
for the dying now gave a merry muted chime to foretell a
wedding. Cleo rose. For she ought to stop in at Simeon's.
With the paper due out tomorrow even his father's passing couldn't keep him away from his desk. It would only
take a few minutes to reach home from his office. After
all, she had left home on an errand of mercy. The strain
of death was unendurable when there was no money for
decent burial. It would hearten Simeon to know he could
make proper arrangements. Besides, she wanted to see
his face when she told him the West End Duchess was
demanding her pound of flesh.

The Duchess held out her hand. "Will you call me
Lenore? I was named for Althea's mother. When — if —
it is settled with Simeon, I will close this house and go
away for his time of mourning. I will stay in a retreat.
Sinner and saint are accepted. When Simeon is free to
join me, we can be quietly married in a civil ceremony in
New York. I want to return to Boston as Mrs. Simeon

Binney." Her voice was low and tremulous. "Yet I will never be married in the eyes of the Church."

Impulsively Cleo pressed her cheek against Lenore's. Here was a woman who wanted the love of God. And she had given her Simeon. A small trickle of shame wet her eyes. Women were better without men. The enemy had made one more victory. She had passed him the spoils.

But Simeon had great intelligence. Lenore had depth and loveliness. Their children would inherit this richness. The race would be strengthened. Lenore belonged to her unborn daughters. Her soul was not hers to give or keep while the life strain was in her loins.

"Good-bye and good luck, Lenore."

Lenore said softly, "Go with God."

CHAPTER 12

SIMEON BINNEY bent over his desk. Behind him, in the dingy back room, the two small presses were noisily clattering. But his ear was turned inward. He was writing his father's obituary. The doctor had said that his father would die before morning. He had felt no shock nor sorrow, and he had come away as soon as Thea returned to relieve him. She would give their father her tears, as he could not.

Simeon had been born in this house when the neighborhood was wholly Caucasian, except for the Binneys, who, according to their neighbors' praise, represented the best in the colored race. They behaved as if they were white. Simeon played with the neighborhood children and sat beside them in Sunday school. But his brownness made him seem different to them, just as Thea's fair skin made her seem the same.

He was darker than either parent, a throwback to a paternal grandfather. He was not an undesirable shade by the standards of his parents' set. Indeed, he was considered the handsomest colored child in Boston. In the usual way, most people made the unamusing witticism that it was a pity that a boy should be prettier than his sister. He was tan, with fine features, great black eyes, and black curls. He was tall for his age and strongly built, in every way giving a manly appearance. Nobody guessed the extent of his sensitiveness, his insecurity in what was considered his safe and happy world.

He felt that he lived in two worlds. There was the world outside, peopled with whites, whites everywhere. He couldn't understand why his parents were proud that he and Thea were always the only colored children in school, in church, in their block. Didn't they know that made him feel lonely? It was good to come into the other world, the narrow nursery world, and play with Thea, and pretend that this was the whole, that he and she alone existed.

He hadn't had any inherent dislike of white children. He hadn't known there was anything special about them at first. For Thea and his father were fair, his mother was very light. He had never noticed that he was darker. Nor had he known that their skin shades were preferable to darker ones.

The five-year-old boy, big enough now to play outside without his Irish nurse's supervision, approached the children on the block with vulnerable innocence. He had never heard any discussions about the difference in man. All that he knew was that there was a favored race of people called Bostonians, and that he was fortunate enough to be one of them.

The group of children he approached stared at him open-mouthed. They were also five-year-olds, and their world had been as prescribed as his. They, too, knew they were little Bostonians, and they thought all little Bostonians looked alike. They were unprepared for the exotic appearance of this brown boy. He might have stepped out of one of their picture books of strange boys in strange lands.

"Hello," Simeon said.

"Hello," they said soberly, somewhat surprised that he spoke their tongue.

"I'm Simeon Binney," he offered cheerfully.

They were silent. They did not know whether they wanted to tell this odd boy their names or not.

Simeon stuck out his hand. He had been taught to do that. And he was used to hearing delighted murmurs at this charming display of grown-up manners.

The boys backed away. They had never seen a brown hand extended. Then one asked shyly, "Will it come off?"

"What?" asked Simeon blankly.

"The brown on your hand," the boy explained.

"It isn't dirt," he said indignantly. Then he felt surprised. What was it?

"Where do you come from?" a pink-cheeked boy asked.

"Over there." He pointed to his house, the corner house, the finest in the block of brownstone dwellings.

"No," the pink-cheeked child said patiently, "I mean, what country?"

"Boston," Simeon answered in a shocked tone, for he had supposed that all Bostonians recognized Bostonians. Certainly he had known without question that these children, whose dress, whose accent, whose houses were identical with his, were his fellow countrymen.

One of the boys drew a sputtering breath. "I think you're a colored boy," he said. It frightened him a little to make this pronouncement, for he didn't know whether it was good or bad.

"I'm a Boston boy," Simeon said with a sob. "Same as you."

Plainly this didn't make sense to them. They looked at each other, shifted self-consciously, and began to sidle away. This was something they wanted explained by a grown-up as soon as they could reach one. They chorused Good-bye, for, after all, he was a small person like themselves, and the inherent humanity of children evoked this gesture of brotherhood.

Simeon played by himself. He could not go in to his mother. He felt ashamed, though he could not explain his feeling. When a reasonable time had passed, he mounted the stone steps quietly and scooted up the back stairs. In the bathroom he scrubbed his hands vigorously, but it was just as he had known it would be, there was no whiteness under the brown. He was not like the other boys. He was not a Bostonian.

He waited for his father to come home and explain to him what a colored boy was. He was reluctant to ask his mother. He knew that she was modest, and did not speak of unseemly things. His father failed him. He was prepared for this moment, and said deftly: "Everybody is colored, Simeon. Some skins are colored lighter than others. Like Thea's. Some look as if they were not colored at all. Like those boys. But put them beside a sheet of white paper, and you will see that they look pale gray. Those boys had never seen a brown boy. Had you been red-haired, they would have asked you if your hair was on fire." Simeon was supposed to smile at this, but his face stayed solemn. For he knew that a red-haired boy wouldn't have smiled either. "You're the color of an Indian, Simeon, and the Indians are the oldest Americans. If any boy ever asks you again why you're brown, you may say it's because your grandfather was a full-blooded Indian."

Simeon accepted this half-truth without enthusiasm. No matter how long the Indians had lived in America, they hadn't lived in Boston. No wonder those boys had asked him what country he came from. He couldn't understand why his father had let the doctor leave a boy who looked like an Indian instead of a boy who looked like a Bostonian.

The next day, when Simeon unwillingly went out to play, the little boys rushed to greet him and vigorously pumped his hand. They, too, had had instructions in correct demeanor from their fathers, who had been preparing for their questions as soon as they saw that the Binney boy looked old enough to come out to play. Their fathers had explained to them that you did not speak of color to colored persons. It hurt their feelings. You must always act as if they had no color at all. God made everybody, and in His infinite wisdom He had made some people brown. It was as rude to ask a colored boy why he was brown as it was to ask a lame boy why he limped. The way for a well-bred Boston boy to behave was with generosity toward those with fewer blessings.

Through the long afternoon Simeon waited to return to the subject of race. He had decided not to say he was an Indian. He was going to stand pat on being a Bostonian. He was going to fight about it if he had to. But the subject was never reopened.

The boys had set out to be bountiful. From that day on, he was never left out of anything. To all outward appearances he was the most popular boy in the block. Yet no boy ever fought him, though they fought each other, no boy called him by a nickname, though they were Fatty and Skinny and Shorty as soon as they left their stoops, and no boy ever contradicted him, though they shouted each other down with "You did!" "I didn't!"

He was never their equal. He was their charge, whom they were honor-bound to treat with charity. They never knew whether they liked him or not. They only knew it was something of a bother to be with him, for the feelings of a colored boy had to be coddled.

When Thea was old enough to go out alone to play, these boys and their sisters treated her as one of themselves, for her pink cheeks and chestnut hair were close enough in color to theirs not to distract them. Their easy acceptance established a loyalty in her that made her unable to understand Simeon's distrust. With Thea, as with Simeon, the first ten years of her life left a profound impression. She was never quite at ease with her own group. Her very fair skin and chestnut hair singled her out, accorded her a special treatment that she was unused to, that pointed out to her how preferable was the status of whites, since even a near-white was made an idol.

When Simeon was twelve and Thea nine, the poorer streets surrounding theirs began to be populated by the black newcomers to the North. They soon learned of the rich colored family living right alongside rich white folks on a near-by street. They took to strolling down this street to see if they could espy their own kind and color riding fat and sassy behind a bang-up coachman. They would stand and gape at the windows, their voices loud and approving and proud. Some would even go so far as to start a conversation with Thea and Simeon.

Thea would toss her chestnut hair and skip away. She was a little bit scared. These people smelled, they wore queer clothes, they spoke a strange tongue, and their blood was black, while hers was blue.

But Simeon sensed that their blood was the same, and he was ashamed. Because he was ashamed, he could not run away like Thea. He had to face them for his own pride. He had to believe that he could stand in the company of these people and still feel confident of the wall of culture between them.

Mr. Binney was completely outraged by the ever-increasing concourse of dark faces within the sacred precincts of his street. He didn't feel at all like a king with worshiping subjects. He felt like a criminal who had been found and tracked down. In his wildest nightmare he had never imagined that his house would be a mecca for lower-class Negroes. They were ruining the character of the street. They were making it a big road. The worst thing of all was that Simeon, who was being so carefully brought up, who scarcely knew the difference between white and colored, whose closest friends had always been white, was making friends with the little black urchins who boldly hung around the back door in the hope of enticing him away from his playmates on the front stoop.

The day Mr. Binney made up his mind to move was the unforgettable Sunday that he heard sounds of battle, rushed to the back window to find Simeon in his new suit engaged in strife. Simeon, who had never fought in his life, was rolling all over the alley with a ruffian who had never worn shoes until he came North. It was spring. Windows were open. Neighbors were witnessing this unholy spectacle of young Binney so demeaning himself as to fight with a boy beneath his station. It put them both in the same class.

Mr. Binney so far forgot himself as to bellow for his son. Simeon disentangled himself, shook his opponent's hand, and bounded into the house. He felt wonderfully elated, and he was scared but happy that his father had witnessed the fight. His father had never seen him fight in his life.

"Come in, sir!" his father commanded, leading him into his den. He turned and faced Simeon. "I have never been so ashamed in my life. My son behaving like an alley rat. I've never known you to raise your hand to one of the boys in the block. You've had the reputation of being a perfect young gentleman. Then the whole street sees you and that dirty black imp sprawled all over the alley. Do you know what they said to themselves?" Mr. Binney took a deep breath. He was going to say the worst thing he had ever said to Simeon. But Simeon had to be roundly shocked into full realization of his unpardonable breach of conduct. "They said, 'Isn't that just like niggers?'"

The word had never been used in Simeon's household. Its effect was not explosive. As a matter of fact, Mr. Binney had the uncomfortable feeling that Simeon accepted the ugly word as if he supposed it was part of his father's vocabulary.

"I know," said Simeon quietly. "I suppose they said 'colored' instead of 'nigger,' but that doesn't matter. I've always known they've never seen me as like themselves. They fight with each other, Father. Not in the alley, and not on Sunday. But I have to fight when I can. It mayn't make sense to you, Father, but Scipio Johnson" — Mr. Binney visibly winced — "is the first boy who ever fought me man to man."

It didn't make sense to Mr. Binney. "It is time you learned a hard-and-fast rule, Simeon. A colored man can

never afford to forget himself, no matter what the provo-
cation. He must always be superior to a white man if he
wants to be that white man's equal. We are better fixed
financially than any family on this street. You and Thea
attend private schools. The other children go to public
school. Your manners are superior. Your mother has more
help. We set a finer table. If our manner of living was
exactly like theirs, we would not be considered good
enough to live on this street."

Simeon thought that he and his father had met on common ground. He, too, had something to say that was
better said now. "I don't like white people, Father. I
think I hate them."

His father was shocked and disturbed. "Never say such
an unreasonable thing again. You get that from those
wretched black boys. Do you know why they hate white
people? Because they're lazy and shiftless and poor. They
hate them because they envy them. You are Simeon
Binney. You will never have to envy anyone. You are
being raised like a white man's son. Pay me the courtesy,
sir, of thinking like one."

The Binneys moved to Cambridge. They were the first
family on their street to move away because of the rapid
encroachment of Negroes. They began the general
exodus. Mr. Binney could say with pride, right up to the
day of his death, that he had never lived on a street where
other colored people resided.

Simeon went to Harvard. He ranked among the top
ten in all his classes, because colored men must be among
the first in any field if they are not to be forever lost
among the mediocre millions.

He took the classical courses. Mr. Binney was disap-

pointed that Simeon didn't want to specialize in law or
medicine or dentistry. All of the sons of his friends were
aspiring to the professions. They were the gentlemen
that meant to be titled. Their fathers were gentlemen
without higher education. They had learned their manners and mode of living in service to the rich. They were
ambitious for their sons and instilled in them the Boston
tradition that knowledge has no equal. That there would
be a surfeit of professional men in a city where the majority of Negroes were too poor and ignorant to seek professional services did not deter them. In his heart each
hopeful student supposed that he would be the one to
establish a practice among whites. This was Boston,
where a man was appraised for his worth, and paid in
New England currency accordingly. What they did not
know was that the whites, whom they dreamed of doctor-
ing and advising, were confidently expecting them to attend their own, thereby effecting a painless segregation.

Mr. Binney was somewhat mollified when Simeon explained that he intended to work for a doctorate. At least
Simeon would have a title even if he would never be able
to hang out a shingle on which to display it. Still, he was
worried about the boy. He hoped he did not think he
could be a rich man's idle son. He had the elegance for
it, but now there was not going to be the money. He,
Mr. Binney, could not hold on to his business another
year. The ten-thousand-dollar rent alone was far in excess of last year's profits. He was already drawing heavily
on his capital. There was just enough left to see Thea
through finishing school and Simeon through college.

Simeon would have to work for his living. Perhaps he
would elect to teach. Perhaps it was not too fantastic to

imagine, he might even teach at Harvard. They thought
the world and all of him there. The faculty had the high-
est praise for him. His class respected him. He was even
putting away a fair sum tutoring undergraduates. If
Simeon would just make up his mind to teach, a position
at Harvard should be his for the asking.

Simeon elected to edit a Negro newspaper. It was a
sudden decision arrived at a few weeks before he received
his doctorate. Thea was just home from school. She and
Simeon were out for an evening's stroll in the vicinity of
the Yard. She was holding his arm, and her face, full of
lively affection, was upturned to his. A group of young
men, in freshman caps, approached them. They were not
very steady. They did not know Simeon, nor he them.
They stopped in front of him and Thea and would not let
them pass.

"Watch your step, nigger. Let go that white girl," one
of them said.

"Move out of our way," said Simeon quietly.

"Who's going to make us?"

Simeon said quickly to Thea, "Run home and don't look
back." Then he hunched his shoulders and gave a little
prancing step. "Put up your dukes," he said.

It was not a fair fight. There were three of them, and
they attacked from all sides. But it didn't matter to
Simeon. It was what he'd been wanting since he was
five. A fight with white men. That there were three of
them, that his fists could smash three faces, that his wild,
tortured curses could befoul three pairs of ears, that he
could smell the hated blood that flowed in three hot
streams, made it the moment in his life that satisfied the
long waiting.

He was found unconscious a few minutes later by a passing patrolman. His watch, his wallet were on him. He was carted off to jail as a drunk and thrown into a cell to sleep it off.

When he roused he didn't mind being where he was. His head was throbbing, there were bruises on his face, and blood in his mouth. But it wasn't important. This would wake these sleeping colored Bostonians. They would see they were not a privileged group, that no Negro was immune from a white man's anger when he did not watch his step. These self-styled better Negroes were standing still, sticking their heads in the sand, pretending that liberalism was still alive in Boston. They were using the transplanted Southerner for their scapegoat. It was he, they insisted, who was causing the changed attitude, if one existed, not the changing times. The colored problem began with their coming. It was no wonder. They were coming in such droves. These upper-class Negroes, Simeon argued to himself, didn't have the sense to see that a minority group was never a problem until its numerical strength threatened the dominant race at the polls. What power had the Old Colored Families, sparsely scattered by preference in the many suburbs of Boston? They had none, and they did not know it was desirable. To them the Irish were pushing, and they were proud that they were not. They would have been outraged and astounded if they had been told that they knew their place, and kept it.

All of these things Simeon expected to say in a rousing speech to the press when it was discovered that a Harvard graduate had been beaten by brother Harvardites for no other crime than walking with his sister in the neighborhood of his own house.

Toward midnight he was summoned to the sergeant's desk. His father was there, looking distressed. There was somebody from the dean's office, looking uncomfortable. There were three bloodied freshmen, looking sober and sheepish. The policeman who had made the arrest, looking red-faced. And the sergeant and two reporters, looking bored.

A solution had been arrived at by everyone concerned except Simeon. The unfortunate happening was to be considered a freshman prank, prompted by an overindulgence in strong drink. The freshmen were to apologize, which they did easily and earnestly, thrusting out their well-kept hands, which Simeon ignored until he heard his father's embarrassed plea, "Simeon, remember you are as much a gentleman as these young men," and felt that he would look foolish and childish if he continued to stand on what his father and the others did not recognize as his dignity. The Irish policeman apologized next. He did it gruffly, because he was upset by all the formality and fine English. It made him feel inferior to everybody present, and that was ridiculous since two of them were niggers.

In a few brief minutes it was over. There was general handshaking, with Simeon's hand feeling cold as a clam to whoever touched it. The young men and the dean's representative bowed themselves out, not with obsequiousness, but with the graciousness befitting those who have transgressed against the rule of *noblesse oblige*.

Simeon turned to his father. "I thought you would bring your lawyer," he said.

Mr. Binney looked scandalized. "Fineberg's crudity would have been out of place in a delicate situation like this. He would have made a race issue out of it, and taken it to court."

"It was a race issue," said Simeon stolidly. "They said, 'Nigger, let go that white woman.'"

His father looked racked. Everybody had been carefully avoiding any reference to those unhappy words. "They were drunk, Simeon. They forgot themselves. As soon as they sobered, they were Harvard gentlemen."

"And when they get drunk again, they'll insult some other couple whose juxtaposition doesn't suit them."

"Simeon, be reasonable. You and your sister have walked together through the streets of Cambridge half your lives. Have you ever been insulted before? It isn't likely that you'll be insulted again. They made a very natural mistake. Thea is fair enough to appear white. You must face facts, Simeon. Since that riffraff has come up from the South, their men have run after white women. You see them all over the South End, the worst elements of colored men walking with low-type white women."

"Thea and I are hardly comparable," said Simeon stiffly. He disliked having to say that. It weakened the point of the argument. But his pride could not let that observation pass.

"Of course, you're not," said his father soothingly. "Those young men were the first to say so when they sobered." He patted Simeon's shoulder. "Let's go home now. Your face needs attention. You need rest. You will get your degree in a few weeks. It will be a wonderful occasion for me. Don't spoil it by making a mountain out of a molehill. I want you to look and feel your best."

"I'll be ready in a moment," said Simeon wearily. "I want a word with the reporters. Will you wait for me outside?"

His father's patience broke. "They're not going to print anything, Simeon. They promised. They know how the better class of colored people feel about any story that is derogatory to the race. You're young and headstrong. I won't let you do anything tonight that you'll regret tomorrow. Rest assured that your name will appear in every paper in Boston when you receive your Ph.D. That will be a proud day. Don't do anything to take away from its glory. Give me your promise."

Simeon promised. He supposed he owed his father that much for his education. They walked toward home. Simeon was silent. He knew what he meant to do. He would publish a newspaper for colored people and make them face the facts of their second-class citizenship. He had enough savings to make a down payment on a printing press. His father would not deny him the use of the unoccupied South End house when he convinced him that he would either edit a paper for Negroes or harangue on Boston Common before audiences largely composed of whites.

For two years now Simeon had struggled to keep the paper in circulation. The people who read it were not the people who could pay for subscriptions. There were only occasional ads for church socials and rooms for rent. His bills were mounting. His single helper was underpaid. He himself never had a decent meal unless he ran over to Cleo's. Cambridge was too far away, and there was the carfare, and poor Thea was a rotten cook, with little enough to cook anyway.

If he could not keep the six-page sheet alive, at least he had established the need for a Negro newspaper. It passed around from hand to hand in the South End. On the day of its appearance there were little clusters of shabby people with nickels in their hands, waiting for the shabby newsboy to appear.

Thea did the social column. It was the only thing that kept the better Bostonians even mildly interested. It satisfied their curiosity as to who might have had a party to which they had not been invited, or what person of social prominence from New York, Philadelphia, or Washington was visiting what socially prominent Bostonian at his beautiful home in the suburbs.

Nothing else in the paper met with their approval. Every other word was *colored*. That this was Simeon's concession to their sensibilities did not make it any more palatable. Had he used the word *Negro*, they would have refused to read the paper altogether.

There was far too much, they complained, about the happenings below the Mason-Dixon line. They could be resolved quite easily. The nice colored people should come North. They needn't all come to Boston. There were many other large cities among which they could disperse themselves without dispossessing the already established families. As for the other elements, their extermination was the best thing possible. Every locality had its thieves and cutthroats. In the South they happened to be black. That Simeon should waste his time and talent writing long editorials protesting their punishments, urging the improvement of their conditions, was the folly of hotheaded youth. It was thoughtless cruelty to call attention to the dregs of the colored race.

Simeon, they concluded, was much too race-conscious for a young man who had been brought up exactly as if he were white. His persistence in identifying himself with anybody and everybody who happened to be black just showed what lasting effect those few months of contact with common colored children had had on a growing boy.

Simeon picked up his pencil. "Carter Burrows Binney was born in Boston in the year this once abolitionist city sent its son to liberate the enslaved black souls of the South . . ."

Across the sea England was writing the obit of a Kaiser. The world was at war.

CHAPTER 13

Simeon," said Cleo. She touched his arm.

He lifted his head. His face was drawn with the long dreaming. He rose and ran his fingers through his hair. "Hello, Cleo," he said quietly. "If you mean to stay longer than a minute, shall we go upstairs? There's so much clatter here."

They sat in his dreary sitting room, where the curtains needed washing and everything needed dusting. The furniture had not been considered good enough to take to the Cambridge house, and now it was even older. Simeon was letting it fall apart without the least compunction.

He leaned back in his chair and shut his eyes. One black curl fell over his forehead. Cleo wished that poor little Judy had lovely curls like that. Braids were fine if they fell to your waist. But two braids bobbing on a colored child's shoulder looked like pickaninny hair, no matter how you dressed it up with expensive ribbons.

Simeon said, "Mrs. Hartnett and Cole are with Thea, watching Father die. Have you come to watch with me my paper's demise?" He opened his eyes and stared at her.

"You give me the shivers," Cleo said.

Simeon was such a fancy talker, she thought, feeling her

137

short patience beginning to ebb. She didn't have time to hear him speechify. Mr. Judson was home now, trying to worm things out of Judy. Where did you go today, what did you do, who did you see? And Judy was running off at the mouth. It had never occurred to Cleo that these were natural questions. There were so many secrets in her day that any discussion became an exposure.

Simeon had shut his eyes again. His lips attempted a wry smile. "I suppose I've been wanting Father to die for years. I wanted him to die because he was rich. I didn't know how I would spend his money. But I knew I would spend it differently. Now I shall inherit nothing but two houses. I can't sell the Cambridge house over Thea's head. I can't sell this house either. It is so heavily mort- gaged that the sale would net me nothing." He opened his eyes, and his tired glance swept the dismal room. It had been his world once, his world and Thea's, before he was five, before he knew that a nursery is a child's fantasy.

"The houses are not yours to keep or sell," Cleo said softly.

"I don't understand," he said.

"They belong to the woman they call the Duchess."

Simeon said heavily: "Do you mean Father gambled the houses away, too? But Thea," he asked in a strained voice, "she will have the insurances?"

"He cashed them in and lost that money, too."

Simeon pushed himself to his feet. He strode to Cleo's side and stood above her. His hand struck the packet on the table beside her, and Cleo could not quite meet his eyes. But her expression was one of sympathy.

"Why didn't he tear out Thea's heart at the same time?" Simeon said savagely. "Why did he raise her like a rich man's daughter if he meant to die a pauper? You know how hard it's been for her these last years, trying to make ends meet, trying to keep up appearances. And when she had a chance at happiness with Cole, Father destroyed it along with himself."

"Poor little Thea," said Cleo, feeling genuine indignation.

"Thea's grown used to a certain way of life. Father's tried to bridge three generations in one for her. It would be like throwing her to the wolves to expect her to earn her own living. I cannot face her and tell her that all she has are her health and strength. She had never learned to use them." He turned away and began a restless walking.

"The Duchess is willing to bargain," Cleo said.

He stopped his pacing and answered shortly over his shoulder, "Thea and I have no medium of exchange."

"You have the Binney name."

He whirled and looked at her with faint contempt. "Thea and I and our kind are phenomena who have bloomed and will die in one generation. Our fathers built a social class for us out of tailor shops and barber shops and stables and caterers' coats. We cannot afford its upkeep because they have taught us to think above their profitable occupations. The poor professional is evolving. His sacred shabby circle will be the redcaps who went to Harvard with him. Thea will tell her children, if the fates find a husband able to support her, about their grandfather Binney, and they will be surprised that a man who never went to college could behave like a gentleman."

"But he does," said Cleo stoutly, seeing Mr. Binney's hat, stick, and gloves.

The philosophical intent of Simeon's speech escaped her. She always heard a man out with impatience. A resentment rose in her. If either was going to do the talking, let her do it. When men spoke, she knew that their worlds were larger than hers, their interests broader. She could not bear knowing that there were many things she didn't know; that a man could introduce a subject, and she would have to be silent. Her defense was to shut out of her mind the didactic sound of their voices. "Whatever else your father is, he's a perfect gentleman," she said tartly.

"I don't want to hear your specious reason," Simeon said agreeably. "You're a colored mother. You want to preserve a non-existent world for your child. Women are well enough, but they interfere with a man's honesty. Thea is the flaw in mine. She narrows my vision. I don't hate her helplessness. Perhaps I cherish it because she's my sister. Her minor predicament seems more important than a paper that speaks for the oppressed. That's wicked. That's wrong. I would give my whole soul to see her settled with Cole and off my mind."

Cleo said triumphantly, "The Duchess will exchange everything she has of your father's for your promise to marry her."

She saw him stiffen, saw his hands slowly clench, and his eyes grow black with bitterness. He said finally, "The world is too full of women who feed on men. As the devoted brother of one of them, I have no choice but to accept the terms that will enable Thea to feed on Cole."

Cleo felt deflated. She had expected Simeon to make a mighty holler. Instead he was going to cut his own throat simply on her say-so. Was it because a woman was no more to him than an old she-cat to whom he would give shelter to spare himself the annoyance of hearing her howl outside his window?

She said coldly: "You know the woman I mean? A woman not good enough for Thea to wipe her feet on." This description did not trouble her conscience in the least. She was determined to get a rise out of Simeon.

He was almost amused. "There are so few people who are good enough for Thea that one more hardly increases the problem of her speaking acquaintances."

"I thought you loved your sister so much," Cleo taunted.

"I love her enough to ask the Duchess to be my wife."

"Well, I suppose it's all settled then," Cleo said indecisively. She still felt that Simeon was far too calm about it. Her dramatic sense was unsatisfied. "But how will Thea accept that woman?"

"As my wife," said Simeon simply.

"Even though your father is dying because she beggared him?"

"Thea will hide her feelings from me as I will hide mine from her."

Cleo felt frightened. Judy is going to grow up like that, she thought. She belongs to me. And already I can see her will to belong to herself. I want her to be a Bostonian, but I want her to be me deep down. Judy, her frightened heart cried, be me as my sisters are Mama. Love me enough to let me live forever.

The telephone jangled. Simeon sprang across the room. "Thea," he said. Then tenderly, urgently, "He is happier. Now he has peace. I'm coming at once. Cleo is here. I know she wants to say some word of comfort to you."

Cleo took the receiver from him, and her hand shook a little. Mr. Binney was dead, and now Mr. Binney was everywhere, seeing into the packet, even into her mind, knowing she had sacrificed Simeon, knowing she could have spared Thea an hour of anguish.

"Thea," she said, in a choked voice, "no need to tell you how grieved I am for you. I'll come early tomorrow and stay all day." She could not have stayed in the same house with Mr. Binney's ghost that night. She would sleep away her sins, and rise the next morning, like a child, with a clear conscience. "There's nothing for you to worry about. I'm sending you a message by Simeon." She put the receiver back on the hook.

She turned to Simeon and said unsteadily, "I'm sorry, deeply sorry."

The lines of weariness had deepened in his face. He touched her hand. "Thank you, Cleo." He tried to straighten his shoulders. "I must change and go. What is your message to Thea?"

She passed him the packet. "Tell her I saw the Duchess and was successful. You needn't tell her what a time I had persuading her, and how she wouldn't put this package in my hand until I had sworn on my honor that I wouldn't let go of it until I had your sacred promise to marry her. That was the bitterest thing I've ever had to do."

"Thea has enough with her grief. Do you think I would add to it?" asked Simeon, with a faint smile. "My marriage to Lenore Evans can be a very natural thing. She has money. I haven't. Thea has always approved of me, even when she didn't understand me. She will think I am making this marriage to save my paper. She will not see that I may have lost the South End. She doesn't know that the South End is important. She would never believe that they are the colored population of Boston now."

Cleo didn't either. That was more of Simeon's odd male talk. Living here in the South End he was getting to think just like these poor darkies. Why, the South End was no longer the colored population at all. All the nice people were moving away along with all the whites. Soon it would be solid black. Get a whole lot of poor colored people together, and what did you have? An eyesore of rundown houses and runny-nosed children. She knew. She came from the South. How many women had been like Mama, who kept her children clean and her house clean and made Pa chink up the holes? The thing about Simeon was he didn't know the South and its don't-care-nohow people. You had to be born there . . . And when you were, her thinking ran dreamily, all you remembered were the happy days of your childhood, when being alive was a wild and glorious thing.

She went to the door. Poor little Judy had been promised a dish of ice cream at a drugstore. That was her idea of an adventure. No wonder Bostonians grew up to be Bostonians.

CHAPTER 14

THE WHITE-GOLD MOON rode the summer sky. Cleo lay on her side of the bed, with her face gleaming palely in the soft light. She was dreamily suspended above sleep. In a moment she would slide into the lovely pool of her lost innocence. Down, down she went, feeling the freedom of a wild bird plummeting through time and space. She was hurrying back, falling faster and faster, poised for the swoop into sleep . . . almost . . . there . . .

A gigantic snore like the thunder of brasses and cymbals jerked her awake. On his side of the bed Mr. Judson began to conduct a full-scale orchestra, and every instrument had sat out in the rain.

He was lying on his back with his mouth open. She gave him a shove with her elbow and couldn't budge him. She glared at him furiously, disliking his mustache, his two gold teeth, and his look of supreme good health. He was fifty-two, and he ought to be getting old, but there wasn't a thread of gray in his hair, nor a line in his face. Nobody looking at his powerful shoulders and hands would have believed that Cleo had expected him to be doddering just about now. He was twenty-three years her senior. She had been ignorant enough at eighteen to think she was marrying an old man who would leave her a rich young widow.

144

Bart continued to snore. Cleo hissed at him softly,
wanting him to stir and shift without wholly waking.
They had had no real conversation since her return home,
and she didn't want to start him up now. She had found
him nodding in the easy-chair by the open window where
he was on watch. Judy was asleep on his lap, her plump
hand cupping the emblem of his trade, a gold banana
that dangled from his watch chain.

Mr. Binney's death and its accompanying powers of
observation were still too fresh in her mind for her to be
able to tell Mr. Judson, without an unexplainable display
of uneasiness, that a business acquaintance had died. She
would feel better when God was through asking Carter
Binney about his corner of the earth below, and had
turned his attention to another newcomer, who neither
knew her nor anything bad to say about her. When supper was ready, she fetched her husband and daughter
down, and spun a long story about her childhood to keep
Mr. Judson from getting a word in, and Judy too en-
thralled for him to want to spoil her pleasure.

After supper it was she who took Judy out for her ice
cream, an excursion she would normally have put off with,
"When did I say anything about ice cream? You can have
some tomorrow." After the treat she trotted Judy into
the neighboring green, where they rarely went nowadays
since the sedate little oblong had become the whooping
ground for every little heathen whose Southern mammy
leaned on her heavy breasts and watched him from between her bunched-up curtains.

When they came home, Bart had retired, as Cleo had
hoped he would. At the height of summer he took his
tiredness to bed at sundown. In winter his day began at

four of a bitter Boston morning when he hurried downtown to regulate the temperature of his ripening rooms.
Whatever the season he was ready for bed the minute he
plodded upstairs from supper. He was not a companion.
He was a good provider. Had he tried to be a companion,
Cleo would have said that he talked her to death. As it
was, she said he bored her to death.

There was no help for it except to wake him.

"Mr. Judson," she said furiously. He snorted, stirred.
"Wake up and roll over."

He opened his eyes, blinked, yawned, scratched.
"What's the matter? Was I snoring?"

"Ask anybody within five miles."

"I was lying on my back," he observed. "Never could."
He rolled over on his side.

She settled herself for sleep, hoping to God he wasn't
wholly awake.

"Cleo," he said.

"What?" she said in a resigned voice.

"Judy said you didn't go to the doctor."

"You're always picking her, poor little thing. You keep
on with that child, and you'll teach her to be deceitful."

"Children don't lie unless someone puts them up to it.
Judy's a truthful child. I ask her a question. She's truthful enough to answer it."

"Well, what about the doctor?" she asked belligerently.
"Did you go?"

"I thought you were telling me," she said smartly.

After a moment he said quietly, "There's not going to
be another child, is there?"

"You're still telling me," she reminded him.

His voice shook with resignation. "Cleo, a man gets
sick of foolishness. You never talk straight —— "

"Now you're telling me I'm a liar," she countered.

"And you always wriggle out of things by talking around them."

"Why do you bother to talk to me then?"

"Because a man has to talk to his wife. A man has to trust his wife or he's lost. God joined a man and woman together. If they go flying off in different directions, they might as well never have married. You must work with me, Cleo. If you work against me, you're the child's enemy, and we might as well give up the ghost."

The mention of ghost reminded her. "Did Judy tell you that Thea was here?" Her inventive mind was beginning to function.

"Yes," he said cautiously, for Cleo was never straightforward. "She said you went out right after her on an errand of mercy."

"Oh," she said hurriedly. "I'll tell you about that later. But the news that'll knock you out of bed is poor Carter Binney's dead as a haddock."

"So Binney's dead," Bart marveled. "When did he die? Wasn't it sudden?"

"When you get through asking me, I'll tell you. He had a shock this morning and died this afternoon. That's why I never got to the doctor's. I came home to leave Judy. She was complaining about being tired. I was going to ask Miss Johnson to keep an eye on her while I went out again. And Thea was here waiting. That's how I found out about Mr. Binney. That poor girl had had to leave her dying father to come here to beg me to buy her a black dress."

"Is that what Judy was trying to tell me? She said you bought some kind of dress. Wasn't black, the way she was telling it."

"Maybe after this you'll stop listening when a child talks," Cleo chided. "They know just enough about grown folks' affairs to tell it all wrong. I bought a dress for myself today. That's the dress Judy was talking about. But after Thea left, I rushed downtown to change it for a black one. That's why I told Judy I had to go on an errand of mercy. I didn't want to tell her I was going to buy Thea a mourning dress. No sense in making her sad."

Bart was still impressed by Mr. Binney's sudden demise. "I remember Carter Binney when you couldn't touch him with a ten-foot pole. And now my wife has to buy his daughter a dress to wear to his funeral."

"And it's not a fine dress either," said Cleo before Mr. Judson could ask her what it cost. "Mr. Binney ought to feel kind of bad that's the best his daughter has to wear to his funeral."

"You should have come back to the store. I'm a man who's careful with money, but I'm not mean. I never refuse when there's need. And death is a time for drawing together." He lay on his back again, staring up at the ceiling. "So Binney kicked the bucket, and you bought his daughter a cheap black dress. I guess there's a lesson there for us all. It don't do for a man to walk too proud. It isn't what you make. It's what you save. It's easy to throw your money around, but it's hard on the family you leave behind."

She said defensively: "Mr. Binney didn't throw his money around. He gave his children a wonderful raising. My opinion is it's better to give your child a good foundation than to save for his future. For the matter of that, Mr. Binney didn't expect to die a poor man. He thought he had a sound business for his children to inherit. He was just as surprised when he failed as you would be if you failed. You follow your own advice about walking proud. Nothing is certain in life except death."

"People have been eating since God made the world," Bart said profoundly. "An automobile can get you places same as a horse, only faster. A readymade suit can cover a man same as a tailor-made suit, only cheaper. But nothing man is apt to think of can substitute for fruit and vegetables. That's what I sell, and I sell the choicest. Man thinks a lot of his stomach, and he wants the best that money can buy."

"You told me yourself," Cleo reminded him, "that some of the men in the market are beginning to worry about the chain stores."

"They're borrowing trouble," Bart said promptly. "Those chains will stick to tea and canned goods. Some of them tried to sell people potatoes, and people complained about the quality. Quality counts. Those chains can't compete with the independents. People aren't going to take their trade from a meat market owned by a butcher who takes pride in his product and give it to a cheap chain store run by somebody who don't even own the block he's chopping on, and don't even care. Same with fruit. Same with everything else that don't come in a can. And the independent retailers are going to stick by the independent wholesalers they know by reputation."

Cleo said crossly, "Now start on yourself and start boasting."

He said earnestly: "It ain't boasting to say that when you buy a stem of bananas from Bart Judson, you know you're buying the best the market offers. And I didn't get that reputation by sitting down. I got it by tending bananas like you would tend a baby. I sent in my bid today for the Navy Yard contract. No reason I shouldn't get it same as last year. Give me a few more years of the business I've been doing in the last few years, and we'll be near enough to Easy Street to see the smoke coming out of the chimneys. Just you help me scrape and save, Cleo, and the day will come when you can spend."

"Mr. Judson," she cried, "can't you see? I'm not old. I'm twenty-nine. You're middle-aged. You've learned patience. To me the race is to the swift. I won't tag along behind. Your god is money. It isn't mine. To me money's just something to exchange for something else. I wasn't born to pinch and sacrifice. Don't try to make me over."

His voice was soothing, fatherly. "You aren't settled yet, Cleo. Judy's so grown for her age, she's not much care, and the Binney girl relieves you of a lot of that. But when you have another child, you'll have your hands full, and your mind won't be so free to think up things to want. By the time the little shaver is sensible size, you'll be older and quieter in your mind."

"Mister Nigger," said Cleo coldly, "who told you I was going to have a little shaver?"

"You address me by name. You told me yourself sitting right in my store."

"I beg to differ, Mister Nigger. You told me."

"Cleo, don't you start that again. Why in the name of God did you take money from me to go to the doctor if you knew it was a fool's errand?"

"I never refuse money when it's offered me," she said imperturbably.

"Cleo," he insisted darkly, "what about your sister

Lily? What about telling me she could help you run that house while you were carrying your baby?"

"I would never," said Cleo indignantly, "talk about carrying an unborn child in the presence of Mr. Christianson. All I have to say to that is, you're a liar."

"Maybe those weren't your words exactly, but that was the sense," Bart pursued.

"All right," said Cleo resignedly. "That house has ten rooms. I'm one woman. I'm your wife. But you don't care if I do the work of a horse, just so long as you can win some old fool argument about who said what." She felt concerned. Her voice shook with fury. "Thea's heartbroken in Cambridge by her father's body, my own sister, Lily, is starving to death in New York. But that's not enough misery for you. You won't be contented until you drive me crazy with questions."

"Now, Cleo," he said in a worried voice, "no need to take on. Just calm yourself. You work yourself up so every time I try to talk to you. Man gets so he'd rather let things slide than see you get so excited."

"But you waked me out of a sound sleep to pick me like you'd pick a bone. Now I'll lie awake the rest of the night." Seeing the face of Mr. Binney floating before me, she thought wretchedly.

"You put your mind on what furniture you want, and think about a real nice Mission parlor set. Bet you'll drop to sleep right off."

"Oh," she said.

His voice was beaming with benevolence. "You meet me tomorrow, and you can start choosing."

"Oh," she said again. She was unprepared to tell him about the furniture the Duchess had given her. Mr.

Binney's death had kept her from getting a likely story together. She had tried to turn her mind away from everything remindful of it. Yet if she did not tell Mr. Judson now, she might find her house filled with Mission furniture, and Simeon's sacrifice would have netted her nothing.

She said as a feeler, "I know where I can get some used furniture for nothing, beautiful pieces good as new, enough to fill a whole house."

"How much do you call nothing?" he asked cautiously.

Until he put it into her mind, she hadn't thought about making any side money. She drew a deep breath and took the plunge. "Two hundred dollars, and worth a small fortune."

"Who's selling it, and why?" And he hated having to ask. She would launch into a long story, and he would be lost in its intricacies. When he had found his way to some fact, he would be swamped in the confusion of what had gone before. A man had to have the patience of Job to live with Cleo. But she was the woman he wanted beside him when he lay dying. God help him, he could not help himself.

"Oh, it's been a day," she said dramatically. "I haven't told you half. After I exchanged that dress, I went to see this woman. Well, it starts with one day last week when Thea — poor Thea — was telling me about this white friend of hers. A lovely girl from a lovely family. Well, she got infatuated with a man who wasn't free to marry her. He set her up in a fine house and furnished it like a palace. Now he's dead, and she's decided to begin a new life. She's getting rid of everything that reminds her of the past."

She briefly paused for second wind and a second stok-
ing. "And that," she fished about, "is where the furniture
comes in. She offered it to Thea for what it would cost
to cart it away. But Thea and Cole will live with his
mother when they're married. So when I called Thea to
rest her mind about her dress being delivered tomorrow,
I asked her for this woman's address. You'd been so good
about Lily, I wanted some way to thank you. I thought
this woman might up and give me her stuff — since she
was so bent on getting shed of it. But I couldn't out and
beg for it. So I offered her two hundred dollars. And
when she accepted, I couldn't back out."

Bart gave a disapproving grunt. "Seems to me I smell a
gyp. Some women are pretty slick customers. I'll go
there tomorrow to see for myself."

"What in God's name do you know about furniture?
All you know about is bananas. And where are you going,
pulling in that white woman's house? You know how
skittish white women are. She'd swear you'd come there
to rob or worse. Just leave things to me."

"I don't like all this monkey business," he protested.
"I've almost a mind to tell you to take two hundred dollars and buy some solid Mission furniture. Only that
wouldn't fill a house. This way it's all smack done. You
get that stuff as soon as possible and see the last of that
woman. Come down tomorrow and get the cash. I don't
want to give you a check. Woman like that would add an
aught, and skip the city with two thousand dollars of my
hard-earned money. I don't sleep on my feet when I'm
dealing with shady characters."

She heaved a long sigh of relief. If you could tell a
bold enough lie, you could get anyone to believe you.

"Looka here," he said suddenly.

She really did jerk her head around, trying to read his expression.

"There's always a catch. We'll still have to buy more bedroom suites. Don't reckon she ran a rooming house."

"I saw a servant or two. I don't suppose they sleep standing up. There'll be beds enough for the bedrooms," she said tartly. "I'm not turning my house into a sleeping stall the very second I cross the threshold. I want a little time to feel like it's mine before I turn it over to strangers. You don't know how I brag to my sisters about the living you give me. Just now I was lying here wishing it wasn't just Lily was coming. Your family's right here. You don't know how it feels to lie awake wondering about your sisters scattered all over the globe."

"If they were in trouble, you'd hear," he consoled her. "Like you heard from Lily."

"That's a man," she said bitterly. "You mean when they're dead, I'll be notified, and you'll give me the fare to go to their funerals. But while we're all alive and young, and the living is easy, I can't invite my own sisters to spend one week in my house."

"Cleo," Bart thundered, "you know I've never said your sisters weren't welcome. Up to now we've had no place to sleep them. I don't care if they come for a week, even two. I'm not pretending to be a poor man. I can feed all your family for a week, two weeks, for that matter. I'll foot the bill for their stay."

"I'll write Serena tomorrow," she said dreamily. "And Charity, too," she added hastily. "It doesn't seem possible we'll all be together again."

"And the minute they leave," Bart reminded her, "we'll

put an 'ad in *The Clarion*. Winter's my slack season. I don't want to be caught in that big house with three or four empty bedrooms that we could use the money from."

"You leave that to me," she said peacefully. "There won't be an empty room in that house. You'll see."

He yawned. "Well, I guess I'm talked out."

She yawned. "Me, too." She felt relaxed and satisfied. The little waves began to lap, the silvery voices of the South began their siren song. Down she went into her well of remembering . . . down . . .

"Cleo?" His voice was soft, with the little hunger behind it. His body rolled toward her.

She raced like a deer for the darkness. And slept.

CHAPTER 15

THE REUNION had been a thing to remember forever. Lily had come first with six-year-old Victoria, or rather Vicky had been the wise hen with the bewildered chick. It was she who had taken charge of the tickets, asked the conductor — with Lily's elbow jabbing her every time he passed — how much longer it was to Boston, fetched Lily water for her seasick pill, smacked her way through the shoe box of sandwiches that she couldn't coax Lily to look at, let alone eat, and lent a protective hand whenever they rocketed through a tunnel or rode over water. Many times Lily gave up the ghost, and was more wretched than relieved to find herself still in the land of the living.

Victor had put her on the Boston train, and both of them remembered how she had balked on that other occasion, but neither thought to read any warning in that early reluctance. He looked at his wife and daughter, and felt very proud. They were dressed in the best that he could afford, everything new from head to toe. There had been a lot of basement-store buying, but the result was a handsome front of furbelows and frills. That the other clothes in the ancient suitcase could not match this showy splendor wouldn't come to light if Lily and Vicky didn't overstay.

There were twenty dollars in Lily's purse, to spend on foolishness, Victor grandly instructed. It was borowed money, but this was Lily's first holiday, and he wanted to send her off in style. Such a sum was not to be sneezed at, he was happily confident. It would allow his wife to make a nice splash, and not have to stay in her rich sister's shade. A week or so ought to see Lily back before she formed the habit of throwing money around. Whatever the trouble was with her sister, it shouldn't take too long to settle it. Women's matters were mostly tempests in teapots. In any case, Lily knew how he felt about finding her always at home. She wouldn't stay a second longer than she had to.

He only hoped that sister of hers wouldn't fill her head with ideas. Every time Cleo wrote, Lily somehow seemed different. She never would read the letters aloud, which made him suspect that Cleo was writing things she shouldn't. Probably saying he wasn't good enough for her sister. Well, by all the signs, Lily was satisfied. She never looked at another man. Acted kind of scared of them, truth to tell. Victor knew without anyone having to tell him that Lily wouldn't leave him for the best man on earth.

When he watched the train pull away, with Lily's and Vicky's faces pressed against the glass, he felt the greatest and queerest wrench. He found quite suddenly that he was the kind of man who could not live without a wife.

Down home Charity was packing a borrowed suitcase, putting her poor best on top, so that she and Penny could make a quick change just before they crossed the line and moved up front with the white folks.

The night was outside, and the lamp was soft in the

room, shrouding the leaning walls, masking the unsightliness of all the mean places, the buckling floor boards, the
rag-stuffed windows, the chairs and tables that had to
be lashed into usableness with rope.

There wasn't any use denying it. Ben was a mellow,
loving man. No way in the world to call him a hard-working husband. Ben liked the bed with a woman beside
him. The days in the fields were just a long wishing for
night to fall, just a deep dreaming of women's bodies that
slowed his hands and feet, that made the overseer speak
sharp, that cut his pay, that too often cost his job. Maybe
he wasn't the kind of man a woman should tie herself to.
Maybe Cleo was right in everything she wrote. But how
tear out of your heart the thing that made it beat?

"You going to miss me, Ben?"

He looked at her, the softness, the roundness, the flush
stealing up her cheeks, the love trembling on her lips.

"What do you think?" he asked lazily. And there was
that thing in his husky voice, that worrisome thing that
melted her limbs, that made her wonder how she was
going to stand the time away from him.

"You going to be true to me, Ben?" There was always
some woman with her heart out for him. Wasn't easy to
look at him and look away. He carried seduction in his
eyes, his voice, his slow caressing smile.

He said with soft taunting, "How long you figure to be
away?"

"You know I'll be back quick as I can. You know I ain't
really wanting to go. But Lily's in trouble, and Cleo's
letter would trouble my conscience if I didn't heed it."

"That Cleo and her letters! That Miss Big Dog!" The
words were spat. "Wouldn't surprise me if it ain't her

back of the bust-up of Lily and her man. I'm giving you warning. You stay out of her clutches. I wouldn't put it past her to turn a baby against its mother's milk."

"Ben, don't talk so loud. You'll wake Penny. Don't talk so harsh. You sound like you're jealous of my sister. It ain't natural for a man to be jealous of a woman. Cleo's our eldest. It's right she sets herself over us."

"She sets herself over me, that's what sticks in my craw. You'd think I wasn't half a man the way she messes in my family business. You'd think the living I give you wasn't good enough." And now there was embarrassment behind his rancor. "It's the best I know how."

She closed the suitcase. She would strap it later. There was time for that. It was too hurting a thing to see this god of love needing assurance of his importance to her. How could she want what Cleo had, a middle-aged man? How could she shame her heart with envy of Cleo's quiet nights?

She crossed the room to Ben, and put her arms tight around him, feeling the quivering begin in her body, and the breathlessness riding her words.

"No Mr. Judson ever come into my life for me to choose between him and you. Nobody ever offered me a living like Cleo's for me to chose between it and mine. But what I have is part of me, is blood and bone. I couldn't no more wish I had different than I could wish I'd never been born to love you."

He swooped her up in his arms, and for a moment only, his face bent away from hers when he blew out the lamp. In the warm dark their bodies merged in perfect oneness, and their island of the passionate night was rich in everything for their needs.

Afterward, she lay in the languor of love, and thought
of the wonder that was over, and said in the stillness,
"Ben, you'll be true to me?"

And again his husky teasing answer, "Depends how
long you figure to be away."

Her breath caught in a little sob. He did not want to
make her cry, but he did not want to lie to her either. He
could no more have denied his desire for women than he
could have denied his belief in God. There was no way
for him to say how long the remembrance of this last
night together would sustain him. He loved her. He had
married her, and he had not married the others. Of all
the women he had known, he wanted her most. But
there were untried women who might surpass her. He did
not want to know.

He let his lashes tickle her cheek, to stop the sob and
make her laugh at his foolishness.

And she did say, "Ben, you're such a fool." Her silvery
laugh shattered the sob. Presently she was fast asleep in
his arms.

Across the moon-washed counties, in the town from
which Ben had ridden away with her sister, Serena was
trying to coax a smile out of Robert. They were alone in
their lamplit night. The little boy, Tim, and Pa were
asleep in the next room.

Pa's sleep was full of little groans. Already his marrow
was missing Serena. He had never been separated from
her before. When Miss Hattie died, Serena had married
a homeless man, and Pa had been glad to give them the
whole of the house but a nook for his bed, so that his last
child would not leave him, as his wives had left him in
the demands of death and his older daughters in the demands of life.

Robert was an orphan man, son of some straw-haired cracker too poor, too uncaring, too conscienceless to feed and clothe his bastard as the bluebloods fed and clothed theirs. Robert had shame in him from as far back as he could remember. He was not the first of his mother's spawn nor the last. His mother was a nomad. He was just one of the droppings left on anybody's doorstep, and one that survived. Where his mother was now was in no one's knowledge. She had long since exhausted the town in which Robert saw birth. He had sustained life in a dozen different holes, wherever there was a hand that held bread. They were hands of whores, of drunks, of the diseased, the outcast to whom a hungry unquestioning child was company in their terrible loneliness of the lost.

Robert had worshiped Serena from the first moment he set eyes on her. White-skinned and fair-haired though he was by the accident of his birth, he was as blackened by grime as a chimney sweep. To him Serena was a walking angel. She was clean. Her hair was combed. She lived with her own folks. She had shoes to wear. She went to school.

In his growing up, Robert learned to do any kind of odd job for a living. There wasn't any chore beneath him so long as it gave him money for a bar of soap, for sleeping space with the decent poor, for the slow and painful acquisition of one good suit to court Serena in. She was the star by which his life was guided. If she would have him, he would have the world.

But even the realization of the dream did not change his nature. He was like a man holding his breath waiting for something to happen. For the shame in him knew he was not good enough for Serena. Cleo wasn't talking

through her hat. Laboriously he had spelled out her letters when Serena wasn't around. That was wrong. But
he didn't know very much about wrong and right. And he
had to know what Serena's rich sister thought about him.
He had to know if he was right in what he thought about
himself.

He was a nothing from the devil's patch. He had stolen
his name from a dying old man who had no more use for
it than for the half-loaf of bread he put in Robert's hand.
In Robert was always the fear that, in some moment of
dreadful illumination, Serena would discover his nothingness and be done with him.

When Pa had that accident with his hand, Robert felt
proud to support him. Pa wasn't any use to the mill until
it healed, and he wasn't their responsibility, for the accident had happened off their property, while Pa was helping fight a neighbor's fire that was plainly in no danger
of spreading to the mill.

With Pa not contributing there was never quite enough
to go around. For Robert was only a handyman. There
was in him a weakness from the years of slow hunger that
would never let him be a strong-bodied man able to work
for a strong man's wages.

Cleo's letters, with the money inside them, saved many
a supper from being turnover bread and boiled peas and
parched-meal coffee. And now here was Cleo's latest
letter, with money in it for fare to Boston, and a few
cluttered lines about Lily and some kind of trouble.
Though nobody said it in words, and nobody wanted to
say it, everybody knew it was almost an act of Providence.
Serena's going and Tim's would ease the strain of these
last weeks, would mean more to eat for everybody.

Robert was ashamed that this was so. For the first time he saw Pa's house as it was, a poor man's home, neat as a pin, the holes chinked up, a cloth on the table, every wick trimmed, every chimney glistening, a rug on the floor, sheets on the bed, and the clothes put away, all starched and mended. But now in his heart Robert knew that nobody but somebody who had never known as good would say they didn't want better. The fear was in him that Serena's rich sister would open her eyes.

Serena saw his grieving. She had learned how to lighten the darkness into which he slipped so easily. A radiance lit her cherry-red mouth. The dimples appeared in her cheeks as if a tender finger had made little hollows to catch the smiles that they would coax from whomever they bewitched.

He had to smile back. Though his lips curved slowly, his despair was no longer inconsolable. He was willing to be comforted.

"Robert, I'll write you every day. I'll write you everything I do. It'll be like I'm here in this room talking your ear off."

The shame that was always just there to be tapped made him say diffidently, "Well, it won't be exactly the same. I can't read but a little bit. I never went to school."

She said with tenderness, "There'll be love in my letters, won't there? All you have to do is watch for it to spill out the envelope, and hold your heart ready to catch it."

"You won't go off and forget to come back?"

"When I forget God's in the sky, I'll forget to come back to you. And there's no way to live and breathe in this world without knowing God's on high."

Again her smile reached for his heart and quieted its trembling.

CHAPTER 16

L<small>ILY SAW</small> C<small>LEO</small> before Cleo saw her. She descended
from the train in helter-skelter fashion, her eyes darting
wildly in every direction, and the worry half of her mind
imagining that Cleo might come to meet her on crutches,
or worse, showing some permanent scar, a razor slash, that
Mr. Judson had inflicted on her lovely face. She forgot
Victoria, panting behind her with the suitcase that she
had forgotten, too. When she spied Cleo — and who
would not know her instantly who had known her once?
For what had changed her, who was still untouched by
time or tribulations? — Lily started running, her hairpins
slipping out of place, her hat dipping crazily, and a garter
going pop as it left its moorings.

When she reached Cleo's side, her joy at seeing her
unblemished brought tears of relief to her eyes. Cleo's
first awareness of Lily was of those drenched eyes,
Mama's doe eyes holding Mama's parting tears. The rest,
the comic angle of the overdecorated hat, the hair escaping to her shoulders, the sagging stocking, the cheap and
wrinkled finery, the people grinning at their tableau, even
Vicky, who put down the suitcase and sat on it to wait
for her mother and new aunt to get through being mushy
— all these irrelevancies were for the moment unnoticed

164

by Cleo in the rush of remembrance those eyes evoked. As they stood tightly embraced, she knew that some part of her interrupted childhood was restored.

But in a moment she gently pushed Lily out of her arms, embarrassed by their public exhibition, mindful now of Lily's crumpled appearance, wishing to God she had fixed herself up before she left the train, and turned away from her in unconscious disavowal to welcome Vicky. Meeting the grave stare, seeing the fine intelligent face, she claimed the child, and briefly wondered where her dumbest sister had got her.

On their way to the waiting room, where Cleo had left Judy with strict instructions not to stir a quarter of an inch, Cleo airily answered Lily's anxious questions. Why, of course, she and Mr. Judson were getting along fine. Whatever gave Lily the idea that they weren't? Her letter? Oh, that! That was when she thought she was going to have a b-a-b-y. Can Victoria spell? They were packed and ready to move, and then she'd been miserable with morning s-i-c-k-n-e-s-s, and hadn't seen how she could manage alone. And it had only been an attack of indigestion. Well, the joker was that Lily's frantic reply had given Cleo the confused impression that Lily was in desperate trouble, too. She had promptly sent for Serena and Charity, thinking three heads would serve better than one in solving Lily's problems. Well, the two of them had certainly made a mountain out of a molehill. But out of the mix-up had come this reunion which was worth whatever distress it had cost.

Before Lily's coming, Cleo had laid down the law to Bart about what his attitude should be. "Don't speak to her about her trouble. Stay off the subject of Victor. Act

like she was just here visiting. Don't make her feel like a
poor relation by setting out to pity her. I want her to have
the same kind of time as the rest of us for as long as all
of us are together."

To Lily Cleo said: "Don't feel bad if Mr. Judson doesn't
ask after Victor. You know how some men act when they
get a little money. Look down their noses at other men,
and forget they're on earth."

Bart's complete avoidance of any mention of Victor
was plain enough proof to shy Lily that a Pullman porter
— and very possibly that porter's wife — was beneath his
consideration. She was tongue-tied in his presence, and
walked on tiptoe that she might disturb him as little as
possible.

Cleo was the one who wept when Charity came, for it
might have been Mama walking toward her. The last
time Cleo saw Mama, she was hardly any older than
Charity was now. She was hardly any different. Almost it
was as if Mama were still alive.

Charity put her arms around Cleo, and her tinkling
laugh tried to stem her sister's tears. But only when little
Penny began to cry in sympathy did Cleo remember that
time had not been standing still.

When Serena reached Boston, her baby sister, with a
baby of her own — though it really was too bad he had
to be a boy — Cleo's created world was complete.

Bart gave the visiting sisters the keys to the city. A
week or so before their coming he had cornered the
banana market. The sinking of the *Lucy Evelyn* by a Ger-
man submarine made his shipment the only bananas to
be had in the whole city of Boston. There was war, but
Germany's rout would be a matter of weeks. The way

Bart figured it, God wouldn't let a long war undo his prosperity.

Every day was a holiday for the Jericho sisters. A breakfast feast began it. There were peaches and cream, butter-soaked muffins, chops, hashed-brown potatoes, broiled bananas, sliced tomatoes, and pie for whoever had the capacity. Serena unashamedly confessed she never had as good on Sunday, and Charity regretfully refused second helpings because Ben liked her round but might not like her fat. A prodigious late snack brought their crowded day to a close. When they took their happy exhaustion to bed, they talked back and forth until gradually Cleo's rich compelling voice predominated. The others listened dreamily to Cleo remembering back in a way that cast a magic spell over the South and their sister.

The visiting cousins spent most of their time under Thea's supervision. It mitigated her mourning to be part of their animation. It improved their speech and manners to mirror her, with the natural imitativeness of children.

They rode on the swan boats in the Public Garden, on which Thea had never ridden as a child, being whisked to the shore at the first sign of summer. They went to Nantasket and rode on real boats, though here, too, the child Thea had never been taken, because it was just a cut above Revere Beach and uncountable cuts below a proper watering place. They visited the landmarks of Boston's history — except small Tim, who was not yet two. They had picnics in the Fens.

Thea preferred their unrepressed companionableness to social exchanges with their bashful mothers, who bewildered her as much as she bewildered them. They just could not think of her as colored with her fine airs, and never got past greeting her and running for cover. She could not think of them as anything but phantoms, and supposed she would never chat over tea with them. She would have liked knowing how people lived who didn't live in Boston.

Cleo had the better part of two hundred dollars burning a hole in her pockets in addition to Bart's nightly bounty. The sisters went shopping every day. Charity and Serena were extravagantly thrilled to walk into any store, to take their turn at any counter, to try on any garment Cleo chose. The thrill got a very good start when they boarded the front of the trolley, expanded through their shopping spree, continued unabated when they ate their ice cream at the time and place of purchase, and increased, if anything, when they walked through the same entrance of the moving-picture palace as anybody else who had paid admission.

Though none of these pleasures, nor the rest of their treats, were unfamiliar to Lily, the money lavished on them was. In her effort to keep up with Cleo, she had spent her twenty dollars in two days, or she supposed she had. She couldn't think whether Cleo had ever given her back the change from a five-dollar bill the time she borrowed it to pay the ice man because Lily's purse was handiest. But instead of Cleo being provoked when her money ran out, Lily was thankful to find that Cleo was even nicer, and tucked her even more securely under her wing.

The sisters wrote glowingly to their husbands, and Serena kept her promise to Robert not to leave out anything. Only once or twice did their accounts falter, when the low point of their day had been an encounter with a visitor. Cleo had talked to them so much about what they should and shouldn't say about their husbands, their husbands' occupations, their homes, their friends, and Pa that the three simple, honest young women, not wishing to embarrass her, yet not wishing to give false impressions either, had sat like deaf-mutes, while Cleo spoke for them in her characteristic way of taking a nub of truth and stretching it out of all proportion.

On the day that Miss Eleanor Elliot came to call, their heads spun briskly for hours afterward. When the spinning stopped, common sense advised them, even Serena, to let her visit go entirely unrecorded.

Miss Eleanor Elliot, a Vassar graduate, was the maiden daughter of a Negro district attorney, now deceased, whose brilliance had won him high prestige and a house among the rich. He had trotted Miss Elliot all over Europe on his summer vacations, where she had unhappily discovered that after Vassar, and now this, she could never marry a colored man. Marriage did not enter the minds of the European men she met, not because she was a colored American, but because she was not a rich American.

She was not rich now. She had been brought up with too expensive tastes to husband her modest inheritance. It was gone. Miss Elliot's Back Bay drawing room was now the setting for a Saturday dancing class. Weekly in winter a hand-picked collection of little boys in white gloves and little girls in best dresses formed a double line and made their bows and curtsies to Miss Templeton, their teacher. Miss Templeton was white, genteel, exquisitely tactful, and still a little surprised that Miss Elliot's offer had been irresistible.

While the installation of the parlor graces went on behind her disinterested back, Miss Elliot's ringed hands
called the tunes from her polished piano, and her thoughts
revolved around Vassar and Capri. Her unseeing eyes
mirrored the great stone houses outside her window,
stately houses now desecrated by Room for Rent signs and
new owners. Only Miss Eleanor Elliot and her moulted
elegance remained to represent the better whites who had
preceded these lesser ones.

Thea had proposed Judy's name for Miss Elliot's class.
An acceptance was given official stamp with Miss Elliot's
visit of state. As she reached the house, she met Thea
leaving it with the four little cousins. Miss Elliot, who
had met handsome Mrs. Judson but not her daughter, immediately addressed Penny as Judith, because she was so
pretty. When Penny's surprised expression pointed out
her error, she turned her beam on Vicky because she was
Cleo's color. Judy, who was quite used to having her
mother denied her, quietly stepped forward to assert her
closer kinship.

Miss Elliot cloaked her chagrin with a delicate clearing
of the throat, and submitted to being properly introduced.
She was enchanted with Vicky's and Penny's attractive-
ness, and proposed to ask Mrs. Judson how long they were
staying. She was deeply sorry that bright-haired Tim was
too young to be invited to be her most impressive pupil.

Cleo's sisters could not escape Miss Elliot. She demanded the pleasure of meeting them, with no intention
of leaving until she had seen what they looked like. She
was not disappointed, though their accents distressed her.
She took it for granted that they were the cream of the
South because they were the right color. It seemed to her

a great pity that their sparing speech had a noticeable flavor of illiteracy. In Miss Elliot's opinion the mammy system of the South should be abolished. The nicest children sat at its knee and were taught to maltreat their mother tongue.

"We," said Miss Elliot, who had formed the habit of saying "we" when her father was living, because it made her feel there was really no difference between being a noted district attorney and being a noted district attorney's daughter, "we do hope you'll make a long stay with us."

"Well, my husband — " began Lily, blushing furiously as she did nowadays when mention of Victor was unavoidable.

"Is much easier in his mind with Lily here," Cleo interrupted smoothly. "His work takes him out of town at least half of the year. There's no need for Lily to hurry home to an empty house."

"Pa — " said Serena, wondering if he was able to help a little around the house, or whether Robert still had all the cooking and cleaning to do.

"Father," Cleo gently corrected, "is more Serena's baby than she is his. She wore herself thin waiting hand and foot on him when he was ill. It's time for Serena to think of herself, or let me think for her. I've made up my mind to keep her here until I can get some flesh on her."

"Then, of course," urged Miss Elliot, turning brightly to Charity, "you won't want to leave such pleasant company."

"Ben — he's my husband — " said Charity valiantly — "he ain't the kind of man to leave alone for long."

"She means," said Cleo, with a hard look at her sister,

"Ben's not the kind of man to keep house for himself. It
will take Charity weeks to straighten out the confusion.
That's why I tell her there's no reason to rush. Dirt can
wait."

Miss Elliot turned a compelling eye on Cleo's sisters.
"Dear Mrs. Judson does right to persuade," she said
earnestly. "With so many of the unfortunates of our race
migrating to Boston, we find ourselves becoming cru-
saders for our beloved city. We may soon be outnum-
bered by the South-Enders, or worse, diminished in the
estimation of our better whites who hardly thought of us
as colored before their coming. We Bostonians have
been a little hidebound. But now we are eager to open
our ranks to whoever will help us in our fight for survival."
She rose. Her voice was unsteady. "When we see lovely
children like yours, we hate to see them leave our city
while the South-End children stay. Forgive a woman
no longer young for wanting to preserve her father's
world."

Cleo gave a hasty glance around the circle of her sisters,
who, she saw, had comprehended enough to look uncomfortable. Without appearing to, she sped Miss Elliot's
departure. When she returned from seeing her to the
door, she said lightly, her eyes not quite meeting theirs,
"Don't ask me what that poor stuck-up soul was talking
about. I wasn't half listening. I was thinking what I'd
fix for us to eat before we go out."

"Well, I'm ready to eat," Charity admitted. "I know
that lady meant well, but what she was saying kinda left
a bad taste in my mouth. She talks so big doing, I
couldn't catch everything. But it sounded to me like she
ain't got much use for poor people."

"Why, she's poor herself," Cleo said, with a little laugh. "Couldn't you tell by her old-time clothes? You must have misunderstood her. Well, what does it matter? She'll be a long time dead while we're alive and kicking.

"Looka here." She contorted her limber body into bosom and bustle, pitched her voice to a falsetto elegance, and launched into an imitation of Miss Eleanor Elliot that had her sisters chuckling in reminiscence all through the many dishes of their meal.

CHAPTER 17

After two intoxicating weeks Cleo's sisters began their preparations for departure. She urged them to stay a little longer for the children's sake. They were enjoying each other so much. It seemed a shame to separate them. Her sisters said sincerely that they wished they didn't have to go, feeling a not unnatural reluctance at leaving the scenes of their wonderfully good times. But already they were living them in retrospect, and anticipating the telling of their adventures to their husbands. Though Cleo's whole heart was behind her plea, only a lesser part of theirs was behind their regret.

Cleo fell ill. Her illness was not feigned. She, who had been so alive, lay listless in bed, her hot dry hands twitching on the sheet, the vibrant voice a thin whimper. She could neither eat nor sleep. In her will-less body was only the emptiness left by the deathblow to her heart. She was pining away.

The baffled doctor said it looked like a nervous collapse, perhaps brought on by the summer heat. Cleo had never been sick a day in her life except for Judy's easy birth. Bart was scared out of his wits. He begged her sisters not to leave her. In his excited frame of mind he was heartbreakingly certain they might never again see Cleo alive.

Their disappointed husbands wrote with some indignation that if Mr. Judson was as rich as he was cracked up to be, he could afford to hire a raft of nurses to take care of his wife, and when were they coming home to take care of their husbands?

When her sisters gave Cleo their watered versions, she suffered a relapse. With an excess of family loyalty, seeing the wasting form of their oldest, their brightest, their beautiful sister, they notified their heartless husbands that they would return when Cleo took a change for the better, and not a second sooner. Whoever didn't like it would have to lump it.

Lily, who stayed tearfully certain that Cleo was going to die, suggested that Vicky and Penny start school with Judy. She did not want her daughter, who was not a quiet child, to speed her sister's end. She was far too bashful, however, to carry through her own idea. It was Charity, looking trim and pretty in her newest dress, who shepherded the three little girls off to first grade, inwardly repeating by rote the necessary falsehoods concerning her non-resident daughter and niece in which Cleo, showing her first interest in days, had coached her.

Then it was that Cleo really began to mend. She could take nourishment. Her hands could lie still. She could listen with eagerness for the children's return from school, and be lulled to sleep by the sound of their happy chatter.

On the day that Cleo went downstairs for the first time and sat at the kitchen table, inhaling the tantalizing odors of Charity's cooking, the postman's ring sent Charity, who was already on her feet, to the door.

She returned with a pleased smile and a letter from Ben. She was already writing the answer in her mind:

Cleo is up and about. Me and Penny will be starting for home any minute now. She would not add what was understood — as soon as Cleo gives me the money.

She sat down at the table with her sisters and opened her letter. It was short, specific, and brutal, written by a mellow, loving man with a passionate woman looking over his shoulder, her wet mouth pursed to press against his whenever his stub of pencil faltered. A postscript added that the rags she and Penny had left behind were already on their way.

Wordlessly she passed the letter to Cleo, pushed back her chair, stumbled out of the kitchen in a daze, and blindly went up the back stairs, her breath pushing hard against her chest.

Cleo digested the letter at a glance. Calling down curses on Ben's black soul, she tore it into shreds. With a fierce protective strength flowing into her, she followed swiftly after Charity.

As she bent over her lacerated sister, a great swell of love and pity restored her heart to pulsing life. Her voice was like a 'cello, deep, rich, dramatic. "I won't watch one of my sisters cry for any man on earth. Ben's a bad lot. I say good riddance. You've always got a home with me."

"I love him, Cleo. I can't live without him."

"That's wicked talk. Think of your child. Think of your sisters. Think of me. You've got us to live for."

"But Ben — I ain't got the words to describe him. He's a man made for women to love. There was always some woman I had to watch out for. Wasn't his fault. Wasn't theirs. He looks at you, and you want to melt into him. You want — no use my trying to lie about it — you want him to blow out the lamp. I been missing his loving, Cleo, no use my lying."

"You're a mother, Charity. A colored mother bears a child, she 's got no time for wringing and twisting in bed. She's got to put her whole mind on raising that child right."

"You can talk," said Charity bitterly. "You can get in Mr. Judson's bed whenever you've a mind to."

"I haven't been near that nigger's room since my sisters walked into this house."

"It ain't easy to explain myself, Cleo. I'm no hand with words. It ain't just the loving in the night. That part's the heaven part, like nothing on earth. But there's the living part that's maybe harder to do without. It's the sight of your man across the table, the sound of him washing his face in the basin; it's hearing your child call him 'Daddy,' knowing 'twas him put her in your body; it's watching him turn in his sleep on Sunday morning."

Cleo sat down on the edge of the bed. Her face was cold. "Charity, I'm going to talk harsh to help you over the hurt. That dog did you so dirty it makes you think you lost the moon and the stars. All you lost was a nigger who didn't have a dime when you married him and's got no more now. I've been wanting to say this for years. You were always too good for him."

"Ain't nothing you can find to say can make me stop grieving. You married money. I married love. We both did our picking with our eyes wide open. What you ain't had, I reckon you never wanted. Was I to tell you, you wouldn't listen."

Cleo said hotly: "I've thought, and planned, and lied, and juggled Mr. Judson's money for this sister and that, so I could always know there was no one of my kin who didn't have food in her belly or clothes on her back. What name you give to that?"

Charity's hand touched hers, almost compassionately. "You've been a good sister. Wasn't a letter you ever wrote me since the day you got married didn't have something inside it. Wasn't a birthday or Christmas passed without your big box. But that ain't the love I'm talking about." Her breath came hard, and now her hand curled in Cleo's for comfort. "You think if I go back to Ben, he'd put that woman out?"

"Go back for her to cut you in ribbons? Go back to hear Ben say what it came near killing you to read? How could I live with my conscience if I sent my own sister into a cage of lions?"

Charity's hand fell away. She said dully, "I'll get me a job soon's I can. Mr. Judson may know some nice white people who want a good worker."

"You think I want to see my sister slaving in somebody's kitchen? I'll take care of you and Penny as long as I draw breath."

"But Mr. Judson — ? Men and their in-laws don't mix."

"He was going to take Lily in, wasn't he? He promised me someone to help with this house. No difference to him if it's Lily or you."

She stood up. Her expression was wise and tender. "I'm going down to get you a man-size breakfast. This wouldn't have hit you so hard if you hadn't been empty."

She would not let Lily or Serena help her with the laden tray. She was entirely confident of her strength. She returned, settled the tray on the side of Charity's bed, and drew up a chair.

"I'm not going to stir till you eat every scrap."

As Charity reluctantly ate the huge breakfast, sometimes stopping for a sob, sometimes lying back to keep her stomach steady, the hot food was like a heating pad on her pain. The twisted places in her body unwound and felt like flesh again. Only her heart, that was no longer a whole heart, refused to return to an even beat.

After the storm of weeping, after the massive breakfast, she felt sleepy. She could even smile tremulously at Cleo. No use crying over spilt milk. What had happened to her happened to other women. They went on living in their twilight. If you kept your stomach full, looked like nothing seemed so bad as when your stomach was empty.

That night Cleo cooked an excellent supper of the things Bart liked best, and served him first. Afterward, at a prearranged signal, her sisters fell over their feet getting out of the kitchen, and Cleo told Bart about Charity.

"Life's funny," she concluded. "Lily was the one we were worried about. But Lily and Victor got patched up, I guess. I haven't wanted to mind her business and ask her. But she was going with the others before I took sick, so she must have had a husband to go to. Now it's poor Charity who's got no home but mine."

Bart said with pity: "I felt there was something. I saw how that girl was shoveling down her supper. Like a starved dog. I reckon the emptiness in her will take a long time to fill. Well, I reckon, too, it don't make much difference which one stays, so long as the others go. I'm glad you gave them a good time. I'm glad they repaid you by seeing you through your sickness. But winter's not too long away. We got to start cutting down. We got to start renting their rooms."

Bart had called time. Cleo had to work fast. She went to work at once on Lily. She got Lily so stirred up that she was afraid to open Victor's next letter. As if it were a hot coal, she handed it to Cleo to open for her.

Cleo read Victor's abject hope that Lily would soon be heading for home without expression.

Lily began to shake all over. "What does he say?" she asked fearfully.

Cleo expelled a long sigh. "Well, he doesn't say what Ben said. But he says enough. He's not messed up with any woman. But he's fixing to mess you up as soon as he sees you. I won't tell you what he said word for word. No sense in scaring you. But I wouldn't trust him not to beat your brains out. That's why I was sorry when you married him. You never know when a low-class man is going to get ugly. My advice to you is to sit tight until his temper cools off."

She made a motion of passing the letter to Lily.

Lily jumped back. "I don't want to see it. Tear it up."

There were two more beseeching letters from Victor which went unanswered. Then there was Victor himself. He had had the unwisdom to steel himself with a double whiskey. He was afraid of Cleo. He knew he would have to fight her for his wife. And he did not know who would win.

He sat in Cleo's parlor with the smell of whiskey on his breath. He wasn't drunk, but from Lily's frightened expression he might as well have been. She crowded beside Cleo on the sofa, remembering the stories Cleo had told her about low-class men who went crazy with drink.

Victor stared at her from across the room, a brown man looking almost black with the anger in his cheeks. Lily paled and thought about Simeon and Thea, who, Cleo said, had both been beaten to a pulp in quiet Cambridge just for walking together. God alone knew what had kept her and Victor from being killed outright in the wickeder city of New York. She pressed closer to her sister.

"You see, it is useless to try to persuade her," said Cleo. "Her mind is made up."

But the double whiskey was potent inside Victor. "I came for my wife and my child, and I won't leave without them." He felt crazy talking to Cleo, with Lily sitting full-grown beside her. "Get up and go pack," he said savagely.

She began to cry softly. Her only movement was her visible quivering.

He leaped to his feet and started toward her. He walked slowly, for he was mad enough to shake her for shrinking against her sister as if she expected him to hit her. He was trying to rid himself of the impulse before he reached her. He had never touched a woman, and he didn't want to start now.

To Lily his slow-paced step was the sound of doom. Cleo knew from his relaxing hands that it was not. One out of ten thousand men went berserk. It wasn't likely that Lily would ever die by violence.

"Get away from my sister," she blazed. "Don't come one step nearer. If you put your hand on her, I'll call the police."

Lily was terrifyingly aware that if Victor advanced another step, Cleo would run out of the house to scream for a policeman. She would be alone in this room with Victor. When Cleo returned, help would be too late.

Lily's back was against the wall, and it stiffened. The meanest creature will fight for life, and Lily already felt Victor's fist in her face.

She jumped to her feet and sprang at him. She was a wild fury. Her fingernails tore down his face. Her voice shrilled and cracked and spat out a stream of ugly, unforgivable words that she had absorbed from hearing Cleo in her caustic sessions with Bart. They were part of Cleo's personality. They had never been part of Lily's. And Victor was not Bart. What one man can stomach may act as poison on another. The words rushing from her throat were an avalanche of rock that pulverized Victor's self-respect. Lily had never called him "black nigger" in all their married life.

He knew what it was with her now. The sum of it was this sister of hers had taught her to hate her dark husband. For the first time since his blind entrance, he was savagely conscious of Lily's white skin and the golden skin of her sister. Two goddamned color-struck hussies! Heard tell yellow fever was common in Boston. God, let him get out of this house before his little honey-colored daughter came home from school and backed away from her own daddy because he was dark.

He picked up his hat, walked out of his marriage, and left Lily to her destruction. And Lily promptly had hysterics because she had just escaped it.

When Cleo graphically told Bart about Victor's attempt to kill Lily, he said heavily: "Looks like when one blow falls, there's a rain of them. First Charity, now Lily. There's some ill star hanging over your sisters. God knows what's in store for Serena. I know you hate letting her go when her comfort's needed. But Godamighty, Cleo, you got to put her on the train before whatever's due to happen, happens here."

It was mid-October, but there had been no word from Robert since the long, misspelled, chaotic letter that had been his answer to Serena's rash declaration of devotion to Cleo. He hadn't reproached her or begged her to relent. He had urged her to stay. Queer thing was, he had had it in mind to tell her. Their letters almost crossed. He had a real job now, a good steady job, paying good steady money. The reason he hadn't sent her any of it was because he was paying down on a house. The house was fresh-painted inside and out, the roof was new-shingled, the porch was sound, the furniture was part of the sale and looking like it had never been used, the well was just outside the door, no more carting water from the spring. Soon as he paid a third, they could move in. She wasn't to worry if he didn't write again until it was time to send her the money to come. He had sat up till midnight three nights in a row to work on this letter. Writing wore him out, and with the house well-nigh his, he didn't want to lose it sleeping on the job.

Serena had been torn between believing him and knowing he was lying. Knowing there was shame and torment in every line. But maybe God had wrought a miracle, and Robert had a real job. That wasn't too much to make up to him for the times God had seemed to turn His back. For Robert's sake, she would have faith.

The day his letter came — with Cleo too sick and uncaring for Serena to trouble her to listen to it, or for Bart to bother her with the rent money — that day Bart left forty-five dollars with Serena to give to Mr. Van Ryper when he called. But Mr. Van Ryper said there must be some mistake, and gave her back twenty dollars. For a terrible moment Serena didn't want to waste time on faith, she wanted to steal that twenty dollars, grab up Tim, go as far south as she could on it, and walk to Robert the rest of the way. But she had never stolen in her life, and she could not bring herself to steal from Mr. Judson, whose bread she had eaten.

That had been September. And now in October Serena wanted to write some neighbor to take a peep at Robert and Pa and tell her how things were with them. Cleo, who on recovery had read Robert's lies for what they were, said with quiet reproach: "Where's your faith in the husband you claim you love? Why would you send a neighbor to nose in his business? Robert told you plain he'd tell you when to come. It takes time and money to buy a house. You're young and impatient. Don't make Robert think you're trying to push him beyond his strength. You always say he's a shamefaced man. Don't shame his pride. Let him know you're satisfied to stay with me for as long as need be."

Serena looked as if she was trapped between two fires. "But how can I go on staying here in Mr. Judson's house? How can one man's shoulders stand so many burdens?"

"It's my house!" Cleo cried angrily. "Mr. Judson and I got that settled between us the night before I rented it. He runs his store, I run my house without interference." Her voice softened. "Don't ever call yourself a burden again. How can my baby sister be a burden? You don't eat more than a bird, for all my pleading. And a little boy like Tim can't put away but so much, no matter how much he eats. If Mr. Judson didn't want you here, he'd tell me quick enough. He wouldn't bite his tongue. And after all, I'm his wife, as well as your sister. I wouldn't do anything to hurt his pocketbook. Don't forget he's a rich man. He can afford to throw away what you'd set aside for Sunday dinner. Just you put your faith in me and Robert, and let time take care of the rest."

In November there was one more letter from Robert. The bandage was off Pa's hand. He could use it good enough to do for himself. And Robert was leaving town. That job hadn't turned out as steady as the boss had promised it would. He was going to get a better one some place where folks didn't know him and what he was used to working for. There were only a few more payments due on the house before it was theirs. That's why he wasn't going to tarry, taking piddling jobs here and there. She'd hear from him as soon as he got wherever there were good wages. If she could hold on a while longer, he'd send for her and Tim in time for Christmas.

December came, and no word from Robert. And Pa couldn't write even without his bandage. Serena had taught him to sign his name. But the rest of a letter would have to stay blank if Pa was the one had to fill it in. He didn't know how to spell the words he wanted to spell, and Serena wished she had taught him. Three easy words — I miss you.

Every once in a while Cleo gave her a dollar or two to put in an envelope for Pa. The doctor had cautioned him that his hand couldn't earn before January. And Cleo said easily, "Pa's eating, isn't he? What more can he want unless he wants you to come and feed him like a baby."

Soon it was mid-December, and Cleo said gaily: "Christmas is right on top of us. The children's first Christmas together. Serena, don't let them see you with a long face. Don't spoil their happiness."

Then it was Christmas Eve. Serena, standing at the window, trying to see across the world, knew in her anguished heart that wherever Robert was, he was homeless. He who had been conceived as carelessly as if two dogs had met, whose growing had been slow starvation, whose life had been shadowed by his shame, God, help him, Serena prayed, God, give him a home in your bosom.

CHAPTER 18

T HE DUCHESS stood at her bedroom window in the Cambridge house, dressed in white brocade, with her pale hair in a Psyche knot. Her wedding ring had been Simeon's mother's. She had left it to him to give to the woman he would choose for a wife. On the day of his choice, in all probability she had revolved in her grave. Above her wedding band the Duchess wore a diamond of singular beauty. The solitaire on her right hand was of the same size and flawlessness. They were only a fractional part of the treasure that Corinne had acquired in those months when she designed her daughter's destiny.

Outside, the snow was beginning to fall in a blinding swirl, obscuring the sky and the star which had guided the wise men. Between heaven and earth there was now a white shroud. The Duchess could not discern which way wisdom would travel that night.

Behind her, blue flames glowed in hand-painted globes, giving light and heightened shadow to the room. Nothing had been changed since the first Lenore had died on the massive bed, with her namesake and her namesake's mother far removed from the lofty thoughts her last earthly moments inspired. The Duchess had added to the room only the crucifix on the wall and the Virgin Mother enshrined, she who had conceived without benefit of

banns, holding in her arms the child, whom Joseph had
not sired, who would have been nameless if God had not
named him God the Son.

The Duchess was a bride of less than a month. Simeon
had come to propose the day after his father's funeral.
His mood was somber as befitting both occasions. For
there were three burials in a row, the least in importance
Carter Binney's, because it was only his mortal remains,
and second, Simeon's single blessedness, because from its
dust was formed the man of compromise, and first, because of its frightfulness, the Catholic heart that was
buried alive.

Listening to Simeon's proposal the Duchess poised her
soul between good and evil, as she saw them, knowing,
from knowing her mother, that there is no interlocking of
separated worlds, but inescapably forced to make the
choice that would cause the most suffering, that would
flog her spirit to its utmost humility, that would burden
her with the cross.

But there was nothing in the imperial eyes to indicate
this inherited disposition to suffer. Simeon, looking at her
without awe, but using the same yardstick of her bearing
and ash-blondness by which Cleo measured her aloofness
— Simeon thought that she was immune to emotion.

When the brief exchanges were over, the Duchess said,
"I hope you will consent to a joint account. I want very
much to help *The Clarion*."

Simeon rose. He said stiffly: "I am not marrying you
for your money. However it may seem to you, I came to
discharge a debt, not to add to it."

She rose, too. The faintest color was in her cheeks. "I
had no intention of being presumptuous. It was Mrs.
Judson who suggested — "

"If you don't mind," Simeon interrupted, "I prefer not
to discuss it further." He crossed to her and formally extended his hand. "I hope we will make the best of our
bargain."

Her hand lay in his and he saw its exquisite modeling.
A delicate fragrance came from her hair. Her dark-blue
eyes and dark lashes accented her ivory skin. She was
as lovely as a woman in a dream.

"I must go," he said abruptly.

"Of course." She withdrew her hand. "It was good of
you to come at all."

Their wedding night was spent in a cheap hotel in an
unsavory section of New York, where they found over-
night shelter after being refused at a half-dozen other
places in a descending order of desirability. Simeon had
come down from Boston a few days before to file their
marriage intentions. The Duchess, too, came down from
her upstate retreat to change from her sobriety to the
magnificent costume that a French modiste had been
fashioning for her in a celebrated establishment.

In the days preceding their marriage, the Duchess and
Simeon met daily for dinner, she arriving from the
Brevoort, he from the ghetto of San Juan Hill. The worried waiters tried to make themselves believe that Simeon
was a visiting Arab, and hoped the equally worried pa-
trons wouldn't overhear his Boston accent. The sparing
speech that passed between him and his bride-to-be
brought them no nearer to understanding, but their suc-
cessive meetings brought them nearer to a desire for
understanding.

They were married on a snowy afternoon, and evening
found them stranded in Grand Central Station. Train

service to Boston was suspended. The storm had grown to blizzard size, and the tracks were blocked. As they went from one hotel to another in the furious night, the Duchess saw the open contempt in the eyes of the desk clerks. She saw that it was directed at her. Though reason told her that they refused to accept her as Simeon's wife, not because of her church, but because of her color, as reason had tried to tell her earlier that the outraged eye of the justice of the peace was directed at her, not because she was marrying a Protestant without a dispensation or a priest, but because she was white mating with black, still the Duchess let her conscience badger her into believing that these scornful men had second sight and saw that she had sinned.

Watching the leering bellboy back out of the bedroom door, reading in his impudent eyes his lascivious expectation of her corruption, she knew that she was no more Simeon's wife than her mother had been Thad Tewksbury's. She would not let Simeon relieve her of her coat. She sat as far away from him as the small room permitted to wait for day and the first train to Boston.

Simeon sat down on the lumpy bed, and felt no surprise that she did not propose to share it. Their luggage stood side by side in a corner, and staring at the soft richness of one and the rough-grained shabbiness of the other, he was struck by their dissimilarity. Looking across the room at the Duchess, he could not help but pity her for being in this sordid place, even for being his wife.

To take her mind off where she was, to shorten the hours for her, he began to talk. Because the night's expedition was uppermost in his mind, he told her of *The Clarion,* and why and how it had come into being. He

talked of the agonies and hopes of blacks, of the courage
and cowardice of whites, and of his passion to work
toward man's salvation.

The Duchess listened with the stillness that had become
part of her in the quiet of the convent, in the empty days
after her homecoming, in the nights when men were too
intent on the turn of a wheel to know her beyond her
imperial presence, and so recently in the retreat. And
this stillness spread out like a delicate net to enmesh
Simeon's mind. His thoughts tumbled into it. In this
strange room, with this woman who was almost a stranger,
he felt a peace he had never before experienced. He felt
close to something he could not identify.

In the weeks since their marriage, Simeon had come to
look forward to his quiet evenings with his wife. She
listened with compassion and increasing understanding
when he described the poor and oppressed and his moral
responsibility to rouse the ingrown intelligence of colored
Bostonians to a consciousness of the brotherhood of black
men and their common fate.

He felt that if he could reach Lenore, whose life, as he
saw it, had been devoted to selfish ends, he need not
despair of persuading the others to emerge from the
narrow rut of Negro society to a larger perception of
social man. The South End, which had accepted his
marriage to the notorious Duchess with a sullen expectation that she would turn him to her ways, would see that
he had brought her to the hard knowledge of hunger.

The Duchess never referred to her money again. A time
must come when the needs of the poor would take precedence over his pride. Simeon was converting her. And
there was beginning to grow in her the tremulous hope
that she might convert him. She would wait until he had

learned to love her. It was conceivable now that he would. When he was ready for their lives to be wholly shared, she would unearth her Catholic heart. She would persuade him to a priest. She would confess her sin. They would have a true marriage. They would have children. Then would begin the abundant life of the family. The world would be shut out.

Belowstairs the bellpull sounded. The Duchess heard Simeon's quick step in the hall outstrip the maid's unexcited pace. The front door was flung open. There was a rush of cold air. Simeon's voice rose with it to the upper floor.

"Thea, come in, come in. It's turned into a wretched night. Cole, shut the door, old fellow. Thea's shivering."

Upstairs the Duchess shivered a little, too. Then she went out into the hall and down the stairs to meet her new sister-in-law.

The season but not its spirit had prompted Thea to come to dinner. She and the Duchess were to be guests at Cleo's Christmas night. She did not want to be introduced to her sister-in-law before interested onlookers who would relish their first meeting. Her opinion of the Duchess was her private affair.

Cleo's invitation was the first that the Duchess had accepted. It was the first that had been extended. Simeon had never been a social person, and hostesses had grown tired of his ignoring their bids. His unannounced marriage had obligated no one to entertain for his bride.

Thea's social life had been almost wholly curtailed since her father's death. Her quiet marriage to Cole had occurred sooner than planned because of the illness of Cole's mother, who wanted to see them married before she died. But Mrs. Hartnett's illness had not proved fatal. Death had settled for slow decay. Her fretful invalidism, which had made such a stylish start with a day and night nurse, now had to content itself with Thea's well-intentioned but middling care. For the most part Thea fluttered helplessly over her helpless patient.

She had handled her inheritance with the same incompetence. Simeon had refused to touch a penny. He was marrying a rich woman. She was marrying a poor doctor. She put the money in the bank and accepted a checkbook. That, of course, was her undoing. She was not ungenerous. On one of her weekly visits to *The Clarion* to turn in her copy of society jottings, she sent Simeon out on some pretext and industriously wrote checks for a sheaf of overdue bills. She hired a day and night nurse for Mrs. Hartnett. Then had to hire someone to help her cook, because, with the nurses' trays and Mrs. Hartnett's special diet and Cole's meals, she hovered near collapse. When Mrs. Hartnett's infirmity turned into a lingering one, the night nurse was let go, but Thea increased the cook's wages to include cleaning. The back and front parlors were being turned into inner and outer offices for Cole. They would have to be kept immaculate, which was quite beyond Thea's powers. But before the inner office was completely equipped, an irate salesman returned a check marked No Funds.

Now the nurse was gone, the cook-housekeeper was gone, and their duties devolved upon Thea. And she did not even have a new dress to make her look better than she felt. The money had vanished before she had had time to buy anything for herself.

As the Duchess descended the stairs, Thea saw the beauty of her carriage and her gown, the lovely hair and magnificent eyes, the blazing diamonds, and felt neither envy nor admiration, and very little curiosity. She had been born a Binney, and the Duchess would only die one.

The Duchess, seeing the proud indifference on Thea's face, seeing Simeon's eyes on his sister and his inscrutable smile, prayed silently, Merciful God, let Simeon never have to choose between us.

She came forward with her hand outstretched, but she was not offering an olive branch. She was simply prepared to conceal from Simeon any hesitation on Thea's part to extend her hand first.

Their hands clasped lightly. The Duchess said composedly, "We do not need to be introduced. I am glad that you could come."

"You are very kind," Thea said mechanically.

Cole took the Duchess's hand in the second that Thea meant to leave it dangling. He owed his education to his hostess. He had not forgotten. "May I give you my tardy but very best wishes for many years of happiness?"

Simeon said, again with that half-amused smile, "There's an excellent fire in the library, and some excellent whiskey. I think Thea could do with a little more thawing."

The whiskey had a most agreeable effect on Cole, who never had any money to spend on sociability. He leaned back in his chair in an attitude of unconstraint that had become rare with him in the past month or so of mental stress.

Cole had a dream of healing, of giving his heart and soul to the study of cancer. He preferred the laboratory and the poor ward of the hospital, where he spent most of his time, to keeping his office hours and building up a general practice. But the dream was dying inside him. His helpless wife and his helpless mother could not be fed with the experiments that were his only sustenance.

He said, the drink expanding inside him, and the subject dearest to him seeming an exciting conversational
piece, "I made a rather remarkable discovery in the lab
today. One of my rabbits — "

Thea, her own tongue loosening, said sharply: "It's
Christmas Eve, Cole. I don't want to hear about your sick
rabbits. Cole forgets," she explained piteously to Simeon,
"that most of my time is spent with his sick mother and
the rest with his sick patients, hearing them tell me their
symptoms while they wait for the doctor. I don't want to
complain. I'm proud to be a doctor's wife. But living in
Brighton, as we do, we're near none of our friends. I look
forward to the evenings with Cole. And Cole comes home
and talks shop."

"I'm really very sorry, Thea," Cole said tightly. "I shall
try to remember to keep my mouth shut." He straightened
up and took a generous gulp of his drink, but it had no
potency. The feeling of good-fellowship was gone.

Simeon said paternally: "You're both under strain. The
first year of marriage, the first year of struggle to establish a practice in a white neighborhood are full of trials
that will not seem so formidable in retrospect. I'm very
glad that Jewish neighbor will stay with Mrs. Hartnett
again tomorrow. It will do you good to see your friends
and forget your problems for an evening."

"I hope," said Thea, who was not entirely comforted,
"that Cleo won't hand the evening over to this dean of
yours. He'll talk shop, too, and I shan't be interested. I
know nothing about colored colleges except that I don't
approve of segregation. I shouldn't mind if the storm held
him up. When is he due?"

"He'll telephone me tomorrow from South Station,"

Simeon answered. "His first letter gave an earlier date, but then there was a second letter, a rather guarded one. I gathered he'd had a little difficulty getting a ticket North. As for his talking shop, I'm hoping the man will be a spellbinder."

He got up and began to move about the room, too fired with enthusiasm to sit still. "I could read enough between the lines to know that something big is in preparation. I wouldn't be surprised — indeed, I'm expecting that the whole student body and every faculty member are planning to strike against some injustice of the South. You don't believe in segregation, Thea. Neither do colored Southerners. If Dean Galloway has some plan of action, I am very much at his service."

The Duchess felt his passion. "I will be impatient, too, Simeon, until Dean Galloway is actually here. I am not surprised that Mrs. Judson consented so readily to arrange a gathering. She is a woman of great sympathy. And she and the dean are fellow Southerners. I think she is persuasive enough to pledge her guests to whatever cause he has come on."

While they were at dinner the snow fell thicker and faster for all the small Bostonians who believed that Santa Claus came by sleigh. When it was time for Thea and Cole to leave, the white city made walking to the trolley stop an unpleasant excursion.

Simeon had never made use of the Duchess's motorcar. He would not let himself be chauffeur-driven to the shabby offices of *The Clarion*. Seeing Thea's inadequate rubbers, he remembered how he had chided her a week ago for coming out in just such weather without her arctics. Now he inwardly cursed his obtuseness, and his voice was almost savage when he said to the Duchess, "I think you might offer to have Thea and Cole driven home."

The Duchess paled. She had not been unaware of the motorcar in the carriage house. She had simply had no knowledge of the direction Simeon's pride would take. It was a moment or two before she could trust her voice. "Clark has already been told that he might be needed tonight."

Simeon turned to Cole. "Thea's neglected to wear her arctics all winter. After this, you really should see to it."

Cole's smile was wry. "I'll put a pair of arctics in the top drawer of my mind."

The car pulled away from the door. The Duchess could not catch back her sigh that had the sound of a little sob. She murmured good night to Simeon and left him. He watched her go. There had been no other night when they had not said good night reluctantly. But there had been no other night when anyone had come to test the fragile ties of their marriage. When would they ever make those ties secure?

Abruptly he swung his mind away, turned into the library, and poured himself a stiff whiskey. But he could not drown the image of the Duchess. He poured another whiskey, but her image persisted. With a violent motion he smashed the glass against the hearth, and went out of the room, and up the stairs.

Outside the Duchess's door he paused, took a step past it, then turned back and rapped softly.

After a moment she said, "Come in."

He entered her room. She was sitting very erect on the side of the bed in a blue dressing gown, but the coverlet plainly showed where she had flung herself across it in a storm of weeping. A silver hairbrush gleamed on the

carpet. She raised her hands to push back her pale un-
bound hair, and the gesture was lovely and feminine.

"Lenore," Simeon said remorsefully, and then raggedly,
"Lenore."

He crossed to her, and seized her shoulders, and his
mouth came down hard on hers. Then gently he pressed
her back on the bed, and lay beside her, and took her in
his arms.

She could not let it happen this way, however her body
yearned. Now was the time to let her body suffer for her
sins. Now was the time for atonement. She freed herself
from Simeon's arms, and the wrench was as terrible as
tearing flesh apart. Agony was engraved on her face. He
got up and stood away from her.

His voice was even, cold. "I came in to offer you an
apology. There is no better time than now."

She rose, too, and a tremor shook her body. He saw it
as revulsion. He turned and walked to the door.

"Simeon, wait."

He half-turned. "Is there anything more to say?"

"I am a Catholic, Simeon."

"Are you reminding me of your Irish grandmother?
Are you going to tell me next about your Anglo-Saxon
father?"

"I am trying to tell you I have sinned in God's eyes."

"What is this cant of Church and God? What are you
hiding behind them?"

"I am hiding nothing, Simeon. I am showing you my
heart."

His look was sardonic. He opened the door. "It is not
nearly as interesting as what I had anticipated."

The door closed behind him.

CHAPTER 19

CLEO HAD TOLD THEM that they could wake up at six. At six the first streaks of light were in the winter sky. But they had all been awake since just past five when Bart had staggered up out of his snatch of sleep to shake the furnace and pile her on heavy that the house might be good and hot for the children on Christmas morning. The three little girls had won the concession to forego the lengthy business of dressing themselves in their long drawers, long-sleeved shirts, body waists, bloomers, flannel under-petticoats, linen top-petticoats, heavy stockings, serge skirts, blouses, sweaters, and knee-high storm shoes with laces that seemed a mile long on school mornings. Small Tim was unable to dress himself, but it was sufficiently tedious for him to have to stand still and be burdened with the woolen layers that were piled on him because it was winter in Boston.

Victoria was the first to scamper out of bed, where she lay beside Lily, her mother. Vicky was seven, a tall, butter-colored, red-cheeked child, whose seniority of six months over Penny and ten months over Judy made her the unquestioned leader of the little girls.

Across the hall, Penny, hearing Vicky's scurrying sounds, eased herself away from Charity and got into her bathrobe and slippers, adjusting the belt of the robe until the ends were exactly even. Penny was as contented with herself as a cat, and spent long hours basking in her own beauty. Having acquired it at a very early age, she now had no other ambition except to get big enough to wear long dresses.

Together she and Vicky padded softly down the hall to rout out Judy. They had not been cautioned to be quiet, but they did not want the Big People to enter into their Christmas world in the first moments of rapture. Big People were fine for some things. They performed certain commonplace tasks that were necessary to daily living. But aside from that, they were best avoided. Either they told you what to do, like Cleo, or they told you to ask Cleo what to do, which was the same thing.

Judy slid away from Cleo. She still felt surprised that she shared a bed with her mother. She supposed it was all right for her cousins to sleep with their mothers. Their fathers were far away. But it seemed odd to her that she should sleep with Cleo with Papa right here in the house. Papa slept in the small back room on the second floor. Cleo had put him there when the aunts came. They were only going to stay two weeks, she had told Papa, and it would be nice for them to have the top floor to themselves, so they could talk from their beds until they fell asleep. She would take Judy in with her, and Serena and Tim could have Judy's room for the short time they were going to be here.

Judy could never decide whether or not she liked to sleep with Cleo. Vicky said how could she stand seeing Cleo all day and then sleeping with her all night. But if somebody was your mother, that was the difference between how you felt and how Vicky felt, even though Vicky was probably right.

In a way it was interesting to sleep in Cleo's room. The four little cousins fell asleep as soon as they tired of giggling back and forth and running in and out of each other's rooms — except Tim, who was trapped in a crib — until Cleo screamed up to them to stop that fool noise and go to sleep at once, or she'd come upstairs with a hairbrush and wear them out one by one. But when Cleo and her sisters came up to retire, Judy waked.

Cleo would enter softly enough, and start to bank the coal fire for the night. But the little pot-bellied stove was giving out so much cheerful warmth that it seemed a shame to leave it and go to bed. She would call her sisters to come in and undress by her stove, for there were only registers in their rooms. And the furnace heat, which was never really adequate in any Boston house because of New England thrift and addiction to sweaters, had a hard enough time spreading itself around the two lower floors to be of any use to anybody when it reached the top.

The sisters would come in gratefully, giving a look at the sleeping child and talking in whispers. Cleo would urge them to go ahead and sit down, it's just ten o'clock, draw up those rockers, we can't wake Judy, children sleep so sound; besides, I never finished telling you about Ant Rena Robinson, and the time Josie Beauchamp and I dressed up in sheets and scared the poor soul most to death.

It was always Cleo's laugh that waked Judy. Cleo's laugh rising out of the well of her joy, growing, swelling, infecting her sisters, great Negro laughter, rich, belly-deep, body-shaking, with the little gasps for breath, and then another gale, and everybody's eyes wet, and everybody saying, Cleo, if you tell another one of your fool stories, you'll kill me right in this rocker. I got a stitch in my side. I ain't laughed so much since you left the South and took your lies with you.

Judy kept her eyes shut and her body still, though she was quivering inside to share this mirth that had its beginning before she was born. She was not quite sure what was funny, for she was on the sober side, and the picture of poor Ant Rena Robinson, with her basket balanced on her head, being scared out of her wits in the lonesome woods at the apparition of Cleo and Josie Beauchamp draped in Mrs. Beauchamp's fine linen sheets made her feel quite sorry. Ant Rena Robinson had had to wash and iron everything all over again. For the basket fell off her head, and she said, Give me room, ghosts, and God A'mighty, give me wings, and kicked the basket up in the air to give herself a clear path. Ant Rena weighed three hundred pounds. Once around her was twice around Boston Common. But she beat every bird going in her direction, and reached home long before her shadow did. Poor shadow had to hang around outside until Ant Rena's husband came home and let it in. It never really fit Ant Rena after that. She lost near fifty pounds from being so scared and running so fast, and never could eat it back, because her teeth had knocked each other out chattering so hard.

Cleo would start another outrageous story. Judy would lie there listening, half amused, half moved, and wholly confused in her feelings for Cleo by her admixture of fiction and fact. She made it so hard to know what to believe. Why did she never tell the whole truth? Why

didn't anyone ever stop her? Was it her voice? Did they
like to listen to her talk just to hear the music sounds she
made? Was it because she was so full of life that she
made things move inside you, tears or laughter or anger,
and when she went out of a room something like something alive left with her?

Even Vicky and Penny talked about her more than
they talked about their own mothers. They never said
anything nice, but they said a whole lot. It was funny,
but Cleo was the boss of everybody. It was like she was
the boss of the house. Papa wasn't.

Sometimes Judy felt guilty pretending to be asleep, for
she knew that the Big People's tongues were unguarded.
They did not always tell funny stories. They talked about
everything under the sun, sad things, solemn things,
Negro things. And it seemed to the child that Big People
had made a strange world for themselves. There was no
more happiness in it than in a child's world. They did not
know what tomorrow would bring any more than children
did.

When she made her regular reports to her cousins on the
Big People's business, they felt baffled and impatient trying to draw conclusions. If the Big People wanted their
husbands, why didn't they go back to them? If they hated
to see their children forget their fathers, why had they
brought them away? If they thought Papa was so wonderful, why didn't they stand up for him? If they didn't
want Cleo to boss them, why did they let her?

They sat in solemn conclave on the Big People, and
they were glad of each other. They had almost forgotten
what it was like not to live together. As young as they
were, five months had seemed like five years. They had

decided, after giving the matter much thought, to bring up themselves. They did not want to be brought up by teachers and Cleo.

When Judy joined Vicky and Penny, they held a hurried consultation about Tim. At this hour of the morning, he was sure to be wet. They did not mind, but Cleo would make a fuss if he left a wet spot on her rug. If they waked Serena and asked her to dress him, she would cry because it was Christmas. And if she cried loud enough, she would wake up the rest of the Big People.

It was decided that Judy should fetch a towel to tie around Tim while Vicky fetched him. In a moment or two Vicky reappeared with the twenty-two-month-old blond boy. When Judy approached, his solemn little face began to stretch into an enormous smile, and his great brown eyes filled with the image of his idol. Judy was his favorite of all the world. Before Judy he could not remember any real existence. She had taught him to walk and talk. Serena had never wanted a baby, and Cleo was still not reconciled to his being male. He refused to eat anything except what Judy left on her plate. Cleo fought a losing battle with him every day. The only word he ever said to her was "no."

Judy wrapped the towel around his waist and made a bow that looked like bunny ears. Half of the towel formed a train behind him. He stood for it soberly. Judy was his life and love, and he did not care what she did to him. When she was through, he put his trusting hand in hers. The cousins descended the stairs.

The towering tree was in the second-floor sitting room with its Brussels carpet and Hepplewhite desk, now somewhat marred by ink spots and scratches which spankings

had not erased. The children crowded inside the doorway and stood very still, their tender mouths falling open,
their innocent eyes full of awe. The perennial magic of
the Christmas tree choked their throats, their hearts
shook with happiness.

In the early light the great boughs glistened under
their load of sparkling snow nestling on cotton puffs that
looked as lovely and flyaway as thistle. The gleaming
golden star shone down on them, and they lifted their
shining faces, alight with the wondrous belief that Bart
had really found the falling star that he had promised
them. The fragile colored baubles like balls for fairies'
babies, the silvery tinsel threading in and out, the little
candles on the branch tips waiting for first dark, the little
presents in ribbon and tissue tucked here and there and
held firmly in place by the tree's witchery, and the big
presents, the unwrapped presents, the dolls, the sleds, the
tea sets, the teddy bear, the tricycle, the four little rocking chairs, and strung along the mantel the four filled
stockings — these were the evidences that renewed their
faith in the disturbing world that could stop for Christmas
and give little children a day to cherish.

All their Christmas Eve doubts and little fears dissolved.
Santa Claus loved them! Santa didn't care if children
were white or colored. He didn't care if Judy was the
richest or Tim was the littlest. She was not first, and he
was not least. If everybody could be like Santa Claus,
good, and just, and generous, there would never be a day
when children were not happy.

"He came," said Vicky reverently.

They advanced into the room, Tim stumbling over his
towel, with no shred of his bliss disturbed.

"Oh, what shall we play with first, Vicky?" pleaded
Penny, her placidity upset by so many choices.

"Our stockings," Vicky said softly. "And we'll just pat
the other things and not play with anything until the
Big People see what Santa Claus brought us." She
yearned now to share their joy with the Big People. Her
Christmas heart was expanding rapidly. All of her feelings
were tender and loving, and she was ashamed that they
were not always so. She squeezed her eyes shut and said
a rapid little prayer that Santa Claus had stopped at the
house of Bill Aloysius Barry. She had been praying that
he wouldn't, because Bill Aloysius Barry had won their
last fight when the school bell rung while she was down
and he was up.

"I'd liefer let them look, too," said Penny. She had a
penchant for picking up Irish expressions. After a grueling
two months with Thea between school and supper, automatically she adopted any unfamiliar word or inflection
because she supposed it was expected of her. With the
urge of children to conform to the accepted standard, the
speech of Judy's cousins was becoming almost indistin-
guishable from hers. But Penny's accent was always going to be a little Irish.

"I want the Big People to see everything, too," said
Judy, wishing she had sewed her pot-holders for Cleo a
little more carefully.

"Me do," said Tim, who was always her echo.

They made a rush for the mantel then, with Tim falling
flat and scrambling up to fall and rise again. With their
stockings clutched tightly to their overflowing hearts, and
their tongues like torrents, they made the circuit of the
tree, touching and talking to the large gifts, trying to

guess what lay concealed behind the bright wrappings of
the small ones.

With happy sighs of complete contentment they sank to
the floor and began the exploration of their stockings.
Tim's towel was somewhat askew, and his excited sat-
urated bottom made a new wet spot each time he shifted.
The shiny apples, oranges, tangerines, bananas, the ten-
cent whistles, the paper-backed picture books, the peppermint sticks, the nuts, and tissue-wrapped raisins were
thrilling discoveries as their laps filled with these precious
treasures that Santa Claus had selected with no thought
of the time and trouble it was taking him.

Anxiously Judy and Penny watched Vicky's wavering
hand, and Tim watched Judy's. Vicky picked up her
apple. They picked up theirs. The sideboard held a bowl
of identical fruit, but they would never have been persuaded to this fact. No child wanted to be the only one
eating his hallowed apple or other fruit, and find it entirely consumed by the time his cousin began on his. For
a long moment there was no sound but the loud smacking
of thorough savoring.

Vicky struggled to suppress a thought. It was not a
proper Christmas thought, but it refused to settle. Suddenly it exploded, with Vicky feeling a small rush of
shame that her period of being wholly loving had been
so short-lived.

"I'm going to brag to the white children when I go
back to school," she said.

"Me, too," said Penny shamelessly.

"It isn't nice to brag," said Judy in a small voice, for
it was her function to serve as their conscience.

"Not nice," said Tim severely.

"They're going to brag to us," Vicky reminded her.

"Our tree is the biggest in the whole world," said Penny, believing it. "It isn't bragging if it's true."

"But it isn't polite to make people feel bad," said Judy in distress, for Cleo had impressed it upon her that she must never let her cousins feel that she was rich and they weren't.

"Po-lite," said Tim emphatically, picking out Judy's emphasized word, and thinking he was saying two.

"Feel bad," echoed Vicky scornfully, for this was the core of the matter to her. "I've seen the white children make you feel bad."

They had never made Vicky feel bad. She hated the white children and was therefore impervious to inner pain. She would not have hated them if it had not been for Judy. She did not dislike them because they were white. Being one of a household that was vari-hued, from very dark Bart to very blond Tim, she had no color prejudice or preference. Not being Bostonian by birth or inclination, she had no contempt for the Irish, whose red hair and freckles and monkey faces appealed to her fanciful mind. She was by nature a leader. The little sheep who now called her "nigger" would have followed her blindly in the imaginative games of her devising if she had ever stopped scorning them long enough to let them. But her fierce loyalty made her despise whoever could make Judy cry.

The white children never made Penny cry. She was indifferent to them. They were part of the school world, and she lumped everything connected with school in an unused crevice in her mind. She had never envisioned anything but a colored world, and even that she had nar-

rowed considerably until she saw only the bright places
of laughter and ladies in long dresses. She shrugged off
the white kids' shafts that could not pierce the armor of
her innocent conceit and self-assurance.

The first day at school, when all the first-graders were
scared and unsure, the white children had not been reluctant to cling to the light-colored hands of Vicky and
Penny at Teacher's command. But as frightened as they
were of the vast expanse of the schoolyard, so enormous,
so uncharted beside the familiar four corners of their own
back yards, Judy's appearance among them provoked a
feeling of betrayal that even little people could assume
the color associated with nighttime terrors.

The cousins had been escorted to and from school for
a month by a rotation of mothers. But Vicky put her foot
down finally. She was spoiling for a fight. Walking home
with a mother offered no opportunity. In the first few
weeks of the tremendous adventure of three little colored
girls walking unattended in a largely Irish neighborhood,
there was a daily battle. It began the moment the march-
ing children left their formation outside the school gate
and coalesced into a circle for Vicky and whatever bigger
girl or boy had made her maddest.

Penny fought with sublime indifference to Queensberry
rules. She did not want to soil her hands on these white
kids. She waded in when Vicky appeared to be losing,
using her teeth and the stub toes of her storm shoes. The
children shouted, "No fairsies, no fairsies!" But Penny's
imperturbable face gave no sign that she heard. She
wanted to go home and play dress-up in front of the
mirror. She wanted Vicky to come home unbruised. She
did not want to have to listen to Cleo lecture about how

that old Thea and that old Simeon played so nice with white children when they were growing up.

If someone called you "nigger," Cleo had told them, you should say in answer, "A nigger is a mean low person. And only a mean low person would use that word." Did she think those old white children would stop calling names long enough to listen? Didn't the cousins chant, "Yah, yah, yah, go wash your paddy face in the frying pan," to cover the chant of the Irish children's, "Nigger, nigger, pull the trigger," until one or the other side got bored and ran home to play, with each side pretending not to have heard the other?

Judy didn't fight at all. She was wrung with shame that Vicky was doing her fighting for her, since she knew quite well that most of their schoolmates' meannesses were directed at her because she was darkest. But there was nothing in her that could make her strike out. She had been schooled too well by Thea in ladylike behavior. She was unprepared for the dog-eat-dog of public school, and had no impulse for revenge. She loved gentle Jesus devotedly, but was doubtful of her affection for His Father who handed down such pronouncements as an eye for an eye.

"I don't really cry, just my eyes get wet," Judy protested, with a suspicion of tears in her voice. For she did not like knowing she sometimes showed her feelings. "And anyway, the white children don't make me cry. I cry because I can't make myself fight them."

Two tears formed on Tim's long lashes. He crowded close to Judy. Whatever she suffered was his pain. Whatever her mood was his.

"We don't want you to fight," said Vicky staunchly.

"We don't think you're a coward." She chose the odious word deliberately, because she knew that was troubling Judy's mind. "You're good, but you're not goody-good," she said kindly. "Anyway," she said quickly, cramming her mouth full of apple, "last one to finish is a piece of cheese."

Everyone burst out laughing. The little white teeth flew in and out of the apples.

Deep-rooted in Judy was a quality of goodness, which Tim instinctively recognized, and Vicky and Penny felt in a way that they could not explain. They knew that they could not bear it if Judy ever told a lie, or acted mean, or spoke harshly. Fun-loving Penny had never known she could love anyone who was younger and not exciting. Intense, imaginative, restless Vicky, who set no such limitations on love, nonetheless had not supposed her quiet cousin would fill her unsuspected need for interludes of peace. There was a strength and stability beneath Judy's shy exterior that made their independent spirits feel a strange dependency when she was near. She was the fountainhead of their search for truth.

CHAPTER 20

CLEO DRIFTED UP OUT OF SLEEP. Charity's hard breathing had waked her. "Come in here and dress by the fire," she commanded drowsily.

"Soon's I get myself together," Charity said between little gasps. She had just puffed upstairs from her bath. Bart's Christmas supply of heat was keeping the water so red-hot that everybody could have a bath, not just the children who had a prior right, because children, Cleo said, were always frisking themselves in people's faces.

Presently Charity entered with her ponderous walk. The weight of her body was vast, and her small feet steadily ached. Her bloated face was beet-red and a little moist from the effort expended on her slightest movement. She had long since given up trying to find a becoming dress. The search was too unrewarding, and her abnormal addition of pounds burst the stoutest seams in a week. She wore Mother Hubbards exclusively, for in her painful consciousness of her obesity she no longer left the house.

"Lord," she said, bending forward in her chair to button her shoes and struggling upright again with a grunt and a groan and the hard rush of breath, "I could eat a horse. Up till near morning like we was. Remember how Pa used to play Santa Claus? I wonder what he's doing right now? Seems funny he didn't get someone to send a Christmas card for him."

Cleo flung the covers back and swung out of bed. "Oh, you all make me sick, always talking about Pa. Nobody ever mentions Mama except me."

"Mama's been dead twelve years," Charity protested mildly. "She's a happy angel in heaven. But Pa by hisself, first Christmas alone in his life. Don't seem right somehow."

Cleo crossed her arms and scratched her shoulders luxuriously. "Well, his second wife should have stayed alive to keep him company. Shouldn't have married her anyway. Bringing another woman in Mama's house. I haven't had much use for Pa since."

"Why, Mama always liked Miss Hattie," Charity said, pulling her petticoat over her head. "And God knows," she panted inside its folds, "Miss Hattie made Pa a good wife." Her rumpled hair and hotly flushed face began to emerge. "You weren't there to see his loneliness when Mama died. Was me talked him into marrying again." The petticoat slowly began to settle as Charity tugged and twisted. "Lily was always kinda skittish around Miss Hattie, what with you writing her don't let Miss Hattie make you do this and that. But me and Serena thought the world and all of her."

"Oh, you and Serena," said Cleo good-naturedly. "You'd like anybody'd pass Pa a glass of water." She crossed to the marble washstand, stoppered it, and turned the hotwater tap. "I'll take my bath later. Lily's in there now. If I go in after her, she'll spend the day apologizing for not letting me go in before her."

"Poor Lily," said Charity in gentle exasperation, "she's scared of everything and everybody."

Cleo chuckled. "Lord, I can't remember half the lies I used to tell her."

Charity shook her head, and made her easy entrance into her Mother Hubbard. "Cleo, sometimes I do believe you got a devil in you somewheres. Serena told me it hurt Pa's feelings you never once wrote him all these years."

"Well, Pa can't read or write," said Cleo indignantly, and she slapped the hot-water tap. The water was only a slow trickle. "This tap's been acting funny for a week."

"Serena did Pa's reading and writing. You knew that," said Charity. She heaved a great sigh. "Poor Serena. She mopes over Pa more than the rest of us, her and Robert and Pa living all together like they did. She saw how Pa aged after Miss Hattie died. And now with Robert God knows where, Serena don't rest a minute in her mind. She said last night it sure didn't feel like Christmas."

"But it is Christmas," said Cleo firmly — "a wonderful white Christmas." She soaped her face vigorously, then rinsed it in her cupped hands. She reached for her towel. "I was worried last night. It was snowing so steady I was afraid it might snow today and keep people away from my party."

"Lord," said Charity quickly, "let me get downstairs and start breakfast. I promised Mr. Judson some hot bread."

"You spoil that nigger," said Cleo indifferently, soaping her armpits. "You thought what you going to wear to-night?"

"I'm not coming down tonight," said Charity quietly.

"Charity," Cleo cried in alarm, "you got to come down. It's different when a friend drops in. It's easy to excuse you. But how will it look my first party my own sister not there?"

"Look at me," said Charity.

"I been looking at you five months," said Cleo, with a little nervous laugh. She did not turn around.

"Look at me," said Charity hoarsely, and her breath was so harsh that her body shook.

Slowly Cleo turned around, and her heart hammered. The sight of Charity hurt her and humbled her. The look of Mama was no longer there, yet she loved this grotesque creature more than she had loved her in all the years of her gentle prettiness.

"You want me at your party? You want to introduce this mass of flesh as your sister? You want me to come in a Mother Hubbard?"

"I want you any time and any way. There's nobody coming tonight is as good as your little finger."

But Charity did not hear her or did not heed her. "Ben could pass me and not know me. This time last year him and Penny and me was coming home from sunrise service. They was hollering for their breakfast, and I was too full of happiness to be hungry." She shook herself like a great dog shakes. "Lord, let me get downstairs and put on the pot. My poor old stomach's growling so, any minute now it's fixing to bite." Her laugh was like Christmas bells. She propelled her great body out of the room. The sound of her small unsure feet and her hand sliding down the bannister for balance had the running accompaniment of her hard breathing.

CHAPTER 21

Lᴵʟʏ ᴡᴀs ᴍᴏᴠɪɴɢ ᴀʙᴏᴜᴛ in the next room, her thin, tuneless voice lifted in song. "Jingle bells, jingle bells, jingle all the way, Can't you hear the Christmas bells ring out on Christmas Da-ay!" The children had been singing it all week, their caroling voices issuing from angel throats. But as the week progressed, Serena spoke for almost everybody when she said that if she had to hear that song one more time, she'd lose what was left of her mind.

Then Lily had picked it up unconsciously. She never really knew she was singing until Cleo or Serena yelled at her, For God's sake shut up! which she did at once, only to start up again as soon as she forgot.

Cleo rapped on the wall. The singing stopped. "Lily, come on in here where it's hot and finish dressing." She didn't want to get irritated with Lily the first thing Christmas morning.

"It ain't cold in here, house is hot all over this morning. But I'm coming," she called hastily.

She came so quickly that Cleo felt startled. She had not taken the time to fasten her garters. Her stockings were slipping down her legs. Her fresh underwear and clean house frock were bunched in her arms.

"I didn't call you because the house was on fire," said Cleo dryly, jerking the comb through her soft hair. There were times when she was unhappily aware that the sister she could influence easiest was the sister with the least spirit.

Lily gave her a sheepish smile, put her pile of clothes on the bed, then snatched them up and bundled them in a chair. "I can't help running when somebody calls me, either to them or from them." She smiled shamefacedly again, seeing herself on the street, and somebody quite innocuous halting her to ask a direction, and herself taking wings as if the hounds of hell had been loosed behind her.

The comb was arrested. "You were born a fool," said Cleo, not unkindly, "and you ought to thank God you've got me to look after you."

"I do," said Lily gratefully. "When I was in New York so much alone with Vicky, I kept that child at my heels. Wouldn't walk down my own dark hall to my own kitchen without her. I guess that's why she's not scared of nothing. I guess she saw I was a fool, too, and made up her mind not to be like me."

"Well, all I ask you," said Cleo briskly, "is not to be a fool tonight. Not a soul coming is going to bite."

"You mean," said Lily fearfully, "the party?"

"I swear before God —" began Cleo ominously.

Lily began to race into her clothes, her fingers thumbs at the thought of the decision she had been dreading for days. The sound of an automobile crunching to a halt across the street sent her rushing to the window in the hope that a visitor from Mars would alight to distract Cleo's attention.

She reported over her shoulder: "It's the doctor again, at that big corner house. He's going up the steps. The maid's letting him in, guess it's the maid, can't see without pulling the curtains back, and I know you don't want me to do that." She paused and parroted dutifully, "This is a nice street, and it's up to us to help keep it nice." Then she returned to her speculations. "Wonder how the old lady is today? Old folks don't outlast each other. She won't live another month now that he's gone. Wonder who'll move in? Hope no whole lot of people move in. It was nice having two old people who never made a peep. If young folks lived in that big house, I wouldn't half sleep for worrying whether they'd keep us awake with loud parties."

She paled. She had talked too much. She turned away from the window. Her doe eyes searched Cleo's face with the pleading expression of a child.

Cleo gave a final twist to her hair. She, too, had a rather desperate look. She glowered at Lily darkly.

"Lily, it's time you got over being scared of your shadow. I could understand when you were in wicked New York. But this is Boston. Like my party tonight, won't be a soul here like the railroad men Victor used to drag in to play cards and drink. You've seen enough of my friends to know that."

"But I've never seen so many of them at once," said Lily miserably. "I'd be so bashful before a room full of high-toned folks, I'd faint."

"Well, God have mercy," said Cleo helplessly. "You were scared to death of ordinary niggers, scared they were going to start cussing and cutting. Now you're bashful of my Boston friends because they act like ladies and gentlemen."

The sisters stared at each other. Cleo's eyes faltered first. There was nothing to do about Lily's being Lily, and they both knew it.

"All right," Cleo snapped. "Suit yourself." She was struck by the fact that though Lily was pliable, there was nothing really to work on except a mass of fears. Her hand had been largely instrumental in Lily's sorry making, and now she could not remold her into spine and sinew.

"You ready to go down?" she said.

Lily's fingers faltered on her braid of hair. Quickly she flung it over her shoulder where it began to loosen at once. Her hair was flyaway. Hairpins could not confine it. They were always dropping down her back, scaring a scream out of her, which startled everyone else.

"I'm ready," she said hastily.

"Your braid's coming loose," said Cleo patiently. "Where's your rubber band?"

"Here," said Lily, jerking it off her finger, where she had wound it, and emitting a little "ouch!"

"Put it on. I swear to God," Cleo said, with mild amazement, "you're worse than all the children put together. Come on."

Midway on the stairs Lily halted.

Cleo, on the step below, vainly wishing that Lily wouldn't always walk on top of her, said, "Now what?"

"I'm worried about my present to Mr. Judson. Don't seem right to give a good man like him two handkerchiefs, specially since he gave me that five dollars for Christmas on top of all the money he gave you to get as good for my child as you got for his."

"What's five dollars?" said Cleo contemptuously. "I get sick of you sisters. If one isn't talking about Pa, the other's talking about Mr. Judson."

"But after you bought him two pair of socks," Lily persisted, "I couldn't have bought him anything bigger than handkerchiefs. It wouldn't have looked right."

"He ought to be glad we gave him anything," said Cleo impatiently. "You go ahead of me and set the children's table. I'll stop a minute to see how they're getting along."

She stood in the doorway, watching them. Their backs were turned to her. They were sitting in a semicircle around the tree, adoring it. She saw Tim's wet bottom, and did not want to scold him. The sight of his smallness caught her heart. She could not exclude him from her Christmas love. In this quiet moment of contemplation nothing could evoke dismay. She was supremely content. There was nothing more she could want for Christmas. Belowstairs were her sisters, the part of her that was her happiness. And here in this charmed circle was the part of her that was her hope.

There was constant warfare between her and Vicky. Yet Vicky came closest to being her favorite. Their temperaments met head on, struck sparks, and exploded. The love of battle was in them both. Though neither would admit an affinity for the other, they were both stimulated and intrigued by the thought of fresh encounters. When the children went out into the world, it would be Vicky that Cleo would miss most. For Vicky never bored her.

Sometimes Judy bored her. She deplored Judy's gentleness. She supposed it was an agreeable quality, but worried lest it was a sign of softness. She never yearned to spoil her daughter. Her ambition for the little girls was tremendous, and for Judy it was greatest. Out of her egoism she could not imagine that she had not borne a remarkable child. She was determined that Judy should have an abundance of education. She held the firm con-

viction that a plain child was denied the distraction of
prettiness for a noble purpose.

She was afraid that Penny was in danger of being content to be beautiful. This made her impatient, for she
felt that beauty was a dangerous asset without brains.
Too often beauty just got married.

She wanted Vicky, who was a brilliant first-grader, to
be a schoolteacher. Judy, who was showing dexterity with
her first piano lessons, must be a celebrated pianist.
Penny, who exhibited no talent for anything except kicking her heels when the graphophone whirled, could train
for sobering settlement work. Such refined white people
lived and worked at Thaw House. And they were beginning to include a colored face in their personnel. True,
Thaw House was in the South End, but the address could
have a distinguished sound when it was possible to add
that you ate and slept there with better-class whites, and
were paid to treat the Negroes in the neighborhood as
inferiors.

Tim, poor child, thought Cleo, as slow a walker and
talker as he was, he would never be the brightest jewel in
her crown. He might as well go into business. That
didn't take brains, not educated brains, anyway. He could
be apprenticed to Mr. Judson who was always wishing he
had a son. Well, he could take Tim and turn him into
another black banana king.

Judy felt Cleo's presence and turned around. "Mother,"
she said, using her term of endearment, "Santa Claus
came!" She jumped up eagerly.

"Thanta Caus came!" announced Tim, floundering inside his towel in his effort to rise.

"Would you like to see what he brought me?" asked

Vicky, rising carefully to keep from bursting with joy.

"I can see from here," said Cleo quickly. She did not want the children to have a close view of the naked face of her happiness.

"We got dolls," said Penny blissfully. "Mine looks like me except her blue eyes."

"I wanted a colored doll," said Vicky. "But Santa Claus didn't know I was colored. I forgot to tell him in my letter." She hadn't forgotten, but there had been a little persistent fear that even dear kind Santa Claus might have a touch of prejudice.

"What would you want to parade up and down the street with a colored doll for?" asked Cleo in honest bewilderment.

"Because Vicky's colored," explained Judy, who was a trifle pedantic.

"Vicky's colored," said Tim accusingly, hearing the mild reproof in Judy's voice.

"Hush up, Tim. You don't even know what you're talking about. You're four little children. That's all you have to call yourselves. If you think you're different, you'll act different, and people will treat you different. Just remember that brains are the only thing that counts. And brains are not black or white."

There was a little silence. Cleo felt her face reddening and frowned. They were looking at her in astonishment. She knew that they were not surprised at what she had said. They had heard her say it too often. They were just surprised that she was lecturing them on Christmas morning. That even on Christmas she was an old crank. Some day they would learn that her Spartan discipline was for their good. If she let her heart go, it would flood with pity because they were little colored children. And what would she use then to bolster their pride? But she could not leave them with that betrayed look.

"I haven't had my Christmas kisses," she said recklessly, advancing into the room.

Their mouths fell open, except for Tim's, which began to pucker.

"We haven't brushed our teeth," said Judy politely, for Cleo had taught them that unclean teeth were an unpardonable breach of etiquette.

"Me kiss you," said Tim, his first digression, because he was affectionate and Cleo's kisses were rare. He held up his arms.

Vicky jerked them down. "He hasn't brushed his teeth either," she said firmly.

The blush deepened in Cleo's cheeks. She took a step backward. "Then go and brush them," she said tartly. "And take that towel off Tim. And don't let me have to call you twice to come to breakfast."

This was the Cleo they understood. Cleo with her Christmas love embarrassed them. They filed past her, giving sly peeps at her set face, giggling foolishly the moment they reached the safety zone of themselves.

Cleo was alone in the room. She stared unseeingly at the splendid array of expensive toys. Something was missing in the room, something that had been there the night before when she and her sisters trimmed the tree. The thing was a sense of oneness. Now some part of her felt severed, her self-identity with her child.

There was a little girl, and then there were three little girls and a boy. And now in Cleo was the core of fear that there were no children at all.

CHAPTER 22

C LEO started down the back stairs to the kitchen, from where there floated up to her the merry sounds of her sisters and Mr. Judson in conversation. She smiled benignly, shaking her head with the wonder of it. They could talk to Mr. Judson as if they enjoyed it. She didn't see where they got the patience. She got the fidgets after five minutes.

She paused and sniffed the air. Why in the name of God did they have to fry onions today of all days? She clattered down the rest of the stairs and sailed into the sunny room, her eyes flashing green sparks.

"I declare to God," she said dramatically, "if I turn my back for a second, this house runs on three wheels. Whoever wanted onions must have wanted them for meanness."

"Was me asked Serena to fry me some," Bart said peaceably. "I been shoveling snow two hours. Onions is the best thing to keep out a cold."

"I know a stink smell doesn't bother you," Cleo snapped at him. She swung around to Serena. "But I thought you'd have more consideration for your own sister."

Serena's lower lip trembled. "You're a rich man's wife, Cleo. Talk is cheap to you. I'm a poor relation. I can't afford to bite the hand that's feeding me."

223

She turned her back and began to shake the pan vigorously to conceal her own quivering.

Cleo's eyes changed to gray. There was no green in them, no smoldering fire. Gentleness lay in the curve of her mouth. Serena was not herself. She did not even look the same. The dimples never showed in her too thin cheeks. The smudges under her eyes, the deepening lines from nose to mouth, the hollow in her throat were an unlikeness to her old self.

"Serena," said Cleo, in a rich and tender voice, "no need to stir up a hornet's nest over a pan of onions. No need to take out on those who love you your worry over a no-account nigger. I could have told you long ago what would happen when Robert left Camden. That letter before he left about going away to get a good job so he could give you a decent house. That was nothing but talk. These past years he thought Pa's rattletrap place was good enough for you. Don't tell me it took all that time to open his eyes."

"It was my doing," Serena said brokenly. "Me writing about your fine house, your fine furniture. I made him ashamed of himself. I made him think I had to have money. He lit out to get me some. And now the earth's swallowed him up. And as if my cup ain't full enough, I can't hear from Pa. Last year this time we were thanking God we'd all been spared to share another Christmas. This year every one of us is scattered to the four winds."

Charity heaved herself out of her chair and pounded across the floor. Her bread was not ready, and she knew that it was not. But she could not sit still with Serena's sorrow. She rested her hands on her knees as she bent to examine her baking, and her breath scraped her throat like a file.

Lily hung back cravenly in the pantry, where she had retired at Cleo's stormy entrance to busy herself rattling dishes. She was happy in Mr. Judson's house. She did not want him to notice that she was a poor relation and send her back to Victor to die like a dog.

Cleo went to Serena and pried her stiff fingers from the sputtering pan. Gently she took her by the arm, and as her hand circled the scant flesh on the delicate bones, her heart shrank. This was her baby sister, whose little fat body had curled against hers in the old bed down home. She led her away from the stove and forced her unyielding body into a chair. She stood above her, trying to will her strength into Serena's stubborn frailty.

"Serena, you've got to take hold of yourself. You're the only one grieving yourself to death. Pa's probably courting another woman to put in Mama's place. And Robert, I know what happened to him. Those yellow-haired niggers start passing for white and forget they were ever colored."

Bart saw Serena recoil as if Cleo had struck her. He tugged at his mustache, not wanting to interfere. Cleo embarrassed his manhood by calling him down before the girls whenever he put a word in. And if she provoked him to the point of his thundering back, the girls were the ones went to pieces. A man might as well be living with a parcel of kittens. Or a nest of baby birds with their mouths open.

The war was spreading. No need sticking his head in the sand. Might as well say the banana trade had stopped. Might as well say there'd be hard sledding from now on. The living wouldn't be like it had been. Dollars wouldn't come easy as dimes. Food wouldn't fall from trees. The

Saturday night exchange would soon be a thing of the
past. Time was when he could bring home all the meat
and fancy canned goods he could carry, and a five-pound
box of fine chocolates for the price of passing the time of
day and some choice fruit. Saturday nights he had looked
like a pack horse getting off the trolley. Now he and the
other wholesalers, the importers in particular, were ex-
changing without heartiness.

He rubbed his back against the chair reflectively, and
scratched one stocking-shod foot against the other. The
habit of years made him acutely conscious that he had
not been down to the store. But the great banana rooms
were empty, and the few crates of other produce needed
no special cosseting. The Christmas sales had exhausted
the last of the golden fruit, and another small, slow shipment from the narrowing area of untroubled seas would
not be due for God knew when. In the meantime there
was always the overhead. There was more going out than
coming in.

It was a blessed morning, a morning a man could ease
the worry on his mind and listen to the laughter of little
children. And Cleo, God help her, was standing between
himself and the sun. Peace was no part of her. She was
born to bedevil. God pity her, she would cut off her arm
for these sisters of hers with the same knife she held at
the tenderest spot in their hearts.

"Cleo," he said, "you got more to do besides talk. You
got a raft of people coming tonight, and a mess of cooking ahead of you. Why don't you let us eat and get it over,
so you and the girls can start?"

"Bread'll be ready time we sit down," said Charity.
"Mr. Judson, you draw up. I hear the children coming

down the back stairs. Lily, you serve them. Serena'll pass you their plates through the pantry slide. You sit down, Cleo. You going to be standing most all day and all tonight."

Cleo frowned at Charity's unconscious assumption of her prerogative. "You children," she shouted commandingly, "come down the back stairs. I don't want one foot on the front stairs today. Mr. Judson, you're not drawing up to my table till you put on your shoes. Serena, you serve the children. Lily'd just act helpless if they didn't behave instead of slapping them down. I'll sit down when I'm ready, Charity. I can't bear to be talked to like I was a child. You sit down yourself. I'll dish up. You've told me a dozen times this morning you're starving to death."

Bart, bending over his shoes, raised his head and smiled. "Reminds me how my mother used to say, Feed your stomach and promise your back. Never promise your stomach."

"While we're on the subject of clothes," said Cleo, "you lay out yours before tonight. Don't come worrying me the last minute to help you find a clean shirt."

Bart began to lace his shoes, which he hadn't intended to do. But he had no intention of meeting Cleo's eye either.

"Well, now, about tonight, Cleo. You know I'm a man will fall asleep anywhere soon as the sun goes down. You don't want me falling asleep at your party. I'll sneak off to bed before folks start coming. You all," he added largely, "have a nice time."

He raised his head, stole a look at Cleo's glowing green eyes, and swallowed hard.

"Well, I'll finish calling the roll," she said, with deadly calm. "Serena, what fool excuse you got to give me?"

"About what?" asked Serena abstractedly, turning back from the door.

"Just tell me plain out, yes or no, you coming downstairs tonight like a civilized person or not?"

"No," Serena said.

"You can stand there and tell me 'no' as plain as that?" asked Cleo passionately.

"You asked me to," Serena said stubbornly.

"I declare before God, I have to pull the weight of this whole house."

"We'll be leaning over the upstairs bannisters," said Lily helpfully. "I sure want to see everybody that comes."

"That's right," said Cleo witheringly. "Be second-class niggers leaning over the fence looking at first-class folks. Nobody thinks of the children but me. Mr. Judson only cares if their bellies are full. The rest of you only care if they keep themselves clean. I'm the only one cares to see them walk proud. If they don't learn to hold their heads up in the colored world, how they ever going to know to hold their heads up in the white world?"

She saw that they were staring at her just as the children had stared at her.

"Charity, pass your plate," she said resignedly.

CHAPTER 23

T HE COUSINS sat at the dining-room table, too excited
and too full of fruit and forbidden-before-breakfast candy
to want their cereal and eggs and bacon. They ate
stoically, so that there need be no nonsense from Cleo
about nobody can get up from this table until every plate
is clean. The little girls had even persuaded Tim to eat
from his own dish. He ate with his eyes on Judy. When
she took a mouthful, he did.

A dinner napkin was tied around his neck, giving him a
bunny look again. He would not wear bibs because Judy
did not, and he was beginning to demand that his napkin
be laid across his lap. This morning his insistence had
not been too mulish because he felt dressed up in his best
linen rompers and new white stockings and shoes, and did
not want to soil them.

The little girls wore their embroidered serges and the
Mary Janes that they customarily carried in their dancing-
school bags on Saturdays. They sat with their ankles
crossed as Miss Templeton had taught them, but their feet
swung back and forth against the Chippendale chairs in
their nervous eagerness.

They were listening to Bart's resonant voice, making
itself heard above Cleo's, and they wanted to go in and

lean against him. They saw so many women faces in all
the departments of their day that they were wonderfully
glad to see Bart's dark face at dusk. They liked to feel
his mustache tickle when they laid their smooth cheeks
against his lips, the only form of kissing that Cleo permitted in her effort to wipe out all the world's germs.

The adults leaned back from the kitchen table, replete
with steak and onions and hominy and hot bread. Bart
had a match in the corner of his mouth, the extent of
Cleo's permission of the practice of picking teeth at table.
As he talked the match teetered on his lip in a way that
captivated Lily. Serena and Charity were captivated, too,
though the match was only a minor attraction. They were
listening to Bart talk about his life before they knew him.
They had not lived with him long enough for his tales to
be twice-told. Though his stories were old, they were
new to them, and enthralling.

"I hate to hear a lot of talk about old used-to," Cleo
said impatiently. She wanted to tell her own story about
the time she cut off her braids and told poor Mama old
Ant Sooky had conjured them off.

"Don't keep interrupting him," begged Serena. Mr.
Judson was easing the morning for her.

"Well, like I was saying," Bart resumed, "Ma and I sold
out in the South and came to Springfield, Massachusetts.
Reason we came to Springfield was Ma's only known kin
was there. I was just going to visit awhile, then come on
to Boston and send for Ma. But I'm a man can't go a day
without working. I was made for work, and work was
made for me. I want to die in harness."

"Oh, hush up, Mr. Judson," Cleo said sharply. "Don't
talk about dying. You'll bury me. You'll be too mean to
die and leave me your money."

Behind her screen of anger was a strange feeling of desolation. She did not want to imagine him dead. She had never believed that a man could be part of the living substance of a house. All the same, she found herself listening with the others for the sound of his key in the door. Although her greeting was never more than Oh, it's you, nonetheless on the nights when he fell asleep on the trolley and rode to the end of the line, her life was suspended and her heart quickened to every footfall outside. Her sisters and the children were within call, but the completeness she had felt all day slowly began to crumble away until Mr. Judson returned to the house, where she had no place for him, to restore it.

"Cleo," said Bart, looking into her eyes, "you make a mighty bellow for a woman. But you always did remind me of a barking dog. Your bite ain't really in it, just your cussedness."

Her eyes fell. "Nobody asked for your opinion."

"About Springfield," Bart said blandly, "like I said, I came to stay a week and got a smell of the market. My second day there I was learning my trade from a Mr. Lapham, had a wholesale place, taught me everything he knew about fruit except how to ripen bananas. I taught myself and then I taught him. Wasn't so many bananas those days. If Mr. Lapham had as much as fifty bunches and sold forty before they rotted, he called himself lucky.

"I worked up to be his buyer, then I left him and opened a retail store with the money I'd been saving to take to Boston. I put Noble Tilman in charge. He was the grandson of Ma's uncle. Wasn't much to him, but he was a relative, and I thought I could trust him because he was. I've always been a man liked the buying end. I got to be out roaming the market, waiting for boats to dock or trains to pull in, smelling the sea and the cinders, and testing produce with these hands of mine that God has blessed to see the heart of fruit."

"You ought to learn to stay in your store and watch your cash box," Cleo said darkly. "Money is an awful temptation. Noble Tilman stole from you right and left. Persuaded you to open that ice-cream parlor so he could steal more. You letting him bank for you and keep your books, and he was banking in his pocket and keeping a white woman. Now a body has to beg you for every dollar. It makes my blood boil to hear Noble Tilman's name."

"Let the dead rest," Bart said. "God punished Noble when He struck him down with galloping consumption. And Noble made his peace before he died. Spent his last night on earth on his knees in prayer behind his locked door, begging God for a vision. Never will forget that Saturday night. None of us could sleep a wink. When we did fall asleep, it was daylight. And when we woke and went to see Noble, he was gone. And some bug-eyed child come running to tell us Noble was in church preaching the word of God.

"When we got there, Noble was near purification. His face was shining like a star. 'Vanity, all is vanity. I will destroy and make desolate.' Those were his last known words. He came down from the pulpit and walked down the aisle. Nobody stirred. Nobody put out a hand to stop him. He was God's messenger. Ma was the one started the singing. She could sing long meter till you'd want to cry. I reckon forty sinners got up and hit the trail.

"Noble went down to my stores and took his fists and

smashed the plate-glass window in my ice-cream parlor. Then he climbed inside and tore through my two stores like God's wrath. In half an hour he destroyed everything in his path. When the policemen finally got there, wasn't nothing left standing. And Noble was dead when they put him in the wagon.

"It took every penny I could rake and scrape together to pay my creditors. And Ma was never really the same after that. I think what it was, she was worried in her conscience. I was her son and she grieved for me, but Noble had done God's bidding, and she wouldn't condemn God's mysterious ways. I buried her in the spring, and came on to Boston with my faith and five dollars. I been after the Almighty Dollar all my life, and I'll sprinkle salt on its tail before I die."

Lily looked happy. She believed in Mr. Judson completely. He was a wonderful man. He didn't drink or smoke or swear bad. He was kind to women and children. He came home at dusk before she could grow afraid of the dark. If she never got in his way and did her best to please him, she would be safe forever under his wing.

To Charity this was Cleo's man talking, not hers. She was a poor relation. She and her child were nameless. It was as if they had sprung into being in Boston, one to be called Cleo's sister, the other Judy's cousin. And there was no help for it, nowhere to go.

Serena jumped up and said earnestly: "Mr. Judson I'm going to get a job. Watching for the postman isn't feeding me or my child. Cleo's always preaching pride. It's time I got some and took my hand out of your pocket."

"We-ell," Bart said cautiously, "it might help to take your mind off your troubles. Work's been many a man's salvation."

Cleo rose, too, and began to pile the plates with vicious bangs. Lily made a nervous start toward helping, but Cleo's angry eye glued her back to her chair. Cleo leaned over the table and reached for Bart's plate. Her knuckles were white as she gripped it. Her face was very close to his, and, as always, in her hot anger her beauty had a look of abandon. Bart felt his own rage rising that she wore this look when hate was in her, and contempt was on her tongue.

"Mister Nigger," she said venomously, "why don't you speak out plain instead of hiding behind pious words? Yes, encourage Serena to go to work and leave her child for me to take care of. I've got my own child to bring up, and this big house besides, and a hard spell of sickness behind me. But what do you care so long as Serena brings home a few dirty dollars for you to snatch from her." She added accusingly, "You were the one was going to pay Lily so fast. That was last summer, and from that time to this you haven't paid her one penny."

"Good God," thundered Bart, "with all of you here together, that makes a mighty difference."

"Oh, it does," agreed Lily wretchedly. "Oh, Cleo, what you want to stir up Mr. Judson for? First I heard tell about any money. Don't think I put Cleo up to asking, Mr. Judson. The little I do in this house I'm paid a hundred times over."

"Oh, hush up, both of you," said Cleo, who was highly annoyed that Bart and Lily were chewing on a part of her argument that she had just thrown in for meanness. Lily wouldn't have got the money anyway, wouldn't even have known it was hers to have. So why didn't she mind her own business? She picked up the pile of dishes and flung away to the sink, where Serena had the dishpan waiting, leaving Lily in an agony to help to show Mr. Judson her industry, but not quite daring to cross Cleo's line of vision.

"Serena," said Cleo, "it isn't your fault Pa was poor, and all of us had to get out and scuffle before we had enough schooling. But all you know, all any of us know, is how to cook and clean for white folks. I don't want the children to see us humbled. Mr. Judson's been talking poor mouth ever since I married him. It's like this every winter. And there never was a winter that didn't ease into spring."

"Cleo," Bart said quietly, "it's different this winter. There's a war."

"My God," said Cleo, in complete exasperation, "what has a war way over in Europe got to do with a handful of niggers in a house in Boston?"

There was a sudden sob from Serena. She flung the dishcloth in the pan and beat her hands on the sink.

"Serena!" said Cleo sharply. The others stared in horror.

"Why did I ever have Tim? I never wanted a baby. I knew me and Robert was too poor. And then like a fool I got caught. After that it was struggle, struggle, struggle. Even Tim had to struggle to live. He cost us more than Robert could make. I got so I lived for Cleo's letters. I let Robert see I lived for them. There was old ladies would nurse Tim for a dollar a week while I went out to work. But most of the time I sat on my lazy bottom and waited for the postman. It took me these months of easy living to learn that I wish I was back down home working steady in the white folks kitchen, knowing at night I was coming home to my husband."

"A woman and man ain't nothing apart. You mighty right," said Bart.

Cleo's eyes narrowed suspiciously. Whenever Serena and Bart agreed on whatever subject, she saw them as connivers. She had never got over, and never would get over, Serena's supreme duplicity in giving to Bart the twenty dollars that Mr. Van Ryper had refused as in excess of the rent. Anyone with a grain of common sense would have brought that twenty dollars upstairs and slipped it under her sick sister's pillow, and kept her mouth shut about a matter that was none of her business. Serena had cut off a source of revenue that she might have made use of for months before Mr. Judson caught up with her.

"Oh, hush up," she said crossly. "Here come the children. I get tired of them hearing you all running off at the mouth."

CHAPTER 24

THE CHILDREN hung over Bart, Tim between his knees, giving little pats to the loved face, Vicky on the back rung of his chair, with her arms around his neck and her butterfly kisses lighting on his bald spot whenever Cleo's eyes were elsewhere, and Penny and Judy nestling in the crook of his arms.

"Anybody would think you were molasses," said Cleo, drying dishes vigorously and passing them to Lily, who always made a little prayer that she would not drop them.

Bart, reading her mind, said placatingly, "They only hang around me to hear my harmonica."

"Play for us," coaxed Vicky, leaning over Bart's head to reach into his vest pocket. Her hair fell over his face, and he wriggled his nose where it tickled, to Tim's extravagant enjoyment.

Vicky produced the harmonica and stuck it between his teeth. He freed his arms, made some lovely flute sounds, then asked, "What you want the professor to play?"

"Jingle bells," they chorused.

Charity laughed merrily from her seat at the kitchen table where she was dicing celery.

"I was hoping you'd ask me to play my best piece," Bart said gravely.

"I will, Papa," said Judy quickly. "Please play 'The Mocking Bird.'"

He swung into a spirited rendition. His mustached mouth flew up and down the harmonica, extracting a full orchestration from the reeds and filling the room with grace and gaiety.

The cousins clapped their approval, Vicky almost toppling from her perch.

"I declare, Mr. Judson," said Charity, whose tiny feet had been keeping time, "you make that mouth-organ sing."

"Papa can sing as good as his harmonica," Judy said proudly. "Please sing, Papa."

He hid his smile. "Well, what you want Caruso to sing?"

"'Good Morning Carrie,'" said Penny eagerly, jigging up and down.

"Me first!" shouted Vicky, startling Bart's ear.

"Me second then," said Penny firmly.

"I don't care if I'm last," said Judy, to save her pride. "It's more polite."

"Me, Man?" asked Tim anxiously, because they had explained to him before that "Good Morning, Carrie" was not a song for a boy.

Bart took Tim's fingers and let them travel up his chest to his collarbone. "There. I've got your song right here. No way for it not to come out next."

He played a flourish on his harmonica for effect. Then the love song lilted in his throat with his special variation.

> Good morning, Vicky,
> How you do this morning?
> Been dreaming 'bout you, my pretty maid.

Say look here, Vicky,
When you going to marry me?

And Vicky, who had been breathing excitedly down
Bart's neck in anticipation of her cue, croaked hoarsely,

Long springtime, honey,
Good morning, babe!

When it was time for Tim to be sung to, Bart looked
down at this unwanted tiny one, saw the worship in the
starry eyes, and muted his voice to lullaby tenderness.

Sweetest little feller everybody knows,
Don't know what to call him, he's so mighty lak a rose,
Looking at his mammy, eyes so shiny blue,
Makes you think that heaven is mighty close to you.

"That was me, Man," said Tim, looking beatified. He
climbed on the front rung of Bart's chair, digging his
elbows in Bart's knees for balance, and clasped him tightly around the neck, his arms entangling with Vicky's.

It seemed to Bart that sometimes he had to wade
through a sea of children to get to his own child. And
the little loving hands that clung to him on the way could
not be brushed aside by any man who believed that
Jesus spoke sublimely when He said, Suffer the little
children to come unto me, and forbid them not.

All the same his sleep was troubled. Wasn't anybody
but John D. Rockefeller could support a houseful of folks
and not feel it. And wasn't any real use complaining to
Cleo. She would say he was only getting old and cranky.
Didn't she know what helped to keep a man young?
The nearness of a wife, the falling asleep beside a familiar body, the knowing that this was their island of the
night.

"Well, that's that," said Cleo, hanging the dish towels on the rack. "And if you'll call a halt to your singing bee, Mr. Judson, I'll clear the kitchen of children, and we'll get started."

"Cleo," Penny wooed in her most appealing voice, "may I speak a piece for the company tonight?"

"You'll speak it in bed. I won't take any foolishness tonight. I want you all to go to sleep on the dot of seven."

"May we just peek at Dean Galloway once?" begged Judy.

"What do you know or care about Calloway, or Galloway, whichever it is."

"It's Galloway," said Judy, in her serious way. "He's the dean of a college where everybody's colored. He didn't want to write Simeon a letter, so he came to see him instead. I don't know about what."

"About begging for money," Cleo said, ignoring Judy and addressing the grown-ups. "What else would he come up North for? Nobody coming here tonight is coming for his sake, anyway. They're coming to see Simeon's wife. Poor Thea. Simeon lying on velvet, and Thea lying on straw."

"Well," said Bart practically, "Thea and Cole couldn't hold on to her inheritance."

"That's why I hate to tell you anything. You tell it back so mean-like. They didn't throw away that money. They spent most of it on old Mrs. Hartnett's sickness."

"I still don't see," argued Bart, "how come Cole was making ends meet until Thea married him."

"He was making ends meet by redcapping and gambling. You know that. Now he's just another poor colored doctor."

She was suddenly aware of the gaping children and turned on them angrily. "You children get from under foot and go on upstairs. I declare, when you're off by yourselves, we can't hear ourselves think. But you come around us, and you could hear a pin drop, you're so busy taking it all in."

"I was going to excuse myself, anyway," said Vicky with dignity, though the intention had just popped into her mind. "I have to go to the bathroom. Please excuse me." She turned to leave under her own authority.

"One minute, miss," said Cleo severely. "You've got to get out of that bad habit of going to the bathroom. If you can't control yourself at home, you'll go in public places and get germs. Only men go to the bathroom all the time, anyway."

"I still have to go," said Vicky stubbornly.

"I do, too," said Penny, because all this talk had made her think she wanted to.

"And so do I," said Judy loyally.

"Me do," Tim said stoutly.

"Then run along," said Bart over Cleo's beginning protest. "Quick. March!"

They threw him a look of love and left.

"Letting them go to the bathroom every time they say they have to," Cleo muttered. She turned a cold eye on Bart. "I'll thank you not to spoil them, Mr. Judson."

CHAPTER 25

From the distance came the muffled sound of the sunset cannon. Silently and softly the winter dusk descended. The lamplighter, in the bulge of his woolen wrappings, set his wand to the street and sprinkled his stars in glass globes.

In the Judson house everything was in readiness. The wild disorder in the upstairs sitting room had been cleared away. The best gifts had been left on prominent display, and the lesser ones, in the main Bart's, had been herded toward the rear of the tree. The tree had been lighted for the expectant children at first dark. The dozens of little candles had gleamed five minutes, with the children looking rapt and the grown-ups racked, and had then been snuffed out with unceremonious haste before the house and everybody in it caught fire. This ritual would take place nightly as long as the wretched candles lasted, with the grown-ups wishing Christmas week were a year away instead of now.

With the last rite of the day concluded, the children were tucked by the fire in Cleo's room with supper trays and a sleepy feeling that was going to keep them from staying awake to express defiance of Cleo's curfew.

Bart's bedroom on the second floor, habitually kept

closed from public view because of its ugly meager furnishings that Cleo had bought with haste and disinterest at the shabbiest of second-hand stores, and Bart's fruit smell that was worse in winter with his barred window and his unwillingness to bathe in brisk weather, had been turned into a scented bower for the ladies, with something borrowed from each room upstairs, including Lily's bed.

The bathroom, next Bart's room, stood open, too. Every faucet sparkled, the marble and porcelain glistened. The snowy starched curtains at the window stuck out like ballet skirts. The rug had been beaten with such vigor that the worn spots showed. But the tub did not betray its secret — that the bath water usually refused to flow out until it was given a swoosh with the suction pump past some unyielding toy belonging to Tim.

The money that Cleo squeezed out of Bart for repairs was almost always spent otherwise. And she, who was jack-of-all-trades and master of none, did a poor patch job with makeshift materials.

The playroom, on the other side of the bathroom, with its scuffed floors and washed spots on the wallpaper, showed the hard use to which it had been subjected, despite the spit and polish. The dining-room ceiling beneath bore faint fissures in its plaster from the incredible tonnage of paperweight children and scale-size toys.

The moon, growing bigger and brighter, skimmed toward the center of the sky. At just past eight the guests began to arrive. The storm door was open, the street door was on latch. Cleo, her aliveness like a flame, wore winered velvet with long sleeves and low bodice. Her shining hair was wound in a coronet. There were pearls in her ears, Bart's Christmas gift, a dusting of powder on her face, and her untouched lips and cheeks were glowing with health and happiness.

When she spoke, her accent and inflection showed no detectable flaws. Her silvery chatter, her low, lovely laugh were bright threads weaving her guests together in a comforting assurance that this party might be taking place in a white lady's parlor. Even the caterer's man, who had come with the ices and to serve the highballs and hors d'oeuvres, had got over his initial shock that colored people were briefly his betters, and was passing among them with impeccable politeness, noting behind his bland mask their elegant behavior and supposing they were all very rich and distinguished.

Among the men arriving were the old judge, a man of some distinction at an earlier date; a criminal lawyer with an important practice and a daughter passing for white at Wellesley; a young lawyer with no practice at all and a complete disinterest in the profession his father's butler-wages had bought for him; a doctor who privately hated his growing practice because his patients were the colored poor; a valet whose dress and bearing were superior to that of all the men present; a caterer's helper, on his night off, who accepted a proffered highball with no nervous recognition of a fellow worker; and the man of talent, a violinist, handsome, poor, and gifted.

And among the ladies arriving were Miss Eleanor Elliot in old finery; an auburn-haired social worker, the first of her race at Thaw House — though hardly representative — also distinguished as a Wellesley graduate but who had had no inclination to pass because her family name was honor enough; a schoolteacher, doomed to spinisterhood by Boston's ruling, but too contented with her white pupils to yearn to mother a colored child; and a brilliant teacher of piano, who had a growing list of the best colored children because she had been astute enough to start her enrollment with white students, selected from her neighbors' crop and charged a modest fourth of her dollar fee.

Cleo, along with the caterer's man, was storing impressions. The Rabelaisian half of her mind was faithfully recording every word and gesture for devasting mimicry the moment the storm door shut behind her last guest and she could race upstairs, rout Mr. Judson out of her bed, and summon her sisters, with the low-down laughter starting in her throat, to watch her peerless performance.

But the other half of her mind — that part with which she avidly read the latest books by authors who wrote about the well-born; which she took to the Hollis Street Theater along with Thea where, leaning forward as the houselights dimmed, Thea listened and she learned; which went with her to smart restaurants accompanied by Thea and her tale of woe, to which Cleo closed her ears and absorbed like a sponge the snatches of conversation flowing around her like sparkling fountains — that part of her mind was quite certain that this was the hour which gave her whole life meaning.

Thea and Cole entered, and Cleo went forward with outstretched hands to draw Thea to her and press her cheek against hers. This effusive greeting, contrary to Cleo's custom, served as public proof of the intimacy between her and Mrs. Cole Hartnett, born Binney.

She could sense the excitement Thea's entrance created in the ladies and gentlemen assembled in the parlor.

Thea's unconscious hauteur made them uncertain of her opinion of them and anxious to evoke a good one. She acknowledged their fulsome greetings with charming detachment, her gracious voice, with its little undercurrent of indifference, keeping her firmly fixed on her pedestal, despite her poverty and lack of pretension.

Plain-featured, dark-yellow Cole beside her was considered a fortunate man because he had a doctor's degree and a fair-skinned wife who would give him fair children.

Miss Elliot, descending the stairs, greeted Thea with enthusiasm as they met on Thea's way up to remove her wraps. The young matrons like dear shabby Thea assured the succession of colored society. And the outlanders like handsome Mrs. Judson were bringing their money where it was badly needed.

"It's so good to see our Thea out again," she said warmly to Cleo. "And how are your sisters? We're so sorry not to see them tonight. We hope they're only away for the holidays. The children are becoming such little Bostonians."

"Oh, my sisters are all quite settled here. It was Father's dream to send us to Northern schools. But teachers in small Southern schools have such impossible incomes that Father could never afford it. He made us promise that if we married and had children, we would educate them in Boston."

"Your sisters were very fortunate to marry understanding men," said Miss Elliot, with her eyebrows asking an explanation.

"One is beyond understanding," said Cleo sweetly. "My sister Charity lost her husband in early September. She's now away on a visit to Father. I wanted him to spend

Christmas with us, but the long trip here and back would give him too short a holiday before he returned to his teaching duties. My sister Lily is away, too. Her husband travels for a firm that sells improvements for stubborn hair." She smiled wickedly at Miss Elliot, whose hair was not an asset to the appearance she liked to present.

"He telephoned Lily last night to meet him in New York this morning. He found that he had a free day before he leaves for Chicago. That's why Lily has established her home with me. Her health is rather delicate, and her husband worried at knowing she was alone so much.

"As for my youngest sister — who sends her apologies, Tim's quite feverish from too much Christmas excitement — her husband, who is very fair, is working as white in a very prejudiced part of the South. It means an indefinite separation. But when there's a child to consider, the parents must make almost any sacrifice to insure that child's future."

She smiled brightly at her own ability to taste untruths on her tongue and make no betraying grimace.

The old judge turned away from a group and lumbered over. His voice boomed over the room. "Dear Mrs. Judson, I've the oddest feeling that I've been here before. What is the magic you exercise that makes me feel completely at home in your charming house?"

Miss Codman, the inmate of Thaw House, said ardently, "It's an enviable house, Mrs. Judson. Did you have a decorator, or is your own taste your wonderful talent?"

The interest of the room was aroused. The murmurs of

conversation died. Every eye made open inventory, then came to rest on Cleo expectantly. In the faces of most of the men a puzzled recognition had dawned. In a moment it was overspread with blank amazement. Darting quick uncomfortable glances at their women, and being reassured by their expressions of innocent envy, they turned on Cleo a frankly curious and faintly mocking stare.

The color had deepened in her cheeks. She had never expected to be challenged by so many eyes at one time. For her way was to tell a falsehood to an audience of one, thereby leaving herself an opening for a conscienceless denial whenever it suited her. Now before her was an assembled company that could testify for each other that she had actually said what they heard her say.

She drew a deep breath. "You are very kind, Miss Codman, but my talents are still undiscovered, though I did once yearn to be an actress, and would have made a very poor one. And, my dear Judge, I am not surprised that you recognize a familiar hand in this room. For I am sure that all of you" — she surveyed them with a gentle smile — "knew Lenore Binney before I met her as Simeon's fiancée. With her generous nature she was good enough to give me the benefit of her exquisite taste when I began to furnish my house." Now figure that out to suit yourselves, she told them silently.

Outside a motorcar crunched on the snow. Thea, descending the stairs, at the foot of which Cole stood waiting, knew with the others who it was who could afford that moneyed sound. In a moment Simeon's head and hand briefly appeared. Then Lenore and Dean Galloway entered the open door.

Lenore had seen Cleo only once since their first meeting, and then at a distance, on a day that Cleo and the children had been standing by a car stop after dancing school. The three little girls in their velvet coats and beaver hats and buttoned shoes, with their slipper bags dangling on their arms, had made her want to see the face of their innocence. She had ordered her driver to draw to the curb. But the approaching trolley had swallowed up Cleo and the children before the chauffeur could invite them into her car.

She knew that Thea was Cleo's great friend, and she had no wish to intrude, for she believed that Cleo, with the warm sympathy that she remembered, would insist upon a friendship that might alienate Thea's. But Cleo had made no overtures outside of harmless inquiries to Simeon about her state of health. She felt that Simeon would consider any greater interest in his wife a disloyalty to his sister. She had got from Lenore what she wanted, fine furniture for the children to grow up with. Thea had a good deal more to give them. She had no intention of jeopardizing that for a woman whose acceptance by society was still undetermined.

Lenore had come to Cleo's supper as a courtesy to the Dean. She no longer wanted the rights she had won by her marriage. She had paid too high a price for the privilege of pouring tea. The last years in the West End house and the end toward which she had lived them seemed a nightmare and herself a dreamer slowly struggling awake.

As she stood in Cleo's hall, her smile did not extend beyond her hostess. The men had never been important to her, and the women no longer mattered.

Cleo heard the women's involuntary intake of breath as

they saw the fabulous Duchess for the first time, in chinchilla and French accessories. The Duchess heard the sibilant sound, too. Her face stilled, and over it spread that highborn look that had humbled Cleo the day of their meeting. Cleo read the women's minds perfectly. The Duchess's instant barricade had only excited them further. They had been praying for a cheap blond with some betraying negroid feature. They were overwhelmed with what God had given them instead. In an acute rush of color-consciousness each one wondered nervously if it was she who had caused Mrs. Binney's undisguised disappointment in a gathering of the best people.

"My dear Lenore, the evening is complete," said Cleo triumphantly, and touched the Duchess's cheek with her lips.

Thea came forward with Cole. There was a polite, unrevealing exchange between the Binneys and the Hartnetts, with Thea thinking that Cleo with her unnecessary kiss had really overdone her effort to make the ex-Duchess feel welcome.

When the small flurry of family greetings was over, the dark face of Dean Galloway was brought into focus. The disinterested women, for whom he was an anticlimax, faced away from the door and turned back to their men.

Dean Galloway, with the horror of remembered things rimming his eyes, heard Cleo's brittle accent miscalling him Calloway, felt her brief handclasp, met her indifferent look. He could not believe that this was the woman whose roots Simeon had said were Southern, who would understand his story, and pledge her support of a mass meeting.

CHAPTER 26

THE GREAT SLIDING DOORS between dining room and parlor were open. Both rooms glinted with wax and polish. In the chandeliers the gas-jets flickering green and gold highlighted the somberly glowing furniture and the shining brass of the parlor hearth, and sent shivery streaks along the gleaming surface of glass and silver *objets d'art*. Holly and evergreen, intertwined with Bart's practiced touch, lay along the marble mantel and were reflected in the ornamental mirror, in which the grand piano, the room's dark jewel, gave back its image of truth and beauty.

The dining-room table had been stretched to its full length and spread with embroidered damask linen. Bart's centerpiece on a silver tray was a tumble of polished fruit, balanced with exquisite precision to form a horn of plenty.

A large boiled lobster, its meat removed and replaced, was dramatically couched on a silver platter edged with lettuce. A grapefruit, dotted all over with toothpicks, the ends of which were capped with diced ham and tongue, had been placed at one end of a platter, and at the other a large cucumber, pricked with toothpicks to resemble a porcupine, lay lengthwise, its scooped-out center filled with red seafood sauce. On another similarly sized platter at the opposite end of the table was a molded ginger-ale salad of apples, bananas, celery, carrots, and shredded cabbage. In the center of the mold was a boiled dressing mixed with whipped cream.

Along either side of the table were covered dishes of creamed mushrooms and welsh rarebit, and plates of the startling white of turkey breast and the dark breast of wild duck. There were thin round crackers spread with a spiced mixture of cream cheese and whipped white of egg, toasted bread of triangle and diamond shapes spread with snappy cheese sprinkled with paprika, and caviar, and minced sardine, and baskets of buttered tea rolls. For the ices that were to follow were little cakes and lady-fingers.

In the center of the sideboard was the bowl of claret punch, and at either end were the coffee and demi-tasse services, and the cordials. Dishes of pickles, olives, nuts, and mints completed the supper feast.

To and from the abundant table and buffet filed the enchanted guests. Parlor and dining room hummed with well-being. Cleo moved among the ladies and gentlemen, her cheeks as pink as roses from their praise.

Lenore, who had listened to the little pleasantries of introduction with the feeling that they were mocking, and not wishing to expose herself to further disguised dis-like, sat somewhat apart with Simeon and Dean Galloway. Simeon did not stir from the seat beside her out of a dutiful unwillingness to expose her to its glaring empti-ness should he leave her. Dean Galloway flanked her, too, not because he had any awareness that she needed his protection, but because he needed hers in the face of the inattention his Southern accent and plain appearance had received from the guests who, like Cleo, saw him only as the insignificant peg on which to hang this brilliant party.

Thea, nibbling daintly, knowing that tomorrow Cleo would bring her the leftovers — which would not only keep her from having to cook for a week if she were careful, but would also keep her from having to eat her own burnt offerings — stood in the center of a large group whose lively chatter pleasantly ruffled her amiable detachment. She had entered the opening they automatically made for her, with no inner compulsion to be the focal point of the party, but in her very real desire to give herself to her friends as a queen gives herself to her subjects, while retaining her person inviolate.

In a corner Cole was earnestly talking to a doctor who expected to be bored by Dean Galloway and did not want to be bored by Cole. He didn't think there was any future in cancer. Here was that superb Duchess, looking as if she had just stepped out of a bandbox, and here was poor Thea with a hole in the heel of her stocking. Good God, who came first with Cole? Thea or a lot of nameless people with cancerous growths. The trouble with men like Cole, who had suckled on silver spoons, was that when they got poor they still tried to cling to the noble ideals their prep schools had taught them. Yet Cole had gone with the rest of them to the West End house. A doctor's degree had meant that much to him. Thea should mean more.

"Look, Cole" — he lowered his voice — "I know a white doctor with a practice that's more than he can handle alone. He's looking for someone to help him, preferably

a colored doctor. It makes it easier on his conscience not
to corrupt his own kind."

Cole turned his back.

The other doctor smiled cynically at his threadbare
suit. "The offer is open indefinitely. He wants a very
good man. As a matter of fact, he didn't want me."

Mr. Davies, who, with the departure of the caterer's man,
was now the sole representative of his craft, stretched
out a hand to Cleo as she gave him a sparkling, unseeing
glance on her way across the room. He had been titil-
lated by the sight of her all evening, and he wanted to
hear her warm voice addressing him exclusively. The
quickening her glowing skin and engaging mouth and
lively eyes stirred in him seemed infinitely preferable to
the marble dignity of the blond Duchess or the unap-
proachable apartness of chestnut-haired Thea. There was
something about this golden-skinned Southerner suggestive of excitement. She had no business with a middle-
aged husband, who might as well have married his store.
He was spending the night with his bananas, she had
explained in pretty apology earlier. He had just received
a shipment of them. She scarcely expected him to sleep
at home for a week. No wonder Bart Judson had only
given her one dark daughter, Mr. Davies thought jealously. In that magnificent body were golden sons. In
that heart beneath those lovely lifting breasts was unre-
quited passion. On a night like this she must lie alone and
toss for love.

His voice was full of emotion for her unhappy fate.
"The lobster was delicious, Mrs. Judson."

Her eyes really saw him then and twinkled delightfully.
He was part of her party, a contributing factor to its suc-

cess, and therefore to be regarded with more kindness
than if he were simply a male object in the path of her
progress.

"You make me very happy," she said, in a singing voice.

Mr. Davies went warm with pleasure.

"Lenore" — Cleo stood before her, and the ear and eye
of every woman gave disguised attention — "have you
everything you want?" The question was superficial. She
was simply showing the ladies how easy it was if you
knew how.

"There is nothing more I could want except to see your
lovely babies," said the Duchess, whose innocent words
seemed pointed to the ladies, who felt rather crestfallen.
"Will you bring them to visit me during the holidays? We
will have a tea party."

"They'll be delighted," said Cleo, who knew that they
loved long trolley rides. "Will Wednesday suit you if it's
fair?"

"I shall look forward to Wednesday."

Miss Elliot surged across the room, hoping her age,
that she rarely referred to, would serve her now as a suitable opening.

"Forgive a woman, no longer young, for taking the
liberty of listening. But children are my greatest interest.
I can't resist pricking my ears when they're mentioned.
I'm devoted to Mrs. Judson's dear little girls, and would
so love to be invited to their tea party. In my Saturday
classes I try to teach deportment as well as dancing. It
would be a very real pleasure to me to see them on their
best behavior."

"It is kind of you to want to come," said the Duchess,
thinking that anyone who loved children was not as for-

midable as her first impression had indicated. "I shall expect you at four."

"Now I am quite jealous," said Miss Graham, moving forward. "As the children's music teacher surely I am not to be excluded from their tea party where you may ask them to play?"

"I shall be pleased to have you," said the Duchess, who really was pleased that Miss Graham had a simple heart that could delight in a children's tea party.

"I should like very much to come, too," said Miss Bruce. "After two years of teaching, I'd really like to watch a group that I shan't be expected to instruct."

"Do ask me," said Miss Codman. "I have no excuse to offer except that it's my free afternoon and I'd love to come."

Other voices joined hers. In a very little while both Simeon and Dean Galloway were quite crowded out by all the ladies, who had deserted Thea completely. Simeon seized Galloway's arm and piloted him toward her, with jealousy for his sister filling him with hot, unreasonable anger toward his wife.

"I think," said Cleo to the Duchess, with a merry laugh, "I should bring the children another day. Any other day will suit them equally well. It will be a nicer tea Wednesday without them. I'm afraid they'd show off before so many grown-ups, and spoil an afternoon I very much mean to enjoy."

"Then do bring them Friday," said the Duchess, carefully keeping the regret out of her voice, for these were Simeon's friends who, for his sake, were being kind.

"I beg your pardon, Cleo." It was Simeon's voice, coming across the room, colder than she had ever heard it, commanding. She went to him quickly, not meeting his eyes nor Thea's.

"It is nearly time for Thea to leave," Simeon told her. "You forget her duties begin at dawn. You and Lenore lead somewhat easier lives. Dean Galloway arrived this afternoon. He, too, would like to leave as early as possible."

Cleo turned to him eagerly, escaping Simeon's stern sounds. "We are ready and waiting to hear your little talk. Simeon, put him by the piano where we can all see him." She clapped her hands for attention. "Ladies and gentlemen, our guest of honor, Dean Calloway."

There was a scattering of polite applause. Heads were indifferently turned. Somebody scraped a last mouthful of ice. There was a small clatter at the sideboard.

"It is good to be in Boston," began Dean Galloway, "for the eyes of the nation still regard it as the city of men on the side of justice, regardless of race or creed or color. You know that I am dean of a Negro college. You may not know that our activities are prescribed by the good white people" — he paused, but there was no ripple of laughter — "who support us. Something has happened in my city that happens every day in the South. A Negro is going on trial for his life before a lily-white jury. The man is not important in himself. He is a symbol of the South's injustice to black men."

His listeners shifted nervously. Dean Galloway was really being terribly earnest on top of such an excellent supper. There were even little beads of perspiration on his upper lip. Why had he chosen this roundabout way of asking them to ask their own good white friends for money to help support his school? Poor Mrs. Judson must be quite embarrassed by this fellow Southerner.

Cleo was not embarrassed, for she had not listened beyond his opening words. Having heard his flattery of her
chosen city, she supposed the rest of his little speech
would be the same. She turned to Thea to make amends,
dropping her voice to a whisper.

"Promise me, Thea, you'll come to Lenore's tea. I
know women. They'll deliberately misunderstand if you
don't. They won't say you're snubbing your sister-in-law.
They'll say you're jealous of her."

"I am," said Thea. It was such a new emotion that she
made no attempt to conceal it.

"Nonsense," Cleo hissed. "You'll be over that feeling
before Wednesday."

"I have nothing to wear Wednesday," Thea said, and
felt surprised at saying it. She had never been interested
in clothes. She had worn the best when there was money.
When there wasn't, she had been too sure of herself ever
to wonder if clothes made the woman.

Dean Galloway cleared his throat, and Cleo started
guiltily. But Mr. Galloway was not rebuking her. His
eyes were fixed on the lodestar that had brought him to
Boston.

"We are risking our school and its subsidies. But the
faculty, the students, and I will make a willing sacrifice
of ourselves and our futures to fight the jury system of
our state.

"We need your help. We need the help of *The Clarion*.
If Boston can be aroused, and her mighty voice thunders
against this travesty of justice, the nation will listen, and
even the world."

Cleo again had stopped listening a good while back. "I
can't put my hands on a penny," she fretted. "I can't pawn

these pearls so soon after Christmas. And after this party, I won't get another nickel out of Mr. Judson for weeks. Can't Cole — ?" She glared at him. "He's too married to his old germs to notice if you were buck-naked."

Thea stared at Cole, too. For the first time since their marriage she did not feel proud to be his wife. Without money the thing whose luster she had been most sure of seemed shabby. With money one could buy anything, a chinchilla coat, a servant to clean a house for guests to come to tea, and friends across the tea-table.

Thea's whisper was harsh. "I'll have a new dress to wear to Lenore's and Cole will buy it for me. I'm keeping his house, I'm nursing his mother, I'm denying myself a child. I think all that deserves a new dress. Cole had ways of getting through school. He can find ways of dressing me."

"That's the way to talk to a man," Cleo said, too loudly in her enthusiasm. She gave a quick glance across the room. Simeon was staring at Thea. She said, under her breath, "Guess we'd better let Calloway talk to us."

"Doctor Binney" — and Simeon, too, started guiltily — "will advertise a mass meeting in *The Clarion*. He has promised to write a front-page story that will burn the hearts of Boston. He has told me of his certainty in getting a famous old hall rent-free. He will see the board to-morrow. And when the night is decided on, I urge you to talk this meeting up. You represent colored Boston. You can help to swell the hall with the white and colored friends who look to you, and to Doctor Binney, for the expression of colored opinion in Boston. I and my school can be here only in spirit, but we will be waiting for Doctor Binney's flaming words to light the torch with which we will burn out one of the South's evils."

He looked over his audience. "I beg you who are here tonight to lend your respected names to the formation of a committee for the defense of Robert Jones."

For the first time his eyes singled out Cleo and sought understanding. She was a Southerner, she was his kinswoman. Cleo averted her eyes. She felt slightly embarrassed. Robert Jones. The same old nigger name as Serena's husband. Every poor darkey in the world was named Jackson or Johnson or Jones. Dean Calloway needn't stare at her. He was as bad as white folks who expected all niggers to be one big family. Just because she was from the South didn't make Robert Jones any nearer or dearer to her than to anyone else in the room. Let him pick on somebody else. If he thought she was going to speak up first, he had another thought coming. She wasn't going to stick out her neck at her very first party.

She shifted her eyes around the room. Everyone was looking betrayed because this appeal was not for their money to keep Southerners in Southern schools, but for their virtual alliance with a colored jailbird.

She scowled at Simeon. He had brought this embarrassing man among them. And Simeon was looking unhappy. It served him right. Maybe he would learn after this that his Boston friends had lost patience with his unpopular causes. It was her hard luck that he had picked her party.

Simeon did not feel her hot gaze. Over and over in his mind ran a crazy refrain, Committee for the Defense of Althea Binney. He saw her fine head bent before this unjust jury, who had found her guilty of no crime but poverty. And he was powerless to help her, for all that he had was a profitless newspaper and a wife whose money proud Thea would never touch. She stood alone, with even Cleo, the upstart Southerner, only coming when commanded.

No one had filled Dean Galloway's pause with anything but inward thinking. He began to feel the room's resentment, but there was nothing he could do, there was nothing he wanted to do, but go on.

"Robert Jones's crime was poverty. He was a Negro from South Carolina who came to my city to seek employment."

The color drained from Cleo's face. She listened with every nerve.

"He was fair enough to pass for white. Because wages for white men are higher, he did. There was trouble in our Negro section. A child had been killed by an automobile. And the drunken young driver had not stopped. The Negroes knew his identity. The father of the dead child went to see the young man's father, who said that his son had been ill at home all day. There was even the doctor's visit to prove it. But the doctor had been called at one. And the child had been killed at noon.

"The Negroes grew mean. They began to brush against whites on the street, they grew sullen on their jobs. The white people felt that trouble was coming and swore in extra policemen. Robert Jones was one of them. He armed himself against his brothers for three dollars a day. The need of money can reduce men to the level of beasts who eat their own kind. Two days later, at sundown, the Negroes began a march on the town. And Robert Jones killed a man. He killed a frenzied policeman, a Klansman sworn in that day, who had emptied his gun into the orderly crowd and was reaching in his pocket for another cartridge box.

"The Negroes were not armed. They had not come to kill. It was their plan to march to the center of town to show their unity and their strength. I will tell you that we in our school had been as upset by the smoldering resentment of these poor Negroes as any of the whites. We did not want any trouble either. Nice Negroes never want trouble with whites. But the night we watched that silent march all of us felt ashamed to be inside our darkened school.

"When the white man fell, the Negroes knew their protest march was over. They picked up their dead and wounded and ran.

"Robert Jones ran, too. He crossed the state line that night. At dawn he reached his father-in-law's, and hid there all day. That night the old man tried to help him escape across the river on his flight North.

"But the river was swollen, and the boat capsized. The old man drowned, and Robert Jones reached the shore after hours in the water. He was too weak and ill to move. He was found and extradited.

"And now he sits in a cell in my city. No medical attention has been given him. There has been no attempt to lynch him. My city remembers that unarmed march. They will do nothing to incite an armed one.

"We have won a partial victory in the very fact of the trial. We will win a total victory when every bitter truth is illumined. Robert Jones must not stand trial alone. The poverty of Negroes, their segregation, their terrorization, their wanton murders must go on trial, too. We must talk through Robert Jones for the whole embittered black

South. We must pack that meeting hall. Doctor Binney does not doubt, and I, too, have his faith, that some brilliant fearless lawyer will rise to offer his services to the cause of justice."

Dean Galloway's impassioned voice dropped. Perspiration stood on his forehead. A little rivulet ran down his neck. "There is nothing more to say. Robert Jones refuses to tell beyond what I have told you. The neighbors in his own town will not talk either in their understandable ignorance and fear. There is a wife and child who came North to escape the South's oppressions. He will not reveal their whereabouts. But when his story reaches the farthest corner of this nation, they will step forward to stand by his side."

Dean Galloway took out his large handkerchief and mopped the emotion from his hands and face.

Cleo stepped forward. Her shoulders were very erect and her head very high, her eyes a luminous gray. The others looked at her. They had been moved by Dean Galloway against their will. He had brought the dehumanized South to their doors. They had felt their oneness with Robert Jones. Through the soft iridescence of tear-filled eyes they saw their Southern brothers as themselves. They waited for a straw in the wind.

Cleo spoke. Her voice, in which there was no longer any brittleness, was beautiful and compelling in its depth and quietness.

"Dean Galloway, I am sorry to say I do not see what benefit will be derived from making the name of Robert Jones a household word. He had a reason for killing. But when one colored man commits a crime, the whole race is condemned. Tell Robert Jones's story to the world, and the world will be stirred by the drama and tragedy of the killing. But the rest of the race will be the real martyrs. Wherever white people see them, they will watch them for danger signs. They will be frightened by a dark face, or a slow answer, or a quick step. They will think that all Negroes are armed.

"I am no different from other colored women. And colored men will never understand us. They feel mean and low at every sl⟨i⟩ght, at every setback, and want to weep on the world's shoulder. But colored women can't afford self-pity. They're the ones that raise the children. What kind of children would they raise if they let them see their grief and despair? They'd raise humble dogs or mad dogs. They wouldn't raise human beings.

"Simeon, you know how Boston mothers feel about *The Clarion*. We keep it out of our children's way. If you print the story of a — colored killer, I will never again permit it in my house."

She stepped back and grasped a chair for support, her knuckles showing white and her eyes so luminous that they looked wet.

"Despite your very sympathetic speech, Dean Galloway, I feel I must agree with Mrs. Judson," said Miss Elliot, kindly but firmly. "And the same is true for *The Clarion*, Simeon," she said sternly, as an old friendship should permit. "Our daily papers have treated our race with the utmost consideration. Not one of them has ever splashed the story of a colored murderer across its front pages. It will be an unforgiveable error if your paper should establish the precedent."

"A shame indeed . . . really monstrous . . . a dreadful mistake," the ladies passionately assented. At last the op-

portunity had been given them to tell Simeon in unison
how thoroughly embarrassing was a colored newspaper
that devoted most of its space to exposing the worst elements of the race.

Simeon listened to their open hostility. It was no new
story to hear disapproval expressed. But the barrage had
never been so vigorous. He had never been assailed by
so many people *en masse*. If he printed the story of
Robert Jones, he might alienate them forever. Even Cleo,
whom tonight he had commanded to Thea's side, might
close her ears to him hereafter. She was capable of
cruelty, as were all these women, as they had brutally
demonstrated when they canonized the Duchess, who had
been nothing until he had given her the name that was
Thea's before it was hers.

The Duchess had asked these women to tea. She would
give other affairs. Thea's friends would flock to the house
in which Thea had presided. And the Duchess would win
them over. She had started her campaign tonight. Well,
he would start one of his own. He was handsome, brilliant. Women liked him, had even wanted him. They
would learn that the road to his heart lay through Thea.

"Dean Galloway," said Simeon, forcing his tone to be
frivolous, "I think we must bow to the command of the
ladies of Boston. We made a gallant try. Let us lower our
flag with the same gallantry."

"Bravo, Simeon," said Miss Codman, with Wellesley
élan, and her eyes were soft as they met his.

"May we go now?" said Dean Galloway, moving quietly
to the Duchess. "I haven't your husband's resilience. Perhaps I am too tired."

"I am ready to leave," said the Duchess. "I am sorry

my husband failed you. It is because I have failed him.
A wife should be a man's conscience. I am not his."

A nightcap was suggested. The ladies flew for their
wraps. A toast was proposed to Mrs. Judson for her lovely,
lovely party. And really it had all been delightful despite
the unfortunate injection of Dean Galloway with his sentimental story about some Robert Something-or-other.
Mrs. Judson — Cleo! — had brought Simeon back into the
fold. She had given them that Viking's daughter, Lenore.
She had wined and dined them royally. And, of course,
she herself, with the becoming tired smudges under her
beautiful eyes, with her lashes looking almost wet with
the happiness that was welling inside her, with her smile
almost heartbreaking in its softness — she deserved to
sleep like a weary angel at the end of this exciting evening
that saw her accepted as an integral part of Boston
society.

The storm door closed behind their bright laughter,
their tinkling good nights. Cleo locked the inner door
and crossed the hall to the parlor fire. She stretched out
her hand to it. In the emptied room she felt cold.

Shivering violently she knelt beside the hearth and
wrapped her arms around her body. She saw the drowned
face of her father.

"Pa," she moaned softly. "Pa." But the held-in tears
would not fall.

CHAPTER 27

Upstairs, Bart stirred on Cleo's bed. This begrudged concession had not included his passage between the sheets. He had been instructed to lie on top and cover with a quilt. Children, Cleo had told him shouldn't sleep next to grown people, who sapped their strength. Except the mothers who had borne them, she had added hastily to forestall any discussion of this delicate subject. Her last command had been that Bart must take a bath and put on a fresh nightshirt. Since his last bath he had probably picked up enough germs to kill the hardiest child. And God knew they had a fertile field in which to stay alive.

Bart stirred again and came awake. The sudden silence in the house was as loud as an alarm. He lay and listened and heard no company sounds. He looked down at his daughter, knowing without need of the faint glow cast by the fire her smallness, her roundness, how the long straight lashes lay on her cheeks, how her lips were curved in a smile at the angel that guarded her. He touched her outstretched hand, and his heart shook a little at the wonder of his child.

He wanted to put a coin in her hand. He had put money in her hand from the time that she was born. And

now every morning he emptied his pockets of all his silver
except his trolley-car fare and slid the coins under Cleo's
closed door. There was always the bright pool of silver
for Judy, which Cleo always borrowed before Judy could
put it in her bank. He wanted his daughter never to be
without money. But she, who had handled money before
she knew its worth, would never treat it with respect.
She had been born to a rich man, and he had been born
to a slave. Knowing his furious industry, she took it for
granted that money was not easily come by. She did not
think she would ever care enough about it to want to
work that hard for it.

Gently Bart pressed the palm of her hand, extracting
the blessing. She was his luck, or so he saw her. His
lucky piece, he called her. Unknown to Cleo, it was his
custom to visit at Judy's bedside when the day's receipts
had been exceptional. Waking her, he would pile the
packets of money on her pillow and press her small hand
on the stack. He called that the blessing of his money,
and believed that would help him to double it. He had
the common sense to make the ceremony short, knowing
that Cleo would raise Hail Columbia over his piling germs
on her child's pillow.

He rose, put on his carpet slippers, and padded to the
door. He opened it softly. The girls were asleep behind
their closed doors, shut against exploring guests. He
could hear their peaceful snores. He went to peer over
the bannister. There was no sign of movement below.
Then faintly he heard the soft sibilance of Cleo's suffering, the sighs drawn back into the dry well of her sorrow.

Swiftly he descended the stairs. Something had happened at her party, someone had hurt her. She had

worked so hard for this party, talked so much about it. And it had been a failure. He was filled with pity and anger.

Midway on the last flight of stairs he slowed down, conscious of his nightshirt and bare knees. Maybe that girl, Thea, had stayed to sympathize. No, she had likely walked out with the rest. Cleo thought the world and all of Thea, but women were fickle friends. Thea might have made best friends with her rich sister-in-law right in Cleo's teeth.

"Cleo," he called softly.

Her shivering stopped. She struggled to her feet and faced the door, feeling a painful eagerness to see her husband's face, straining toward the comfort of his voice.

"That you, Mr. Judson? Come on down."

He entered the empty room cautiously. "They all gone?"

Ordinarily she would have called him a fool for such a fool question. Now she said quietly, "Where's your bathrobe? It's cold."

"This house ain't been cold one minute today," he said in an injured voice. "I've kept a red-hot fire. Shook the furnace down good just before time for your party and piled on coal like it cost pennies. Reason you feel cold is all those people made more heat."

She said in that same quiet voice, "You hungry? There's plenty to eat."

"I reckon not. I ain't used to eating so late."

"I guess I'm keeping you out of bed. Don't try to sleep careful in Lily's bed. You sleep how you like."

"Cleo," he said concernedly, "this kind of aimless talk ain't like you. You holding something back. What went wrong with the party?"

"Nothing. Everybody said it was wonderful. It's Pa I got on my mind." Her eyes met his almost imploringly, urging him not to make her say it, not to make it true by the telling.

"What you thinking about him?" he said.

The phrasing of his question gave her a little more time. "Sit down. Pull up that chair by the fire. It's cold. Don't take chances just out of a warm bed."

He dragged a chair to the fire. "Don't you worry none. I ain't going to die till my time comes."

She shied away as if he had struck her.

"Cleo, you skittish as a colt. You had too hard a day, all that fixin' for those folks, and up all last night playing Santa Claus for the children."

She caught the words in her heart. She could feel her breast burning with them, feel the slow trickle beginning in the aridity of her anguish.

"Pa used to play Santa Claus for us. We were poor, but each and every child had a stocking and a store-bought doll. I never saw Pa in a new suit or a new pair of shoes. But he gave Mama money twice a year to make our clothes out of new cloth. Two weeks before Christmas every year God sent, Pa started saying he wasn't hungry when we sat down to supper. The less he ate, the less food he had to buy, and the more he could save for those store-bought dolls. When he saw our faces Christmas morning, I guess he thought it was worth it. Wasn't any happier children in Camden. We figured we had the world."

"I reckon he was born a family man," said Bart.

"I've seen him spend a whole evening patching a doll," she said, with desperate eagerness. I didn't take patience after Pa. I never remember him raising his voice to one of his children. He was the one used to listen out in the night. Mama slept sound. Pa'd sit up all night with one of us in his arms when we had an earache or toothache or some such. We wouldn't take medicine for Mama. We'd always open our mouths for Pa, even me."

She turned away from Bart and looked into the fire, her hands again outstretched to it, its warmth pervading her iciness, her body beginning to yield with her heart.

"He had gray eyes. I guess they were the kindest eyes I ever saw. Wasn't any green in them like in mine. Wasn't any meanness in him like in me. I guess Pa had a beautiful face. I never thought about it. I made myself think I hated his mustache. I made myself think there were germs and things in it. And now I don't want to think of Pa without that mustache. He wouldn't be Pa. You wouldn't be you."

And she thought, They're the same kind of men, the same kind of good men. Pa was poor as Job's turkey, and Mr. Judson could buy him and sell him a dozen times. But Pa was as good a provider. Everything you give a child, if you mix it with love like Pa did, the cup gets filled to running over.

The bubbling began in her chest, the rise and fall of her breast was faster. The hot rush of tears coursing steadily toward release warmed her cold body at last.

"I remember the Christmas we went across the river to Grandma's. Pa was coming Christmas Eve. And Christmas Eve the river rose. Mama told us not to hang up our stockings. She said nobody, not even Santa Claus, could get across that river. We hung up our stockings anyway. Mama cried. She didn't want to see our faith destroyed.

And the next morning our stockings were filled. There were our store-bought dolls. Pa was there, too. He said he'd rowed Santa Claus across. And Mama said it was our love that had kept that boat from capsizing."

Her face contorted. Her shoulders shook convulsively. She hid her face in her hands, and the tears spilled through her fingers.

Bart had seen her cry only once before, the day they had met precipitately in Norumbega Park. But she had been a girl then, crying over a bicycle. Suddenly, after more than ten years, he knew that Cleo would never have cried over a bicycle. She would never cry over anything money could buy. She would put her mind on a way to get it. These were the tears she shed for her dead who were beyond her remorse.

He rose and seized her roughly by the shoulders, swinging her around to face him. "Cleo, was there a telegram? Was that what woke me? Is it your Pa?"

Her hands fell away from her ravaged face. "Pa's dead, drowned in that river. I don't know when. I don't even know if they've — found him. Pa lived so decent. He died so hard."

Gently he forced her into his chair. He kept his voice steady and comforting. "Cleo, I couldn't be no sorrier. I'll go wake the girls and send them down to you. I know you want to tell them alone. I'll be in bed, but I won't be asleep if you need me. And don't you all worry about money. One of you can go South and find out about your father. Seems like Serena's the likely one, and she could search out some clue to Robert."

He turned to leave her, and she clutched his arm. She had no time to wonder why this man of the enemy side

could tell her by speaking her name that his strength
would sustain them both. She knew, and could not take
time to deny it, that in him was a vital power from which
she was renewing her own. His presence was calming her
turbulence, restoring her courage, and clearing her mind
for furious thinking. If he left her alone, some part of
herself that had fastened itself to him with tentacles
would be torn from her.

"Mr. Judson, sit down. I've got something to say isn't
easy said. I can't tell my sisters what I'm going to tell
you. Serena especially. You still not cold?"

He was cold now. For the room's changing temperature, with the last warmth left by the guests now receded
into a party that had taken place a long time ago, made
his single garment a thin protection against the inescapable drafts of a private dwelling in Boston.

"With something worrying you, don't go worrying
about me. I'll put my back to the fire. I'll be all right."

She was silent for a moment, assembling her story, and
freeing her mind of emotion. She had wept her tears for
the dead. They would not bring Pa back. Now she must
think of the children.

"Robert's in jail. That's how Pa drowned, trying to
help him escape across the river. Robert killed a white
policeman. I don't say he was right or wrong. That don't
much matter. A white man's dead, and Robert will hang
for it."

"Cleo, my God, how you hear all that?"

"That Dean Galloway who was here tonight. Him and
I got to talking about the South. I didn't let on I was
Robert's in-law."

"How Robert come to do such a thing? Serena never

talked about him like a man as could have murder in his heart."

"He lost his head and killed a dirty cracker for shooting into a crowd of poor defenseless darkies. If we could get hold of some shrewd lawyer, he could change that murder charge to manslaughter, and save Robert from hanging."

"Cleo, go slow now. You bucking the South. Seems to me that poor girl should go to her husband while there's time."

Her mind was working so fast and feverishly that she could not have stemmed the rapid flow of her words.

"Serena would send him to certain death with her tears and her love. Robert won't talk. That Galloway said he won't open his mouth about his family's whereabouts. He's trying to spare Serena's knowing. That lawyer can say Robert hated niggers. He can say Robert hated his wife. He can say Robert sent her North to her kin so he could go on his own and live as white. He can say Robert grabbed at the chance to shoot niggers, and a white man got in the way of his gun. He can say it was death by accident."

Bart's voice edged with abhorrence. "Cleo, those lies would swell Robert's tongue before he could speak them."

She made an impatient gesture. "All he has to say is 'Yes' or 'No' to whatever his lawyer asks him. Why, a real smart lawyer could even get next to the judge and jury. They're afraid of the colored folks rioting if Robert hangs. They'd grab any way out to keep him off the gallows. There's no reason, as I see it, for any word of that trial ever to reach way up to Boston."

Bart said profoundly, "You got any idea how much a lawyer like that would cost you?"

"Whatever it costs, it's cheap at the price of my child's pride."

"Cleo," he said heavily, "here's something I meant to keep from you, but now's the time you have to know. I been dipping into my capital to keep my store going. I'm not a rich man. I've always tried to tell you that. I've had a big business. That's not the same thing as having stocks and bonds by inheritance. When I can buy, I can sell. When I can't buy, I'm like a man treading water."

She made a harsh sound and strained forward. Perhaps Mr. Judson was really poor. Everything he had ever said to her rushed back to ring in her ears. Why hadn't she heeded him when he tried to teach her the value of money? Why had she spent ten dollars as if it were ten cents. Suppose he was down to his last few hundred? She never imagined a day would come when he couldn't get his hands on a thousand dollars.

"Cleo, what I had has always been between me and my God and my banker. But you're the mother of my child. You got her future at heart same as me. 'Tain't like she's a man-child could inherit my business. I got to leave her money. I never meant to touch my capital. I'm not a young man. I wanted to leave the child fifty thousand dollars, anyway, when it came my time to die. And all I got toward it is fifteen thousand."

Her relief was so great that her expelled breath made a small explosion. Mr. Judson had only been talking poor mouth. Fifteen thousand dollars was more money than most niggers saw in a lifetime. He was as rich as she had always supposed.

She veiled her scorn for his attempted deceit. "You could get any lawyer in Boston for half that amount."

He stared at her. "That money's every cent I have. I'm not talking poor mouth. That's God's truth."

"You mean you're telling me 'No' with that much money in the palm of your hand?"

His words lashed out at her. "I'm telling you I won't wipe out the child's inheritance. You got a way of making a man seem mean. You got a way of marrying a man to your family. God knows I'm sorry for Serena. God knows I wish there was some other way to save Robert. But you're the one that took that girl away from her husband. You're the one kept her away. You got what you wanted. Now ask God's forgiveness for the sin on your soul."

She rose and the blood began to burn in her cheeks. "Talk big, Mister Nigger. You're the one holding the moneybags. Go on and talk. I've got to listen. I can't tell you to take your money and be damned. All I can do is humble myself. All I can do is beg. How do you want me, down on my knees? I never knelt to a man in my life, but I'll kneel to a nigger now."

As she bent her knees, his hands dug into her shoulders. Tears of love and hate and terrible frustration stood in his eyes. He felt his maleness hard against her and pushed her away.

"Cleo, my God, your father's dead, and Robert will die, and you stand there tormenting my soul and my body." He sat down suddenly, and a spasm shook him, not of desire, but of cold emptiness.

She saw that his body had thinned in the last few months. Gray was thick in his hair. The destruction by age had started. Worry had done what all of his years had been unable to do. He would not live forever.

The anger left her. He and her father merged into one

image of goodness. "Go to bed, Mr. Judson. I've worn you out. There's nothing more to talk about can't wait until tomorrow. Serena'll start South as soon as you want to send her. I'd like to go with her to Pa, while she goes on to Robert."

He saw with bitter clarity his position and theirs. Cleo could not go to her dead father nor Serena to her doomed husband unless he gave them a few miserable dollars for train fare. The dependency of women had been the thing he had cherished them for. Yet in this moment he was sharply aware of the brutal weapon dependency wielded.

Tomorrow in the cold light of reason and day, it would seem a monstrous thing that he had clung to money as if it were a life raft, when a man might be spared a hanging, a woman the double grief of his death and the manner of his dying, and a man-child, who must bear his father's shame forever, the pointed finger of cruel men.

Ironically he knew that even half his savings was not an incredible sum. He had made nearly that much in a week and spent nearly that much in a day. That was the thing Cleo never seemed to see. The more he made, the more he spent. Or, perhaps, she did know, after all, that a man in business was a man who had learned to take risks. What greater return than a human life would he ever receive for risking his savings?

This was winter, the season of his habitual unease, when every setback seemed insupportable. He had been underbid for the Navy Yard contract by that new amalgamated group. Well, the years he had got that contract, other wholesalers hadn't, and their worlds hadn't ended. No more should his. That hotel he'd sold to for years, that department-store restaurant, that asylum, they hadn't renewed their agreements with him. But it wasn't as if he'd lost his whole living. Wasn't common sense to think he might have to close his doors because they were buying from the combines. He'd been in business before they became his customers.

And those out-of-town retailers who were giving their trade to that concern that had bought itself those two auto trucks and was making its own deliveries, maybe they were getting goods quicker and cheaper than he could ship them by rail with the new high freight rates and marking time for winter trains, but they weren't getting the quality. People who had tasted his fruit could tell the difference with the first bite. They'd put those retailers out of business.

Thing was, with the war, the retailers were afraid to take a chance on the independents. The independents just weren't getting the goods. There was nowhere really to put the blame. His own broker, Pennywell, liked him fine. But it stood to reason Pennywell wasn't in business for his health. With goods getting scarcer and scarcer, he was selling where he'd get the most for it. These new groups could pay more for one common pin than an independent could pay for a package. And the worst thing was, people weren't protesting the increased retail cost. They were snatching and grabbing.

But spring would come, and summer. The trains would start running on time, the rails would start rolling with Southern produce. The war couldn't last beyond this winter. England would rule the seas again. He would feel the old resurgence of power. Why, it wasn't six months ago he had cornered the banana market. The thing was to believe in himself, to hold on to his faith, to trust God. God would shower down blessings. God might even thrice bless him for doing unto others as he would like to be done unto.

"Cleo, I'll talk to my own lawyer first thing tomorrow. He'll know the best man to take Robert's case. I'll telephone you to meet me and tell him the whole story. Then you can start South to your father sometime tomorrow afternoon. If it's too sad a journey to take alone, you take one of the girls along with you."

"Before you came down," she said, with quiet wonder, "I was near crazy, not knowing which way to turn. Now I feel like myself. I'm going alone. It's better my sisters don't know about anything until Robert's free and Pa's beside Mama. I'll tell them I'm going on business for you. That you got some Richmond property you want to sell to tide you through the winter."

"You suit yourself," he said heavily. "They're your sisters. They're you-all's sorrows."

She put her hand on his arm. "You know I'm not much at saying 'Thank you,' but it's here in my heart."

He got up. He felt stiff and old. "You're my wife, Cleo. Who else a woman got to turn to time of trouble but her husband? She was made of man's rib. She's part of him."

"You go on up. I'll turn out the lights." She added awkwardly, "Good night, Mr. Judson."

He was too tired to feel surprise. "Good night, Cleo. Try to get a good sleep. You got a lot of hard travel ahead of you." He went slowly up the stairs.

She was going down home. She sought for her old images, she tried to reach back to Mama. And she saw her father that Christmas morning at Grandma's. She saw her mother's love-washed face beholding the miracle of his being alive.

Suddenly she was glad that Mama had died before Pa. Mama would have been as sad and lonesome without Pa as she — and slowly her stubborn heart yielded — as she would be without Mr. Judson.

PART TWO

CHAPTER 28

T HE BELLS of the Mission Church chimed the half-hour. The round, full, magnificent notes rolled down Mission Hill, sending splinters of sound to the very beginning of Protestant Brookline. The April sun, however, shone over the whole of Boston. It penetrated the homemade cold-box that was clamped to an outside window-ledge in Cleo's kitchen. But there was nothing in the cold-box to spoil.

There was nothing in the big, battered icebox in the back vestibule either. It had not been in use since summer. Even then it was chiefly a depository for chunks of ice until the iceman stoppered his ears to Cleo's promissory poor-mouth stories. The ice-box had worn itself out by the end of summer, anyway, periodically leaking through all of Cleo's patches. It could not be jarred a quarter of an inch if the ice was to keep its equilibrium. But every hot day the throat-parched children had unraveled Cleo's mumbo-jumbo of rags and putty and splints with the ice pick. And there began the disastrous, ever faster *drip-drip-drip*.

As the last notes thinned into silence, a frown briefly flickered across Cleo's forehead. She sat at the kitchen table with several parts of the kitchen clock spread out before her. She had flung the clock across the room in an outburst of anger. And that anger of the early morning had not yet wound itself back up. Listening to the tolling bells, she could not quite summon sufficient ill-humor to quarrel about the passing of time. A fleeting annoyance touched her face, but not her eyes.

They were the luminous gray of her grief. Underneath her quick surface emotions a sadness had taken deeper root. There could be no more remembering back without the recollection of a Carolina morning when Pa was borne from Potter's Field to a sanctified place beside Mama. Over all her bright images of the South there must remain this bitterest one. It had broken the chain of enchantment. She would never again feel separate from the harshness of down home.

She had not seen Pa's drowned face. Looking down at the plain, clay-encrusted pine box, she had tried to evoke a picture of Pa that would superimpose itself on the knowable ravishment of roaring waters. The picture that rose to her mind and persisted was Pa's reflection on Mama's face the morning of the Christmas miracle.

Had love been the real essence of Mama's beauty? Pa always complained that Mama's tintypes didn't favor her. Mama was bashful before a camera, and all she could think of was getting it over. Yet those tintypes were exactly like her when Pa was nowhere in her thinking.

Why was it that Lily and Serena and Charity had grown more and more unlike her in these last years? Was it because they were manless? Had they lost their look of Mama because they lived without men?

Cleo studied the parts of the clock, concentrating on the order in which she had removed them. She had flung

Little Ben across the room because it was in her hand when she found the forty dollars Bart had left under it. He no longer put money in her hand. That was a rule he would not alter, no matter how she argued. On his way out in the morning, he tucked whatever he could spare under the kitchen clock. He had done so ever since she tore a two-dollar bill into bits because it wasn't the five-dollar bill she had asked for.

Last night she had asked him to leave as much as he could in addition to the rent. She couldn't come right out and tell him it was two months due, and eighty dollars had to be paid by four o'clock today. He would only have demanded to know why she had got behind. And she couldn't remember why now. Last month it had seemed that other things were more urgent.

The trying thing was, Mr. Judson probably thought he was leaving something extra. Though he was first to agree that everything had gone up during the war and was still up, despite the war's end in November, she could tell that he did not quite believe her rent had increased to forty dollars. She could not show him her receipts to prove it, for some months there were none to show, other months there was only a terse acknowledgment of twenty dollars received on account, and once in a while there was a receipt for sixty dollars or so. She did not have one rent receipt that read, Forty dollars, Paid in Full. Even if she had, Mr. Judson would believe she had tampered with the figures. And this harum-scarum way of paying had resulted in yesterday's ultimatum delivered through a dispossess.

"Half-past eleven," said Charity, lifting the lid from a pot on the stove and trying its contents with a fork.

Everything there was in the house had been put together for the children's noon meal. "This ham hock cooked quick. But it wasn't much bigger than my fist. Cabbage feels about done, too. But it ain't any size to speak of. Time I got through cutting off the rotten part, you could put the rest in your eye. I better throw on a chunk or two of wood, though. These little potatoes are still hard as rocks. They must have been frost-bitten. I declare it's a shame the kind of stuff you buy off a team." She paused, smiled reminiscently, and ran her tongue along her lips. "Lord, I remember the potatoes Mr. Judson used to bring home. So mealy they melted in the mouth. Now the poor man don't bring home nothing. The little he's got, he's got to get money for. He's still trying to sell the best, poor man, and we can't afford to eat it."

Cleo, piqued at this reiteration of pity for Mr. Judson, said frostily, "You talk so much I can't think what I'm doing." She cast about for some topic to discourse on herself. "It's time those people got here," she grumbled. "The wife said between eleven and twelve. I want them to decide on the flat before the children come. I wish now I'd told her I had four, and she could like or lump it. I'm sick and tired of people staying a month and moving out because I won't teach the children to take a back seat. Sometimes I feel I'll never put another ad in the paper."

"Plight that dispossess has us in," Charity dryly observed, "we better thank God you didn't feel that way this time. And it wouldn't hurt to thank Him again for having that woman telephone just before the company cut us off."

"Sometimes I despise the first of the month," Cleo said bitterly. "Seems like everybody in Boston starts demanding money. They ought to work out a better system for sending out bills."

Charity clucked in sympathy and bent over the wood-box. Her forearms resembled great hams, though the flesh was no longer solid on her bones. The sorry meals of the past months had not sufficed her insatiate hunger. Now there was scarcely an hour's lapse between her stolen snacks. The craving never stopped. Bread was her opiate. She was bloated with it. Like a drunkard routing out his hidden bottle, stealthily she would open the bread box, cut two huge slices from the loaf, her hands unsteady, her breathing hard, and make a sandwich of whatever she could find, molasses, mustard, cold beans, bacon rind. And upstairs Cleo, forever attuned to the hum of her house, would recognize these surreptitious sounds and move around the room to drown them out and hide from herself this weakness of her sister's flesh.

Charity lifted the stove lids, piled chunks of wood in the pit, hastily replaced the lids, and prayerfully watched and waited. But her faith was not steadfast. In a few moments smoke began to seep from around the rims of the lids. Charity coughed and backed away.

"I declare," she said amiably, "it's first one thing and then another. You cooks with wood to save coal, and you fix to choke to death." She coughed again.

Cleo, who, at the first explosive sound, had dropped a minute screw just as she found the place it would fit, said irritably: "Well, don't stand there coughing in my face. Open a window. I'll have a look at that damper again when the fire goes out. I had it so it could open and shut if you worked it right. You must have fooled with it." But her tone was only mildly accusing, for she remembered perfectly well the day she had lost patience and slammed it so hard that it stuck.

Charity ventured back to the stove to give a look at her eggless, butterless bread pudding. "I'll be glad when summer comes for fair. It's a wonder we don't both catch our deaths with that window wide open on our backs."

"Well, for God's sake, slide it up some. Only a fool would open a window all the way in April." The exasperation suddenly left her voice. She had finally manipulated the diminutive part. She felt that nothing was impossible. "I'll get us a gas stove by some hook or crook, and throw that old coal range on the junk heap."

Charity shut the window, shivering a little inside her old sweater. Outdoors the sun was warming the winter earth, but indoors the floors were still icy. The furnace fire was kept very low to conserve the last scrapings in the bin. Most of the winter the only function it had performed was that of keeping the water from freezing. And it could not do that unaided. On very cold nights little streams of water had been left running from the taps. Early in winter Cleo had pretty thoroughly exhausted her credit with the coal company, which had at last discerned that she was a poor payer to a greater degree than she was a poor woman.

"Lord," Charity mused, "things'd be different if Mr. Van Ryper had lived. If you was paying him forty dollars a month, he'd make all kinds of improvements. Everything's being electrified now. Before I came North, I never thought I'd see by anything but a lamp. And now man's put the sun in a globe. Was a time I'd been scared out of my skin to stick a lighted match to gas. Now everybody's cooking with it."

"You never go anywhere. How do you know?" Cleo said crisply to hide her envy of the everybodies.

"That's what I hear you tell Mr. Judson," Charity answered quietly.

Cleo fitted a final piece in the clock, then tightened the coils of the mainspring, lightly touched the little lever, and the steady ticktock began. But this time she felt no sense of achievement. The clock had lost its glass face long ago, a leg was missing, the long hand had perversely broken off to the length of the short one, the alarm never rang at the hour it was set to ring, and now it was badly dented. Fixing this old clock was just another patch job. Patch, patch, patch, she thought desperately. There were a dozen things in this house that belonged on the junk pile.

"When I moved in this house, I thought I was on top of the world. I used to think I'd have an automobile by now. And I haven't even got a decent clock, let alone a gas stove."

"Old Used-to's dead," said Charity harshly. "You and me and even the children know that." Her voice quieted. "Except Mr. Judson. And many's the night I spend on my knees asking God to let things be with that good man like they was in his heydey."

The Mission bells chimed again, fewer notes for the quarter-hour, but with the same velvet sounds.

"Those niggers aren't coming," Cleo said stormily. "Why did that woman call me up to say they were. Oh, God, I can't bear liars. I thought by now they'd be here and gone, and I'd have twenty-five dollars." She replaced the back of the clock, clamped on the winding caps, and dispiritedly wound them.

Charity sat down at the opposite end of the table and began to cream a mixture of margarine and drippings, which she hoped would taste like butter to the children when she added sugar and lemon, and turned the whole into hard sauce. The pudding itself did not have all the sugar it required, but she expected the hard sauce to disguise this lack.

"Cleo," she said practically, "wait until twelve o'clock to fret. Lord, poor Mr. Judson was all nervous last night, worrying about renewing his lease. And you're all nervous this morning."

"What you wasting pity on Mr. Judson for? What's he got to be nervous about?" With a quick movement she rose and set the clock in its accustomed place as if glad to be freed from sitting still. She turned and faced her sister. "I'm the one to feel sorry for. He's got his rent in his pocket right now. I've got mine to get. If I had just half of what he's carrying around, I'd be downtown buying the children spring clothes. Easter'll be here next week, and they won't have an Easter hat between them."

"If they have a roof over their heads and food in their stomachs, that's all I ask," Charity said earnestly.

"That's fine talk for you," Cleo flung at her. "What do you care about clothes? You haven't put the first foot outside the front door in four years. You've lived for this kitchen. Pretty soon nothing will fit you but a tent. No wonder you're worried about keeping a roof over your head. I'd worry, too, if I thought they'd have to cut a bigger door to get me out."

For a moment of shocked silence both sisters held their breaths, Cleo because she had swung too hard at her mark, Charity because the blow had caught her in the heart. Then a great rasping sigh tore from Charity's throat, and her regular breathing, the hard respiration, began again.

Cleo nervously crossed to the stove and shifted the tea-kettle back and forth to drown out the labored sounds that she never paid any attention to except when, as now, she was made aware that their wellspring was suffering. A drop or two escaped the full spout and sizzled on the hot iron. But in a moment the sizzling subsided, and again there was no barrier between herself and her sister's torment. She lifted the stove lid with a great clatter and poked at the fire. It snapped and crackled, a tiny spark flew against her cheek, but she did not feel it. Her face was already hot with shame. She longed to tell her sister she was sorry, but she had never been able to master the simple words of apology.

Sensing Cleo's humbled pride from the outward signs of her restless movements, seeing her unable to summon speech to cloak her confusion, Charity felt compassion submerge her pain.

Softly, gently, she began to laugh, and the little silver bells rose higher and sweeter, sounding sadder than tears.

"I declare," she said between gasps, "once I got through the door, I'd sure be arrested for blocking the sidewalk."

Cleo whirled. Her eyes were no longer luminous gray. They were green. She said roughly: "Stop making fun of yourself. You're not all that big. I'd be the one arrested. I'd kill the first fool who opened his mouth about my sister's size."

Outside the Ipswich trolley rumbled by. Charity said quickly, seeking escape from the love and hate on Cleo's face, "Guess I'll go see who gets off. I got a feeling it'll be them folks."

She walked down the hall to the front of the house. The crushing weight on her small feet was almost unendurable. Pain stabbed her fallen arches with every step. The loud slap-slap of her carpet slippers was ugly and unsteady. She had lamed herself with her gluttony.

She came back in high excitement. "Lord, Cleo, that house across the way, that big house they've turned into a what's-a-name, you know, where the old lady died."

"I'll die, too, before you get to tell me. You mean the one they've turned into a roadhouse. Well, what about it?"

"Well, I guess they're getting a new stove. I seen them take a nice-looking gas stove out the back door and cart it to the carriage house. Didn't look to be a thing wrong with it, except I guess it's too small for a what's-a-name. It would just do for us. I bet they'd sell it for a song."

"Then you start singing. Though in my opinion they'd rather hear money talk."

The doorbell rang, the polite ring of unfamiliar callers.

"Lord," said Charity, "I was so excited about that stove, I clean forgot to see who got off the trolley. I know that's them people. I'm going to keep praying till they go."

Cleo gave a quick glance at the clock. It was almost twelve. "Keep the children quiet, that's all I ask. If they give you any sass, slap them down. For God's sake, hustle them back here until those people go."

"And this," said Cleo, "is the kitchenette." She had shown her prospective tenants the second-floor sitting room, whose rather worn furnishings gave the appearance of mellowed elegance, except for springs and insecure handles; the old playroom, which was now a large and sunny bedroom, with Lily's bed and bureau permanently borrowed; the bathroom, whose joint sharing always proved to be a chimera in a house with four children; and Bart's former bedroom, the new kitchenette, whose crude fixtures Cleo had had installed in a shady deal with a plumber's assistant working with suspect materials at hours when neither his heart nor his head was in his work.

The disappointing kitchenette did not dissipate the accumulated approval of the two elderly people whose best meals along with their best teeth were behind them. The quiet street, the solid exterior of the house, the shining brass of the doorbell that Cleo had repaired two days before, after Mr. Benjamin had ruined the spring trying to make her let him in, the graceful staircase, the imposing glimpse of the parlor, the immaculateness of everything, the well-bred woman beside them, were all in accord with the genteel requirements of Mr. and Mrs. Kennedy.

Between the two passed a little communicative look which said that this was the proper moment to reveal their decision.

"We'll take it," Mrs. Kennedy said. "We're very dissatisfied in the South End. I'm really reluctant to walk in my neighborhood. There is drunkenness everywhere and vulgar talk. We'd like to move in as soon as possible."

"The flat is quite ready whenever you are," Cleo said graciously. "We live very quietly. My sister and I are here alone most of the day. I'm sure we'll be as satisfied with you as I hope you'll be with us."

Mr. Kennedy made a motion toward his pocket. As he did so, there was a prolonged ear-piercing pull on the doorbell. Cleo recognized that ring. It was the children's SOS. One of them or all of them could hardly wait to race upstairs to the bathroom.

The startled Kennedys stood in frozen attitudes, waiting, as they thought, with Mrs. Judson for some explanation of that outrageous clamor. And the listeners heard Charity, in the kitchen below, stumble out of her chair and knock it over, wheezing and gasping in her terrible haste, her anguished mutterings a wild accompaniment to her grunts and groans, and the ugly slap-slap of her slippers sounding more erratic in her mad scurrying.

Mrs. Kennedy shot a frightened glance at her husband. She was completely certain that the woman downstairs was crazy drunk. That furious tugging at the bell could only mean a drunken friend was demanding entrance.

When the front door opened and several young feet scampered over the threshold, and several young voices chattered at once, though Cleo could have killed the children without tears, the Kennedys felt their tension lessening. But their relief was short-lived. The woman below snapped off the children's greeting. Then one of the children seemed to be trying to ascend the stairs. There was the sound of a hand against tender flesh, and a child's shrill cry that was snuffed out as if that same hand had struck across a tender mouth. Then the young feet were heard in flight to the kitchen, with that woman staggering after them, as if the load of her liquor was too much to carry.

The Kennedys stole a look at Mrs. Judson. Her poise was plainly shaken. She knew that they had guessed her sister's weakness. They would tell her, in a nice way, that this was no house for decent people.

Cleo caught the little sly look the Kennedys sent toward her. Anger rallied her spirits. Who did these half-dead buzzards think they were, to act as if they were scared of children? When was it ever a crime for a child to ring a doorbell because it had to go to the bathroom? She had lived in this house before she knew the Kennedys were on earth. She could find a way of staying here without their rotten money.

Having chosen a nice way, Mrs. Kennedy said, "We didn't know there were children."

"There are four," said Cleo simply and proudly.

Childless Mrs. Kennedy, who adored children and would have been happy to live with a dozen, said carefully: "My husband and I are getting on. We've got set in our ways. Children would make us nervous. Thank you for showing us the flat. And now we'll say good day."

CHAPTER 29

I WOULD LIEFER not eat my dinner, Cleo," said Penny politely. "I would liefer wait to see what we have for supper." She put her fork down and folded her hands in her lap. Besides, she did not like eating in the kitchen. She did not like to be in the same room with cooking smells and soiled dishes.

"You eat up and hush up," Charity commanded. "Cleo's got more on her mind than catering to you."

Penny looked surprised. She was not used to Charity telling her what to do. She rolled her velvet eyes at her mother. Cleo was the only one supposed to make her mind.

She did not respect Charity. Because of her mother's gluttony, she had developed an extreme fastidiousness about food. Charity made her feel ashamed of the normal function of eating. When they ate in the kitchen, she hovered over them, her eyes darting nervously from plate to plate, as she waited for them to finish. The moment one of them laid down a fork, she whisked the plate away, and crossed the floor in choking haste to finish the scraps before she went through the empty motions of surrendering them to the garbage pail.

Charity herself felt no surprise that instead of removing

296

Penny's plate, she had ordered her child to eat what was on it. For the first time in a long time she did not feel hungry. She was worried about Cleo, and this new emotion engaged her whole mind, divorced it from her body.

If Cleo had stormed at her or the children, she could have stood it and understood it. But Cleo had not reproached them. She had just said those people wanted a flat with a gas stove instead of a two-burner plate. Charity had known she was lying. She had heard every word that was said upstairs. She had heard the lady say they would take it just the second before the children made all that racket.

She felt wholly responsible. If she'd used her common sense, she'd have been on watch for the children from the parlor window. But no, she'd been too busy sopping pot liquor behind Cleo's back.

Cleo was thinking hard. Charity saw that. She saw it in Cleo's quietness. Even now Cleo had let her get away with speaking to one of the children. Cleo's mind was on the rent money. With that twenty-five dollars slipping away through her fingers, all she had to count on was Serena's twelve, and added to forty, that wouldn't make eighty. And Charity wished to God she could help. She wished to God she had the gumption to walk out that door and get a job.

Serena was working. Even poor Lily. Poor Lily whose fear of everything on the outside had not been as great as her morbid fear that she could never do enough to retain her protected place inside Mr. Judson's house. She had marched out, unasked, to look for work when his business began going from bad to worse. Now she ceaselessly ran from job to job in her efforts to find one

that paid more than the last. Regularly she lost a day or
two sitting around in employment offices. Being far too
timid to tell her madams she was planning to quit, she
could never produce a reference. This lack of letters of
recommendation resulted in poorer and poorer jobs, with
more work and less pay, plus the growing doubts of the
employment agencies concerning her ability or honesty
or sanity. Still, even poor Lily brought in something.

Charity loosed her frustration on Penny. "Who are you
to act so high and mighty? I ain't paid a cent for what's
on your plate. Beggars can't be choosers. Eat."

Penny's lip quivered. She picked up her fork, but she
could not swallow the morsel she put in her mouth, not
because it was distasteful, but because along with it she
would have to swallow her pride. She was nearly eleven
and exquisite. She was upset if there was a wrinkle in
her stocking or the tiniest spot on her dress. Sometimes
she would wake in the middle of the night in trembling
horror of the rumpled sheets. She would weep softly and
pitifully until Charity grumbled awake and remade the
bed. When she lay down again, she would roll far away
from her mother, hating the proximity of another body
and the smell of sleep.

She was never going to be a scholar. She was in the
fifth grade because Vicky and Judy were. They did her
lessons. She was going to be a great dancer. She could
dance better than anybody in dancing school. But she
wanted to dance by herself. She was sick of being en-
circled by a boy's arm. She wanted to go on the stage
and wear wonderful costumes. And she would not have
to wait until she was eighteen. She looked older than she
was. By the time she was fifteen, she would look old
enough to run away to New York.

Cleo was concerned because strangers thought she was in her teens. Strange men. They looked at her with something hot in their eyes. Sometimes in passing they said sickening things out of the corners of their mouths. And once in a while in the movies or on a trolley they pressed her knee or stood too close.

She was wholly revolted. Because she had no interest in school, Cleo supposed that all of her interest was in boys. She had dismaying visions of Penny eloping with some coltish youth without a dime in his pocket. But Penny had listened to Cleo's belittling descriptions of men, and Cleo's unconcealed contempt intensified her own feeling.

Penny dreamed about growing famous, and having fresh bedding every day and the finest foods in the finest hotels. She was going to have everything she could wish for without any old husband to give it to her. Cleo thought she wasn't so smart. She was going to be smarter than Cleo. She was going to have everything — or almost everything. For she would not have Vicky.

Vicky would not promise to run away with her, even though Penny crossed her heart and vowed to share all her good fortune with her. Vicky had lived in New York. There was nothing there but buildings. She was going to run away and roam the whole world. Slender as a reed, agile as a monkey, wonderfully red-cheeked with radiant health, she was wild and free, and afraid of nothing. She would sleep in the woods sometimes, and in barns sometimes, she confided to her cousins. And she would write poems about everything she saw, and send them to Judy to keep for her.

Restless, fun loving Vicky could be sobered and in-

spired by the simple act of opening a book. She turned
pages tenderly, not wanting to break the ebony thread
that wove itself into a wonderful pattern of words. And
the words were the explanation of life, the key to understanding.

She, the child of Cleo's heart, was the one whose intelligence equaled Cleo's hope. Yet Vicky, for whose stormy
nature Cleo had set no example of restraint, was unable
to discipline her fine mind. She and Cleo battled royally
over her report cards. And on the few occasions when
they were completely creditable, both of them felt oddly
baffled that there was no need for a session of savagery
with each other.

Only with Judy did Vicky feel impelled to the pursuit
of truth. Judy had instilled the need in her, and she had
gone beyond Judy's own instinct for knowledge. Hers
was a larger vision. But she needed Judy to steady the
lighted lamp, to be somewhere near when she wrote.
Away from Judy she could not harness her spirit. But
Judy did not want to roam the world.

Innocently Judy wanted four little boys exactly like
Tim. She did not want to be a concert pianist. She was
tired of practicing in the cold parlor. She had to practice
longer and harder than Vicky or Penny, and she thought
this unfair. In the beginning her whole being had been
illumined directing the black and white keys into chan-
nels of beauty. Music had meant the entry into a people-
less world, where all that made the heart cry could be
blotted out by the evocation of pure sound. Now music
no longer sang inside her. She sat at the piano during
practice hours, playing facilely without thought or emotion. Still music had served her well. It had given her the

distillation of beauty. She could recognize beauty now in whatever form or shape it assumed. And for her it was most manifest in the faces of little children.

She was going to leave home and get married and never come back. She thought it would be an act of folly to return. Cleo would try to turn her against her husband. Cleo would try to take away her children.

Only Tim had not felt Cleo's influence. She did not want a little boy tied to her apron strings. She preferred to have him out of the house as long as the hour and the weather permitted.

He slept with Papa, now that Papa had been moved upstairs, and Serena no longer slept at home. Papa went to bed almost as early as he did. At night they talked man-talk until Papa fell asleep. For a little while Tim lay awake, staring at Papa's dark face in the darkness, his nostrils quivering like a puppy's as he separated Papa's different smells. Presently he was lulled to sleep by Papa's snores, his arm across Papa's chest.

Tim had entered the first grade at four. Cleo thought kindergarten was a foolish waste of time. She passed Tim off for five and a half, explaining, quite truthfully, that he had been born in the South and had no birth certificate. This sudden decision to start him in school had been arrived at on a morning when her patience had stretched its short length and snapped. One more tearful plea from Tim that he be allowed to follow his beloved Judy to the schoolhouse and she would have gone stark mad. She had jammed his hat on his head, jerked his arms through the sleeves of his coat, and carted him off to school with his short legs working like pistons.

At six he was a third-grader, and already had decided

to be a doctor. He expected to go to Harvard. He had
never heard that there was any other university. He was
forever assuring Cleo of his interest in higher education.
She was forever telling him firmly that there were three
ahead of him, and there might not be money for a fourth.
All the same, she had a disheartening expectation of
Penny's putting him in the running.

Before he was three he had made up his mind to be a
doctor with the earnest intent of making Robert well.
He did not want any father but Papa, but he was moved
by Serena's tears. He had never been taken to see Robert
after his arrival at the hospital in Boston. Cleo was afraid
that Tim would bring home a germ form the visit, and
one by one the children would die of galloping consumption.

Their knowing began when Cleo returned from her
sojourn into sorrow to tell her sisters about Pa and Robert,
but not telling even Serena that she was arranging for
Robert to go straight from the train to a hospital. Serena
got her room ready, put Tim at the foot of the bed so he
would get used to sleeping there, and not sulk when
Robert took his place at its head. When the lawyer's
telegram came, Serena and Cleo went to the station. A
long while later they came home alone. Serena found a
sleep-in job the next day. Robert could not stay in Cleo's
house. She could not stay either.

The night that Cleo returned to Boston, and for many
nights thereafter, the low-voiced conversations in her
room, where there had once been so much gargantuan
laughter, centered around Robert's dishonor. Judy lay
still and sick, wanting to tell them that Serena's sobs had
waked her, as later they would wake Tim, but unable to

speak and reveal that already she had heard too much.

Reporting in whispers to Vicky and Penny next day in the playroom, she, too, was unaware that Tim, very busy with his toys, was moving them without sound, was scarcely breathing as he stored up all the incomprehensible words and phrases against that day when he would know their full meanings and their full horror.

He understood everything now, though this dark knowledge was hidden deep inside him, so that no one would ever see it.

He knew, in Cleo's words, that Robert had been a jailbird until a criminal lawyer in Boston, who had never lost a case, went down South and won Robert's. It had cost a lot of money. Papa almost lost his mind when the expenses were listed.

The lawyer entered a plea of Not Guilty. He said that Robert had run from the scene of the killing before the first shot was fired. Seeing himself surrounded by white men with guns, he had suddenly turned into a scared nigger. He knew that white folks were never fooled by white niggers, especially Southern white folks. He thought he was in a trap. He went crazy with fear. He flung down his own gun and started to run for his life. The gun tobogganed to the black side. A nigger picked it up. The nigger witness for the defense was standing right beside him. He saw this man fire, saw the deputy fall, saw the man get his due a second later when the other deputies let loose their guns in self-defense.

Robert was called to the stand only once, and nobody could hear his mumbled answers for his coughing. The cross-examination was very brief, for the district attorney felt very uneasy being sprayed by Robert's germs. The burning spots in Robert's cheeks, his bleary eyes plainly showed that he was hearing and seeing through the thick folds of fever.

It was the nigger witness's day. That nobody had ever seen him before was no concern of the court. For a mob is nameless and faceless and attracts stray dogs.

The court set Robert free on condition that he get out of the South as punishment for the crime of crossing the color line which could lead to unimaginable horrors involving Southern womanhood.

When the bitter tale of Cleo's telling was ended, Serena said miserably, "Why did you have to tell me my Robert committed murder? Why couldn't you have let me believe the story you paid the lawyer to tell?" Cleo said, "I wanted you to know what kind of man you married. I wanted you to see I was right to want to separate you."

Most of Serena's wages paid for Robert's hospitalization. She was general maid in a large house whose only occupant, besides herself, was a harsh old lady who had been blacklisted by all the reputable employment agencies. Her temper was vile, her manner despotic. She believed that servants were thieves and liars. Despite her infirmities, daily she made a microscopic inspection of her house, and her cane lashed across Serena's knuckles whenever it suited her to show her power.

Cleo said Serena was a stubborn fool to slave for an old fool six days and seven nights a week, and then spend her one afternoon off with a crazy fool. But Serena would not have taken an easy place if one had been offered her. She wanted to share Robert's wretched fate in spirit if not in flesh.

On her afternoons off she roamed like a restless cat in

the family circle until visiting hour at the hospital. For
Bart alone she felt no resentment. She saw him rarely.
Unlike the others who saw him regularly, she was aware
of his aging. Because she saw the beginning of his
destruction, she did not have to hate him for Robert's
sake.

Robert had shut his mind to remembering. He would
not look back. Only the now of his nothingness occupied
him. He stayed within his wall of silence, forswearing
all but the meager speech of assent or denial. Over the
growing film on his mind only one image was stretched,
the hated Cleo of his conjuring, she whom he had never
seen, she the enemy who had ravaged him. Serena could
not lead him out of the dark.

CHAPTER 30

CLEO, brooding by the window, praying Serena's old woman wouldn't find some excuse to keep her from taking her afternoon off, wondering how much Serena could be persuaded to part with besides the expected twelve dollars, trying to figure where she could turn for the balance if Serena refused — Cleo heard the sobbing of one of the children, and brought her mind back into the room.

She jerked around and said bitterly: "My God, Charity, I can't turn my back for five minutes without confusion resulting. You see me standing here trying to think. You've got a tongue. Seems to me you could use it to make the children mind. If it weren't for me, this house would fall down." She turned to Penny with a very fierce expression. "What in the name of God is the matter with you? I'll give you something to cry for if you don't stop."

Penny went on sobbing because she had gone too far to stop the freshet at will. But she felt comforted. She had Cleo's attention.

Cleo's voice was deep and scornful. "You call yourself so grown-up. And look at you." Her impulse was to take the child in her arms. But she did not know why Penny was crying. If her pain could be endured, she must learn to endure it. Most of her life lay before her, and life was not easy for anybody.

Penny was able to stop now. She gulped once or twice, then assumed an injured expression. "I don't want this old dinner."

"Well, then, don't eat it," Cleo said calmly, but she held her breath just the same.

Penny was disappointed. "If I do eat it," she bargained, "may I pick out my own Easter dress?" The subject of Easter clothes had not been broached. Easter was a week away. Penny was beginning to be doubtful. Now seemed a very good time to find out which way the wind was blowing.

"I don't take bribes," said Cleo briefly. But she flushed, and her heart lurched a little.

"The Irish children are going to get everything new," Vicky said smartly. "They brag, and we have to brag back. If we don't get everything we told them we were going to get, they'll make fun of us." She hated new clothes, and knew perfectly well that there wouldn't be money for four new outfits. But she felt a pleasurable excitement at this chance to cross swords with Cleo.

"Even the Irish boys are getting dressed up,". Tim put in emphatically, with a wild notion that if Cleo took them downtown to shop, she might be persuaded to let him substitute a cowboy suit.

"Nice people," Judy said soberly, "never wear everything new on Easter Sunday. Only the Irish get all dressed up." Last Easter, when they only had new hats, and the Irish paraded the neighborhood in full panoply, Cleo had consoled them with the observation that nice

people never liked to look as if they had to wear everything new because everything else in their wardrobes
was old.

Her cousins gave Judy a little incredulous look. She
lowered her eyes. She hadn't meant to sound disloyal,
but she had sensed her mother's discomfort. Her cousins
thought Cleo could stand up to anything. But Judy felt
secret pity for her where the others felt secret awe. Cleo
made a big noise to scare people into letting her be boss.
Judy was beginning to see that Cleo was the boss of nothing but the young, the weak, the frightened. She ruled
a pygmy kingdom.

"I want to get all dressed up and go to the colored
church in Cambridge," Penny pouted. "That's where I'd
liefer go at Easter anyway."

They had gone to a white church the previous Sunday
because Cleo said Tim's Sunday shoes were too old to be
seen by people who knew him. Penny was bored in white
churches. Everybody was polite, but everybody stared
at Tim because he was blond. In the Cambridge church
everybody stared at Penny because she was beautiful.

"Easter isn't for showing off," Vicky said firmly to Penny. "It's for Jesus." She understood now why Judy had
lowered her eyes. Cleo was Judy's real mother. Response
stirred in Vicky's heart. Everybody laughed at Lily for
being a fool, but Vicky, too, knew the feeling of secret
pity.

"It ain't only Easter that's for Jesus. It's every Sunday,"
Charity said unexpectedly. "The way you children run
from this church to that, it looks like you're trying to find
God. You were all born good Baptists. You ought to
stick to the Baptist Church."

"You sound like an old ignorant darky," Cleo said scornfully. She was not a church-goer. It made her nervous to sit in church and be talked to about good and evil. "All the nice colored families send their children to the Episcopal Church in Cambridge. You don't have to be a shouting Baptist to be a child of God."

Charity stubbornly pursued her point. "It ain't that I think any other religion is sinful. It's just that I think it's sinful to change from the faith you been baptized in. I was born a Baptist, and I'll die a Baptist, and nobody could persuade me I'd get to heaven any other way." Her voice was aggrieved. "Hasn't nothing to do with my being an ignorant darky. Look at that high-toned friend of yours. You said yourself she'd be dying easier if she could die a Catholic."

"That's just what I said," Cleo countered triumphantly. "I was thinking about poor Lenore when you spoke. Search this city you wouldn't find a living soul with more love for God. That's why you sounded so ignorant running down a dying woman."

Charity was so outraged at this accusation that she could not speak for spluttering. Her face was beet-red with angry blood. She shook like jelly. The children tried hard to pretend they neither heard nor saw her. But Tim caught Vicky's eye, and a giggle escaped him. The contagion of mirth swept the table. Only Penny felt a strange unidentifiable pain around her frigid little heart. She thought it was because she was laughing so hard. She laughed so hard that, to her surprise, the tears came to her eyes.

The doorbell rang imperiously, a sharp, businesslike sound. Both women reacted nervously. Their petty bick-

ering flew out of their minds. Whoever was ringing rang
like a white man.

"I'll go," Vicky offered when neither grown-up moved.

"Sit still," Cleo said in 'cello tones. "Let me think."
Her forehead knitted. "That's not Serena's ring. Charity,
you suppose — " She let her voice trail off because of the
children, and Charity mentally supplied the word
"marshal." "It ought to be too early. Mr. Benjamin gave
me till four o'clock. God, I never knew the day would
come I'd hate to hear a doorbell ring." She shouted at
the children: "Stop listening so hard. I've a good mind
to get stoppers for your ears. Charity, you go to the
door and say I'm not home. If it's — him, tell him I've
just gone to Mr. Benjamin's with it."

Cleo tiptoed out behind Charity, shutting the kitchen
door behind her, and stood in a dark corner of the back
hall, where she could hear.

"Yes, mister?" said Charity, as she opened the door an
inch. Her agitated breathing did not subside at sight of
the shirt-sleeved stranger's attire. He might be one of the
moving men sent in advance by the sheriff to see how
much furniture there was to put on the sidewalk.

"You're the very lady I want to see," the stranger said.
He put his hand on the doorknob.

Charity held firm to her end of it. "No, I'm not. I'm
her sister. She ain't in. She's gone to Mr. Benjamin's with
the rent."

The man looked puzzled and massaged his mustache.
"Ain't you the lady I see at the window so much? That's
the lady I'm after."

Charity swallowed two or three times. "What you after
her for, mister?"

"I'm looking for a cook."

Charity opened the door all the way. Tears beaded her lashes. "Step in, sir. I'm her."

Behind her she heard Cleo's faint hiss. She knew what it meant. Who does that white man think he is coming to my house to look for a cook? Why do you want to say "sir" to white trash?

"Who are you, sir? How you know where to find me? You want to come in the parlor, sir, or you don't want to take the time?" Her voice was terribly eager. Here was her chance to help, to ease Mr. Judson's heavy load, to buy a gas stove for Cleo. This man saw her size and did not reject her. Suddenly she was flooded with pride that he would want her to work in his kitchen.

"I'm Mr. Doran from across the way." His head jerked toward the roadhouse. "We're opening tonight. And this woman was going to cook for me, she just telephoned she burned her hand bad. I see you at the window so much, I figured you wasn't working. On account of you're colored, I figured you could cook."

"Oh, I can, sir, I can! I can cook plain or fancy." She made a little joke to show she wasn't sensitive about her size. "You can see by just looking at me I'll be well at home in a kitchen."

"That's fine," he said briskly. "I'll give you a try. When you come over, we'll talk money. Right now I got to get back. Wish you'd come over as soon as you can. The men are there now putting in a new stove. They can show you how it operates."

"I'll come as soon as I speak to my sister. I won't be long behind you." She took hold of her courage. Her head went up. She felt proud and capable. "Mr. Doran, what you going to do with the small stove? Seeing's I'm going to be working, I wish you'd sell it to me and take it out of my wages."

"Hell," he said, "I guess you can have it."

"No," she said quietly, "I wasn't begging."

"Two dollars then," he said impatiently. "I got to get going." He drew the door nearly shut, then opened it again. "Lady, what's your name?"

"Charity Reid, sir."

"I'll expect you in a few minutes, Mrs. Reid." He was gone.

Cleo came out of the shadows of the back hall. One part of her wanted to rush forward and kick that white man out of her house. Yet another part of her had known that he had brought her children bread, and she could not hurl a stone.

Charity turned and said slowly: "I reckon you heard. God's answered my prayers. I got you a gas stove, and I got me a job."

Cleo said woodenly: "If you know I heard, what you wasting the white man's time telling me for? Why don't you hop to the crack of his whip? Go on if you're going."

"Well, I did tell him I'd be right behind him. I don't have to change. I got nothing to change to. Lily and Serena done wore out everything I got too fat to wear. God sure picked the right place for me to work with no coat or shoes."

She started for the front door. She paused, turned back to Cleo, and said softly, "I kinda hoped you'd be glad."

Cleo said swiftly, bitterly: "Sure I'm glad. You're my last sister. Serena sleeps out. Lily's gone all day. Sure I want to see you go from me, too."

"Cleo, it's just across the way."

"Your breathing's bad," said Cleo, her own breath rasping in her throat. "But the white man wants his pound of flesh. You think he'll let you sit down when you're tired? Sure I want to see my closest sister kill herself."

"I aint much with words, Cleo, but I feel newborn. I don't feel so ashamed of being nothing."

"You're still ashamed of being so fat," Cleo said desperately. "What makes you think you can waddle out that door in carpet slippers and a Mother Hubbard without being the laughing-stock of Brookline? You'll drop dead with embarrassment before your foot hits the sidewalk."

In the kitchen the children were laughing at their own foolery. Their laughter overflowed into the hall, swirled about Charity's feet, rose higher and higher, reached her throat, made her fight for breath like the drowning. She shrank back from the front door and groped her way to the bannister rail that would guide her to some hiding place upstairs.

Cleo yelled savagely toward the kitchen, "You children stop that fool laughing at once, and finish your dinner."

Gently she loosed Charity's clinging fingers from the rail. She looked into the empty face, and it swam before her wet eyes like a face under water.

"Charity, for God Almighty's sake, don't look like that. You tear my heart apart. If you go up those stairs, you'll never come down again. You'll die up there, and I'll have killed you. I never thought the day would come I'd tell one of my sisters to go to work in the white folks' kitchen. But I want you to go. Charity, go, for God's sake, go."

She opened the door. The sun streamed in, the trolley wires sang, the spring birds lifted persuasive throats, the budding trees stretched out their green arms. The world outside swung in its orbit of light. And Charity wakened from her long night.

Cleo, watching that crazy shuffling walk across the street, seeing her sister hoist herself over the curbstone, then straighten, smile, and open the back door, had not felt such pride when her child took her first faltering step out of her animal state into wholeness.

CHAPTER 31

"I TRIED TO GET YOU on the telephone," Thea said with soft reproach, "but the operator said it was disconnected."

She settled back in her chair, stripping her graceful hands of her beautiful, slightly soiled gloves, throwing open her handsome coat to expose the lagging hem of its lining, and carefully crossing her silk-clad ankles, unconscious that a run showed. A delicate odor of flowers emanated from her, but the silk shoulder straps that were visible through her shirtwaist were not very clean, and a safety pin protruded in a place or two.

Old Mrs. Hartnett had done the family mending, thus employing her invalid hours. But she had been dead a year now, and Thea's cluttered bureau was full of unmended underthings. The laundry had piled up, too, for the green girl had left two weeks ago with six weeks' wages unpaid. With an active two-year-old son to care for, Thea had her helpless hands full.

"Oh, that telephone," cried Cleo, assembling her features into an expression of high annoyance. "I suppose that means another stupid mix-up about names. There's another Judson family living near, who, apparently, are very poor payers of their telephone bills. You remember they made this same mistake six months ago. But I assure

315

you," she said firmly, "I'll see to it that they never make it again."

After this there would be Charity's money to help with monthly emergencies. Oh, Lord, she thought distractedly, maybe that's why Serena's so late. Maybe she's trying to telephone me she can't come. Jesus, what am I going to do? Lord Jesus, help me, help me.

"I need your help," sighed Thea. "I don't know what to do. So often I wish I were more like you. You can speak your mind to anybody. You never try to hide your feelings. I want you to talk to Simeon for me. There's something troubling my conscience."

She leaned forward a little, wanting the comfort of Cleo's hand on hers. But Cleo regarded her coolly. She felt that Thea had tricked her. She had opened the door without stopping to think that it mightn't be Serena. She was in no mood to be bothered with Thea. Simeon was doing her thinking for her. Let him do her stewing, too. Still her curiosity was pricked a little. What did Thea have to worry about? Simeon was arranging her divorce from Cole. As soon as the Duchess closed her eyes, Thea would move into the Cambridge house. Certainly she was not distressed because the Duchess was dying, even though it could be said that Simeon was morally responsible. Thea should be accustomed to men killing women for her.

Her distress had been of brief duration when Cole took a woman's life. Simeon had used his influence as an Old Family in Old Boston that never let Old Families down, of whatever color. The daily papers had neither played the episode up nor designated Cole's race in their careful accounts. After all, the unfortunate girl was an immigrant. *The Clarion* hadn't carried the story, though it wouldn't have mattered much. The spineless sheet was read by almost no one now. The poor found no mention of their poverty. Nice people were reluctant to receive a colored paper through the mails or carry it through the streets, for all to see that they did not wholly identify themselves with the majority race.

Simeon kept the dingy office open and a depressed assistant idling with watered ink mainly to cover his erotic activities in the refurnished top-floor flat. Here came the bored and seeking women to run their fingers through his hair, to try to make his somber eyes smile, and his cold mouth soften with love. But they were Simeon's blackmail. The understood price of his discretion was Thea's social leadership.

It had remained his price despite Cole's trial and conviction. He had been Thea's representative at the trial. She had never sat in a courtroom in her life. He saw no salutary reason why she should be subjected to so sordid a hearing.

As an act of Providence old Mrs. Hartnett chose to die from shock on the day her son received a five-year sentence. The intimate friends who called on the bereaved could extend their condolences to Thea without actually referring to Cole.

Those less intimate and less socially secure, who had wondered during Cole's trial what their attitude toward his wife should be if he were sentenced, were profoundly relieved to have it decided for them at the funeral. For it was not Cole's funeral really. It was his mother's. And the old lady's impeccable life demanded their attendance. Thea had been flanked by Simeon and Lenore, whose ash-blond beauty was more startling than ever set off by black. Thea, whom black did not suit, did look a pathetic figure, and everyone had the most generous feelings for her. Thus their first meeting with her after Cole's imprisonment passed off beautifully in perfect surroundings.

Cole's name was never mentioned by Thea. Fortunately she had named her son for her brother, and the boy resembled her. There was then no need to think of Cole when she looked at her son or called his name.

Cole had failed his social class. His magnificent scholarship, his brilliant researches in cancer, his growing reputation at the hospital, and his marriage to Althea Binney were the background he brought to the ignominious rank of abortionist.

His aim had been to save life, his end had been its destruction. He had known from the first that he would never recover the lost ground of his honor. He had known, too, from his growing revulsion that there would come a moment when horror would palsy his hand.

He had never discussed his illegal practice with Thea. Whether she knew or suspected, she never revealed. She was not expected to take any unladylike interest in her husband's occupation. The fact that she wore furs, and could afford a maid and a child, simply meant that Cole was doing his duty by her. His disgrace simply meant that he had failed that duty.

Cleo harbored a dark resentment that Thea still saw herself as impervious to stigma. She could have a jailbird for a husband and not falter in her quiet assumption that being born a Binney was an immunity.

Looking coldly at Thea, Cleo felt enormously cheated that what had cost Judy's inheritance and Serena's happiness had cost Thea no more than a night or two of lost sleep. Remembering Robert, she was aware of time again. It was nearly two. Perhaps Serena was on her way to the hospital. Maybe she wouldn't be home until after four.

I'll give her a few minutes more, her thoughts ran. Then I'll go out and call Mr. Judson. He'll have to let me have the money. My rent is more important than his. There's nothing in his empty store that needs a roof over it. These children can't sleep under the stars. God, you've got your eyes on your sparrows. Look down on my little ones, too.

Thea, seeing Cleo's eyes grow luminous, thought that she had her attention and sympathy.

"I've always thought Simeon was right in everything except his treatment of Lenore. Whatever she was before she was his wife, their marriage made her a Binney. As such she has deserved more respect than Simeon has chosen to give her." That was the nearest that Thea could come to saying she knew about Simeon's women. "He never really loved her. I believe she is dying of a broken heart, though the doctor calls it pernicious anemia."

"It isn't love for Simeon that's breaking her heart," Cleo said heatedly. "Lenore's always seemed to me like a lost saint, trying to find her way back to heaven. If anything, it's Simeon's sin against God's commandment that's killing her. She's lived with sin the best part of her life, from the time she was born in sin to her mother. I guess she just can't live with it any longer."

"That's why I had to see you, Cleo. That's why I want you to talk to Simeon. Lenore wants to make her last confession. She wants the last rites. And Simeon won't call a priest."

Cleo, who had been importuning God all day, and felt closer to Him than she would tomorrow, said resonantly: "Why would Simeon want her to die cut off from God? If she wants her soul to go to heaven her way, who is Simeon to stand in her light? What difference can it make to him if she dies a Catholic?"

Thea's voice was stricken. "When Lenore began to ask for a priest, Simeon was upset out of all reason. He is afraid it is some diabolic plan to leave her money to her Church."

"I remember the time," said Cleo richly, "when Simeon was too proud to touch a penny of the Duchess's money."

Thea said simply, "He wants it for me."

Resentment flared in Cleo again. What right had Thea never to suffer when Serena walked in sorrow? What right had her son to a better life than Tim? Why, Tim was the brightest little boy in Boston. How many other six-year-olds were always begging to go to Harvard? Well, by God, he'd get there. She had a dozen years to dream and scheme how to do it. When he was ready, she would be ready, too!

The Mission bells began to peal. Thea rose. "I must get back to little Simeon. I left him at my neighbor's. But I don't like to leave him there overlong. Her little boy fights him and calls him names. And I don't want to teach him to fight back. I want him to be a gentleman. The neighborhood is running down, filling up with shanty Irish. I'll be relieved to be back in Cambridge while Simeon's growing up."

As they brushed cheeks, Thea said earnestly: "Give me your promise that you will see Simeon today. Tomorrow may be too late. I know how devoted you are

to me. But don't let Simeon persuade you to see his side."
She colored slightly. "Lenore is very low. I'm sure she's
too weak to change her will. Simeon is worrying unneces-
sarily."

"Of course, I'll go," said Cleo. She looked at Thea
with the faint distaste and impatience she always felt
when she compared her with Lenore. A soft feeling, a
superstition, edged her mind. If she procured a priest for
a dying woman, God would make everything right about
the rent.

CHAPTER 32

S<small>HE TURNED AWAY</small> from the doorbell, where she had
stuck the note for Serena, just as the trolley clanged to a
stop. She said a little prayer. When the trolley step was
let down, Serena descended. God was rewarding her
already. Then she gave a little start. Serena's arms were
full of department-store packages.

She waited apprehensively. Serena had gone in town
to shop. That was why she was coming so tardily. She
must have bought Easter things for the children. Cleo
groaned, remembering too late that on Serena's last visit
she had broadly hinted about the children's needs. But
there had been nothing in Serena's faraway look to indicate that she had even heard. O, Lord, how much of her
money had Serena spent?

"Walk up, Serena," she called, when she could stand
the suspense no longer. "It's taking you a year to get from
the carstop to here."

Serena reached the bottom step. "I guess I was thinking," she said so sad and low that Cleo who was not
really listening did not hear.

"I was just on my way out. I wrote a note for you."
She took it out of the bell. "Charity's working across the
street. She went this noon. I said in my note for you to
go see her and give her what money you could spare."

Serena piled her packages on the stoop, and opened her pocketbook. Her movements were jerky, tense. She shivered in the mild wind.

"I won't come in. You're in a hurry. So am I. I'm late getting out to Robert. I went downtown." She thought a minute, then her rare smile lifted a little of the bitterness off her mouth, filled the hollows in her thin cheeks, eased the sorrowing in her eyes. "I'm glad Charity's got a job. She'll be happier out of the house."

Cleo protested hotly: "I had to push her out. I had to make her go. Way you spend your free day with Robert, there's no way for you to know what a time your sisters have together."

"Tomorrow's Robert's birthday," Serena said softly. "That's why I'm late. That's where I've been, buying him presents. She took out a little handful of bills. "I guess I spent more than I realized. There's only eight dollars here," she apologized. "I'll have to owe you four." She put the money in Cleo's hand.

Cleo's voice choked with disappointment. "I was counting on every penny you could spare. What makes you think Robert remembers his birthday? The children are naked, and so are you, and you buy that half-crazy nigger a lot of presents that'll just sit on his table."

Serena said desperately, "Robert don't have to appreciate what I do for him. I can't ever make up for what I done to him."

"But why," Cleo demanded wearily, "did you have to buy him so much? You've got enough here for a dozen birthdays. Robert isn't so crazy he thinks you're Santa Claus."

Serena picked up her packages. Her voice was diffi-

dent. "They're from all of us. I don't want him to know
you all don't care. I'm trying to help him come back to
himself. He don't think he belongs to anybody. I'm trying to teach him he's one of us, no matter what happened
down home."

For a moment she looked at Cleo with eyes so vulnerable that Cleo held back the words of rebuttal that
were hot on her tongue.

"You go on to Robert," she said instead. "I'm going the
other way on my errand. Don't you worry about that four
dollars. It takes more money than that to worry me."

Serena gave her a shy smile. "Well, good-bye until next
week." She started back toward the car stop. She looked
very small in Charity's old coat, very shabby at the heels,
very slight to be carrying her load of doomed love.

"Serena," Cleo said shakily. Serena turned around.
"Tell Robert all of us wish him a happy birthday."

At the other end of the wire, Bart answered Cleo's urgent, "Is that you?" with "Yes, it's me." There was no
one else it could have been.

Miss Muldoon had been let go with regret well over a
year ago. She was not working anywhere. In the last
slow years in Bart's store her skills had slowed down, too.
She made mistakes in totaling, garbled messages, mislaid
mail. She lost the assurance of being indispensable that a
successful business had given her. Bart was spared concern for her welfare, despite her age. Her savings were
sufficient for her few demands. When Cleo felt mean,
it was her opinion that Miss Muldoon ought to have
saved considerably after all the years she had access to
Mr. Judson's till.

Christian Christianson was a fruit broker now with more business than he could handle. His eye and his hand and his intuition had been trained by Bart, and he was considered one of the cleverest brokers in the Market. When he was trying his wings, he had urged Bart to enter a partnership. But Bart was set in the way of his past when he was the Black Banana King. He, who had scoffed at Binney and Hartnett for expecting the tailor-made suit and the horse to survive the mass production of progress, stood in the whirlwind of the mergers, shutting his eyes to his own wreckage. Even Chris, who loved him, had nothing to sell him with the pile of dynamic orders taking precedence on his desk. Bart put his faith in the war's end and the coming of summer's abundance.

Cleo's voice questioned him sharply, "Have you signed your lease yet?"

"No. Seems to be some kind of hitch," Bart said worriedly. He who had once seemed ageless sounded old. There had been nothing to sustain him during the hard years of the war. There had only been Cleo urging him to turn water into wine. When he came home with hollow eyes, she had turned her back on his need for comfort, seeking escape from knowing that things were not the same.

"I expected the agent at half-past two, like I told you," Bart continued in that worried voice.

"I know you told me," Cleo interrupted. "That's why I'm calling you before he comes and takes all your money."

"The agent just telephoned. He said Mr. Bancroft was coming himself."

"Who's Mr. Bancroft?" asked Cleo impatiently. "I never heard of him."

"That's because you never listen," Bart said wryly. "He's only the bank, he's only the owner of my store, of this whole block of stores. He's only been my banker and friend as long as I've been in the Market."

"If he's your friend, what you stewing about?"

"I'm puzzled. I've been in Mr. Bancroft's office more times than I can count. But this is the first time he's ever set foot in my store."

"I'm in a pay booth, Mr. Judson."

"I know that, Cleo. What about it?"

"My nickel will be up while you're telling me Mr. Bancroft's life history."

She could hear him clearing the hurt out of his throat. "What was it you called up to say?"

"Now don't try to jump through the telephone. But I've got a dispossess. I've got to give Mr. Benjamin eighty dollars before four o'clock. Serena came, but she didn't have one penny to give me. She paid the hospital. I've got to get forty dollars from somewhere if you don't want your child to sleep on the street."

He didn't ask any unanswerable questions. He was seasoned to her emergencies. In a three-minute telephone call there was no time, and at any time it was futile, to try to teach her common sense about money.

He expelled a long sigh. "I just have to take it out of my own rent. And God knows I hate to at a time like this."

"That isn't much to take from all that money you've got for Mr. Bancroft," she said defensively. "What's left will still be a lot. If he's such a friend of yours, he'll be nice about it."

"I'll bring the money to you as soon as he goes."

"Why can't I come and get it?"

They both knew why. She would time her coming to Mr. Bancroft's and ask for fifty dollars, because Mr. Bancroft would be nice about it.

"You might miss me," Bart said. "Mr. Bancroft's a busy man. Ten to one he'll call me to come to his office instead. Your best bet is to go home and wait. I'll be up around half-past three."

"All right," she said huffily, and snapped the receiver back on its hook without saying good-bye. She thought it a waste of words to exchange civilities with a husband.

She quitted the booth, and knew that she did not have the patience to go home and wait. With the children at school and her sisters at work, it was too hard a thing to be alone in a great big house. She would rattle around like a pill in a box.

She might as well go to Cambridge to see Simeon. There was nothing else to do that didn't cost more than carfare. Though the thought of sickness depressed her, she really should see the Duchess. She had always meant to see more of her. She had always meant to get to know her better. But there was something about the Duchess that had made her feel uncomfortable on the few occasions when they were briefly alone. She tried to give a name to it, and could not.

CHAPTER 33

CLEO sat beside the great bed where Lenore lay with hands still as hands carved in ivory on the counterpane. Her fine pale hair was in two obedient braids whose tips touched the hem of the turned-back sheet. Her quiet breast made as little stir as would keep her alive for the rest of her endurance. Her skin was so translucent that the poignant mouth could not have borne more color than the thin trace of pink. The blue veins were quite visible. There was no mistaking her right to die a Binney.

The nurse had let Cleo go up. There was no longer any need for her patient to conserve her strength. Simeon and Cleo had greeted each other in the entrance hall with the low-voiced murmurs suitable to the imminence of death. Then Simeon had returned to his nervous waiting in the library.

He did not want to be at home, but the doctor had advised him that it was wiser not to leave. He sat slumped in his father's chair, with his father's decanter at his elbow. The room had been the elder Binney's bulwark, where he had bolstered his delusions with his gentleman's drink of decay. It was unchanged, though there were servants now to keep it spotless. It had become Simeon's barricade against the piety of Lenore.

He had tried to destroy her goodness. It seemed to him that her spirit wrestled with his, despite the stillness that attended all her ways. Evil had ridden him whenever he looked at her. He had wanted to strike her, scream insults, brutalize her. But his hands had been powerless, his tongue had gone dry, as had his loins.

He had tried to destroy her through other women. When he returned to her in the morning after insane nights of lust, his eyes were rimmed with the evil of his adultery, his mouth was slack with the satiation of sin.

Lenore could not live with it. Simeon had profaned their marriage before she could persuade him to sanctify it through her Church. The shamelessness of his women became her shame. When they arrived at her tea-table to still the suspicions of their friends, she sat superbly composed. At the frequent parties Simeon requested for the purpose of making her betray her recognition of his immorality on a wanton face, she gave him no sign of knowing. But the world that she had expected to shut outside the high walls of a sacred union rushed in with a violence that she could not withstand.

Once she had wanted the nunnery and the true marriage. Then in a moment of earthly ambition she had wanted to be a Binney. There was no atonement for this mortal error save the refinement of the spirit through the body's destruction.

Her intense purity seared away her flesh to free her soul for its flight from earth. And Simeon's hatred grew into the gross shape of fear, which expressed itself in his belief that in revengeful spite Lenore would leave her fortune to her Church. The degradation of this thinking was part of his punishment.

"Lenore," Cleo said, with tenderness.

She opened her eyes. They blazed in the white face, the terribly alive blue eyes, belying the body's attitude of repose and resignation.

"I'm glad it's you," she said, in a voice as thin as thread. "You were my first friend. You were not afraid of Thea. You were not afraid of Simeon. Tell me you are not afraid now."

Cleo lifted Lenore's hands from the coverlet. They lay between her palms as weightless as petals. "I've already spoken to Thea. I've come to speak to Simeon."

Two great tears trembled on Lenore's lashes. "I knew," she whispered. "You will intercede for my soul. You are stronger than Simeon. You are good. I have not forgotten. When you talked about your sisters and their children that day, I saw that your life was devoted to others. I know that Simeon must yield to your selflessness."

Gently Cleo released Lenore's hands. She could not stay any longer. Something oppressed her, and she thought, I have never seen anyone die, and I have had enough of seeing it.

Her warm mouth touched Lenore's cold cheek. "I promise you a priest will come."

Softly Cleo quitted the room.

Simeon stood before Cleo, saying expressionlessly: "Once you came to persuade me to marry Lenore to save Thea's happiness. It was not Lenore's asking price. She would have preferred the nobler gesture of freely giving. It would have been more in keeping with her imitation of Christ. Now you have cooked up some story about

Thea's peace of mind. I do not believe you are here on her behalf. You are here for reasons of your own."

She shrugged. "It was Thea who sent me. You can pick up the telephone and ask her."

He made an impatient gesture. "Thea trusts you beyond your worth. If you have already got to her, you have made her believe what suits your ends."

"If you think your sister has no mind of her own, I bow to your opinion," said Cleo coolly. "But if you think she will forget that Lenore was a Binney when you condemned her to wander between heaven and hell, you are mistaken."

"Cleo," Simeon said contemptuously, "what is it to you? I have never suspected you of innocence."

They eyed each other like adversaries.

"I persuaded Lenore to marry you. Now I want to make amends. I've seen my sisters' lives ruined by men. I remember how happy they were before their husbands broke their hearts. Let a priest give Lenore the peace with God she could not find with you."

He said quietly: "Then you did come for private reasons. And you are proposing to sacrifice Thea's one remaining chance to live as she was meant to." He crossed to the door, put his hand on the knob. "You must forgive me for asking you to leave."

She rose. "If you open that door, I'll walk out of this house to the nearest telephone booth. I won't call a priest. I'll call a daily paper."

"And what," he said scornfully, "will you tell them?"

She did not know. She had not thought as far as that. But she gave him look for look while she racked her brain.

"I'll tell them you're a white slaver, that Lenore's been held captive here for four years under the influence of some kind of dope that's finally killing her. Cole's name can appear in the papers again as the one who gave it to you to give to her. Lenore's never said more than two words at a time to anybody. There'll be plenty of hindsight witnesses to say she did act doped. And where are the friends who will help you prove that she's colored? No one of your men friends would tell a reporter they frequented her gambling rooms. None of your women friends ever laid eyes on her before you introduced her as your wife. By the time the mess is straightened out, the Binney name will be mud."

"My dear Cleo," Simeon said dangerously, "have you never heard of libel?"

"Of course. But I shall give the paper your name and address, not mine. The reporters will come. If you refuse to let them see Lenore, they will believe there is some truth in my story. If you let them see her with her ash-blond hair, they will believe it anyway."

There was a pause.

"You win this hand," said Simeon. "But I have a trump card, too. When you walk out of that door, you will never be welcome in this house again."

"That is for Thea to decide when she is mistress here."

"And do you think she will decide against her brother?"

"Certainly not," Cleo said indifferently. "But you will never tell her of this unpleasant scene. It would distress her." She moved to the door. "Will you pick up the telephone, Simeon? I must go."

He picked up the telephone. She heard him ask Information for the nearest Catholic Church. She opened the door and went out.

CHAPTER 34

LILY PULLED THE DOORBELL as violently as the children had done earlier. There was a key somewhere in her bag. But she dared not open it. The man might be waiting for just that opportunity to snatch what was in it. If he put his hands on her, she knew she would scream. And they always killed you if you made an outcry. She could not bear to die for twenty-five cents.

Cleo jerked open the door. "What in the name of God — I thought it was one of the children sent home sick or something."

Lily slipped inside the door and leaned against it, her hat askew, a lock of hair straggling, and her coat buttoned wrong.

"There's a colored man following me," she gasped. "He was on the trolley when I got on. He started to speak to me, but I ran to the back of the car and squeezed between two ladies. But when I got off just now, he got off, too. I ran all the way, but he's right behind me."

The bell rang briskly. Lily jumped away from the door. "That's him," she moaned. "Cleo, save me, save me." She scooted up the front stairs, and Cleo heard her lock the bathroom door and turn the tap in the tub, so that she would not have to hear whatever happened.

Cleo peered through the curtain that covered the glass half of the door, and gave a little snort of disgust that was directed at Lily. She was a born fool and would die one. Cleo opened the door to Lily's husband.

"She didn't have to run from me," Victor said darkly without preliminary. The liquor was stronger on his breath than it had been on that other visit. This time he had fortified himself to excess.

"She wasn't really running from you," Cleo said, feeling as big a fool as Lily. "She didn't recognize you. She thought you were some strange man after her. Come in."

"Well," said Victor, sullenly entering the house and deciding not to remove his hat. "I didn't come after your sister, you can bet your sweet life. I came to get rid of her."

"We don't have to stand in the hall and talk," Cleo said coldly. "Please step in the parlor. I'll go call Lily."

"Sounds like she's washing her carcass," said Victor insultingly. "I seen her scoot upstairs through the glass. Is she trying to wash off where she brushed past me? My color don't come off."

Silently Cleo muttered blasphemies at Lily. "There's really no need for you to be uncouth."

"Or maybe, Mrs. High and Mighty, you've taught her to pass, and she don't want no colored man, in particular her colored husband, speaking to her on a streetcar filled with white folks."

"If you will be good enough to go in and sit down," said Cleo icily, "I'll tell Lily you're here. There is nothing more for us to say to each other. Good day."

Victor wandered into the parlor, and Cleo went upstairs. She rattled the bathroom door.

"Who is it?" Lily quavered.

"You know who it is. Open the door."

"Who is it downstairs?"

"Open the door. It's Victor."

"Oh, my God! Cleo, save me, save me! Has he come to kill me?"

"Lily, will you open this door and let me talk to you?"

"No," said Lily wildly.

"Lily, I could break every bone in your body."

"I don't care. I'd rather you killed me than Victor. Cleo, tell him to go away. You're not afraid of anybody."

"He wants to talk to you."

"You talk to him for me."

"Lily, I'll ask you one more time. Will you open that door and come downstairs?"

"No."

There it was, that once-in-a-year stubbornness of Lily's, when the extremity of her cowardice gave her the courage to take an immovable stand.

"You just wait until I can get my hands on you," Cleo hissed ineffectually, and went back downstairs, feeling more like a fool than ever.

"Lily is bathing," she said, with great dignity, "and begs to be excused. She asks you to give me whatever message you have for her."

Victor dug in his overcoat pockets, then in his suit coat pockets, and finally in the pockets of his trousers. His look was owlish. For a moment Cleo almost believed her own lies. Perhaps he really was fishing for his razor. She sat up straighter, filled her face with a queenly disdain that would cower the heart of the commoner.

A banded roll of bills appeared in Victor's hand.

"Money talks," he said elaborately, and held it out to her.

The width of the room was between them. Neither he nor she rose to cross to the other. They watched each other like alley cats. It was Victor whose eyes wavered first.

"You can tell her I want a divorce. I'm living with a woman who wants us to get married. She's going to have a baby. It'll be a black kid because she's black as me. You can get my yaller kid ready to be ashamed of it."

Cleo rose. "Now that you've got that off your chest, will you be good enough to go?"

Victor sprawled back in his chair and stared at her insolently. "I ain't quite finished. I don't want this divorce business to hang on forever. The quicker I'm rid of your blue-white sister, the better. I don't know the grounds for divorce in Boston, but I don't care what grounds she uses as long as the judge makes it snappy. You can fix up a story for her. You're a first-class liar."

He stood then, and came toward her. She stared at him, her eyes green as sea-water, but his liquor was not in awe of her. He thrust out his hand again and held the money close to her face. "Here. It's two hundred dollars. Take it and go to hell."

She said slowly and venomously, "Get out of my house, Mister Nigger."

He flung the money in her face. In a moment the front door slammed.

Her cheek was as red as blood where the money had struck it. She looked down at the roll of bills and gave it a vicious kick. The action relieved a lot of her anger. Curiosity compelled her thinking. Maybe it was a dummy roll. She crossed the room and picked it up. She slipped off the rubber band. The bills unrolled. They were real. But perhaps there were not really two hundred. That brazen nigger might have cheated. She began to count them.

She did not hear Lily until her soft, anguished voice called down from the upstairs landing, "Cleo, did Victor go? Are you all right? Speak to me, Cleo."

Quickly Cleo took the first hundred dollars that she had counted out and stuffed them down her dress. She rolled up the rest and put the band back around them. Poor people could get divorces for as little as fifty dollars. Let Lily loose with two hundred dollars, and she'd only do something foolish with it. Probably give it to Mr. Judson.

"Come on down, Lily. I'm not wallowing in blood. Victor's gone."

She came downstairs and into the parlor, giving a fearful look around.

"What did he want? Did he want me and Vicky to come back to him?"

Cleo passed her the roll of bills. "He wants a divorce."

"What's this for?" said Lily stupidly, staring at her hand.

"What in the name of God do you think it's for?"

Lily held it gingerly, as if she feared it might explode through some trick of Victor's. "How much is it?"

"That's just the way he gave it to me. Count it and see. He said it was a hundred dollars."

Lily freed the money from the rubber band with the greatest difficulty, and began a slow and halting count, for the money kept rolling back up in her nervous hands.

"Ninety-five dollars," she finally announced.

"Well, the dirty liar," said Cleo sincerely. "Let me count it."

Lily gave the money to her as if she were glad to get rid of it. "Oh, Cleo, I'll die if I have to go down before a judge. I won't know what to say to him. I'd just drop dead of fright."

"You don't have to get the divorce tomorrow. I wouldn't give Victor that much satisfaction. Make him wait. It'll serve him right," she ended acidly, for she could make the count no more than ninety-five dollars either.

"Let's put the money on some bills for a while," begged Lily. She had the idea that if it were spent, she would never have to face the ordeal of going before a great big important person like a judge. And she was quite right.

"Well, there's the rent," said Cleo, thinking fast. "There's the dispossess." Lily didn't want a divorce. It was Victor who wanted one. Let him get one the best way he could.

"Oh, my God, I clean forgot the dispossess with Victor coming. Those people didn't take the flat? How much money you got in all?"

"Serena only had two or three dollars to give me. She spent the rest on presents for Robert's birthday. Those people didn't take the flat. And Mr. Judson only left me one month's rent. It never rains but it pours."

"Well, maybe the Lord sent Victor, after all," Lily suggested shyly. She felt rather proud. She had saved the family from the sidewalk. Mr. Judson would certainly say he wouldn't know what they would do without her.

"Well, the Lord didn't send him a second too soon. You run up to Mr. Benjamin's for me. You've got your things on."

"Oh, Cleo," Lily wailed, "Victor may still be around. You go."

But Cleo had no intention of leaving Lily to explain her whereabouts to Mr. Judson. He would rush right back to his store after he brought her the money. He need never know that she did not rush right out, too, to pay Mr. Benjamin.

"Well, take your choice," she said. "Either stay home and get your throat slit if Victor sneaks back through a window. Or go to Mr. Benjamin's like I asked you. Victor wouldn't be fool enough to slit your throat on the street with people passing."

But Lily was indoors, and it seemed a whole lot safer than the street. "I'll watch the front of the house, and Charity can watch the back. If Victor tries to sneak in, whichever one sees him first can start screaming for help."

"Charity," said Cleo pleasantly, "isn't here. So what will you do all by yourself in this house if Victor comes in one way while you're watching the other way?"

"I'll go," said Lily hopelessly. Then she said in surprise, "Where's Charity? I thought she heard Victor and was hiding upstairs. Oh, Lord, was she taken sick and rushed to the hospital? Like you said, it never rains but it pours."

"Lily," Cleo prophesied, "some day you're going to scare yourself to death. Charity went across the street to work. I thought it was the best thing for her to get her out of herself." Suddenly she was aware that Lily should be at work, too. Lily read her thoughts and lowered her eyes. "Lily, what you doing home so early?"

"The man came home early," Lily said, squirming like a child under Cleo's hard scrutiny.

"What man? My God, you ran home from Victor. Now you think some other man's after you."

"He wasn't after me," Lily said, with dignity. "He didn't even speak to me. That's what made me so nervous. He was so quiet. She went out — my lady, I mean — and he came home early, and went in his room and shut the door, and I couldn't hear a sound."

"Well, how was that your business? You're paid to work, not to listen for sounds."

Lily said sheepishly, "But he looked so kinda sick when he came in."

"Well, God have mercy, that's why he came home early then. If you're going to be scared of men, be scared of the well ones."

"I thought he must have died," Lily said in a low, ashamed voice, for it did seem rather ridiculous now. "I thought I was all alone with a dead man."

"You take the cake," Cleo admitted, with a weary shake of the head. "What are you going to tell your lady tomorrow?"

"I guess I won't go back. I kinda hate to face her. I guess I'll go to the agency tomorrow." Her eyes implored Cleo not to be harsh.

"Well, time's wasting while I listen to you tell me you're a fool," Cleo said mildly. "It's half-past three. Go catch the next trolley."

In her eagerness to make amends for being jobless, Lily turned and stampeded to the front door.

"Lord God," shouted Cleo, in extreme exasperation, 'where you going without the money? Here, I'll give you eighty out of this. I won't waste more time going up-stairs to get my pocketbook."

Lily took the money. "You keep what's left," she offered shyly. "I know it ain't much. But it'll help to keep things running till I'm working again."

Cleo tucked the fifteen dollars down her dress. In her purse and on her person she had one hundred and sixty-three dollars, and Mr. Judson was bringing her forty more. Her eyes blurred with grateful tears. God had answered her prayers beyond her hopes. It never rained but it poured.

CHAPTER 35

Five minutes later the Brookline trolley, out-bound for the Village, where Mr. Benjamin's office was, came to a halt at the car stop. Cleo, who was at the window serving as lookout for Lily's safety, saw her sister scramble aboard and tangle with a man with a load of groceries who was trying to assert his right to get off first. The man was Mr. Judson. Cleo held her breath. But he and Lily had no time to exchange anything but a look of surprise before the motorman shut the door and drew up the step.

Bart came toward the house as loaded down as a pack horse. He hadn't come home looking like that since hard times. He had enough food to feed a regiment. He must have stopped at every store in the Market.

Cleo's thoughts chased each other around like birds. What had happened between her husband and Mr. Bancroft? Maybe when Mr. Judson had explained about the forty dollars Mr. Bancroft had made him keep some more. Maybe Mr. Bancroft, as his onetime banker, had come to tell him about an inheritance from some long-forgotten relative. Maybe Mr. Bancroft, as his friend, had brought him a great big check to help him build up his business again. Whatever had happened, the way Mr. Judson was loaded down, it looked like good times were back.

Impulsively she rapped on the window. She was not given to acknowledging her husband's arrival home. But today she wanted him to know that they pulled in harness together.

He was bent under his load, and his head was down. He raised it briefly when she rapped, gave her a little salute with his eyes, and lowered his head again.

She felt a little flutter of anxiety. He oughtn't to try to carry so much as old as he was. For in that momentary glimpse of his haggard face, she was shocked by the showing of age. That fear of his dying oppressed her heart. Men were nuisances to have in a house. They got in your way wherever you walked. You wanted to talk, and they did, too. You fixed a snack, and they felt hungry. You had the children's big wash to do, and they wanted clean clothes. But you could get used to anything in time, and you got used to having a husband. It was no use denying that nothing would seem the same if you couldn't hear his key in the lock and his voice calling up, "I'm home."

She had the door open when he reached the stoop. He came heavily into the house, and she held out her hands to share his burden.

"You got enough food here for a week," she said happily, and led the way back to the kitchen.

"I tried to get a week's supply," he said.

"Well, this was too much load for one man to carry," she scolded over her shoulder. "After this, you take a taxi straight to the door. Never count the cost when it's a question of saving your strength."

She put her bundles down and began to divest him of his, for he could not have released his arms without toppling the pyramid. A ham took shape in her hands, a great thick steak, a leg of lamb, a roast by the feel of it, a slab of bacon, boxes of sausages and frankfurters. The pyramid's base was a small crate filled with choice fruits and vegetables.

She said, with emotion, "When times are good, God knows you're the best provider in Boston."

His look was ravaged, but he quietly promised, "They're going to be good again."

"They're good now," she protested happily. But he gave her no answering smile, and she was aware again of his aging. He looked ten years older than he had last night.

"You're all worn out. Sit down. I'll fix something for you before you go back to the store." She reached for the steak. It was his favorite. For once, let the children have second choice. He needed red meat as much as they did. He was the one made the wheels go round. If he ever took sick, the earth would tremble.

"I can't stop, Cleo. I got to wind up at the store. I just took a minute to bring you this money."

He took an envelope out of his pocket and passed it to her. It felt like more than forty dollars. It felt like a fortune. She opened the flap. There were fives and tens and even twenties. There must be nearly three hundred dollars. The downpour had turned into a deluge.

She said joyously, "Is all this mine?"

He answered soberly, "You're the boss now."

The rush of joy drained from her. She put the envelope on the table. She did not want the money. Her mouth was dry. "What you mean?"

"I lost my store. I'm leaving Boston. Stretch that money until I can send some more."

"But Mr. Bancroft," she said wildly. "He was your friend. You said so yourself," she accused him.

"That's why he came. He wanted to be the one to tell me. The Dexter Packing Company bought the whole block."

She picked up the envelope and said eagerly, "Take this and rent another place."

"Wouldn't be no use. My credit's gone. You can't run a business without it."

She drew the money out of her dress. "Here's more. Lily's husband came and gave it to me for being so good to her and Vicky. There was more besides, and I sent Lily up to pay the rent. All this is clear. I want you to have it. It'll help with your bills. You won't have to leave Boston."

His smile was gentle. "That's a drop in the bucket. You hold on to it. I'm finished here. Last night I saw a star fall from heaven. I know now that was a sign from God. But there are other stars in the sky. I'll shine among them again."

She let the money fall from her hands. It scattered over the mounds of meat, and she looked at everything with revulsion.

"Where will you go, what will you do?" she said deeply.

"I'll start at the bottom and work to the top. That's how I started in Springfield. That's how I started in Boston. I can do it again in New York."

"New York?" It seemed a world away, the rest of her life away. "You're getting old. You need a wife to look out for you. Let me go with you."

"No," he said quietly. "I don't want the child knocking around. And I wouldn't let you leave her. Boston's the best place to bring her up. Just look out for her. That's all I ask."

She went to him and put her arms around him. The smell of fruit and earth and sweat was sharp in her nostrils, but she did not turn her head away. She lifted her face to his, scanning his eyes for some response, her own eyes luminous with tenderness.

He took her arms away. His voice was immeasurably sad. "Take care of the child. That's all I ask. I've grown too old to ask anything else."

He moved away. "It's getting on four. I don't want to take the time to pack. Send my few rags when I send an address. I want to get out before Judy comes. I know you, Cleo. You'd use her to keep me. And I couldn't stand shutting the door on her tears."

She held back her own tears. "Don't wait till you get some money to write. Write as soon as you get there. Let me know you're all right."

He did not answer. He would never write her a letter unless he had something to put in it. He thought she would tear it up without reading it.

He felt in his pocket for his doorkey. "No need for me to take this with me." He laid it on the table. For a moment he looked lost. He had lived with her a long time in fair and foul weather. She was his wife. He wanted to die with her beside him. He did not know now if he would.

"Well, I guess I'll be going. Don't come to the door. Let me say good-bye inside the house." He brushed her cheek with his lips. He knew that she did not like to be kissed on the mouth.

He was gone. The front door shut softly on her manlessness.

She could not just stand there gripping the table. "Who is there now to love me best? Who?" cried her frightened heart.

Blindly she gathered up the money, tucked it between her breasts, but her heart was not comforted.

Listlessly she unwrapped the meat, and her heart had no relish for it.

"But who will love me best? Who?" The lonely cry re-echoed.

Judy and Vicky and Penny were sufficient to each other. Serena and Lily and Charity cherished their fears and sorrows.

"Then who will put me first? Who?" the piteous heart pleaded.

Tim — ? He might learn to love her best. He would be lonesome sleeping alone. Judy was big enough to have a room of her own. She could change with Tim. Girls were always their father's children, but boys always seemed to cling to women.

The heart began to beat strongly. "Make Tim love me best of all the world. Of all the world," it commanded.

Tim, who tried so hard to be like Bart. Tim, who would try to be the man of the house.

THE END

AFTERWORD
Adelaide M. Cromwell

I first met Dorothy West over thirty-five years ago as we were picking blueberries on Martha's Vineyard. I had read her recently published novel, *The Living Is Easy*, in connection with my research on the black upper class in Boston, and I was eager to talk with her. This was the beginning of our friendship—a friendship strengthened by our common love of Martha's Vineyard (now Dorothy's permanent home) and our common interest in Boston as it was for blacks from the turn of the century until just after World War I.

It seemed incredible to me at the time that so lively, attractive, and talented a woman could have, in a sense, retreated to the Vineyard and remained relatively unknown to younger writers. I wondered then and I still wonder why this seems to have been the fate of so many black women writers—certainly those who wrote their major work before the 1960s—Ann Petry, Nella Larsen, Pauli Murray, Jessie Fausett, Zora Neale Hurston, and Dorothy West.[1] Their talent earns them places beside Lorraine Hansberry and such younger writers as Paule Marshall and Toni Morrison.

Over the summers our friendship grew. In the early 1970s, having started a graduate program in Afro-

American Studies at Boston University, I invited Dorothy
to give a lecture to our students. Although at first she was
uncertain, she came, and the effect was electrifying. These
college students had never seen anyone who had been
part of the Harlem Renaissance, who knew Langston
Hughes (Lang, she called him) or Richard Barthé
(Barthé), Countee Cullen (always Countee), or Wallace
Thurman (Wallie, naturally), or Zora Neale Hurston,
whose apartment she had once borrowed, or Paul and
Eslanda Robeson, in whose London home she had been a
guest. And Dorothy took heart in sharing these memories
in a way she had not been able to do with contemporaries
on the Island, or elsewhere. This was an awakening for
her, a prologue to her rediscovery.

Martha's Vineyard was just the right place for
Dorothy's retreat. It was intimate yet aloof—complex yet
simple. There she has spent more than twenty years away
from New York, even from Boston—living, writing, and
remembering. Until the late 1960s, she continued, as she
had for twenty years, to write two short stories a month
for the *New York Daily News*, and she worked, as she still
does, on her next novel, *The Wedding*, set on the Island.

In October 1965 Dorothy took a job handling
subscriptions and billing for the popular and highly
respected *Vineyard Gazette*. Her fellow employees
enjoyed hearing her stories so much that when one of the
regular reporters went on leave, Dorothy was invited to
take over her column. As "The Highlands Water Boy,"
she wrote for some time about the bird life she saw from
her own window. Later, overcoming her initial reluctance, she began to write a weekly column on people and
events in the large black summer colony in Oak Bluffs.

She called it "The Cottagers' Corner," after a club organized by a group of black women who were summer residents. In 1975, the *Gazette* asked Dorothy to cover the year-round activities of everyone who lived in Oak Bluffs. "Oak Bluffs," the new column, has taken its place beside the three other regular columns on Island news in the *Gazette*. Dorothy West writes in the *Gazette* with a keen eye for facts, but her columns also reflect her skill as a story teller, conveying the drama and interest of the most mundane events and giving them the appeal of fiction.

Dorothy West's association with the *Gazette* has kept her busy and made her an Island personnage, but it has not supported her adequately. Since 1969, she has supplemented her income with a job from May to October as a cashier at Harborside, a popular restaurant in Edgartown. Dorothy takes pride in holding a position of fiscal accountability. During the winter, she is able to write, although her work on the *Gazette* has delayed the completion of *The Wedding*.

Dorothy West was born in 1912, the daughter of Isaac Christopher West, an early twentieth-century black businessman, and his wife, Rachel West. A thoroughly-bred Bostonian, she grew up at 478 Brookline Avenue and studied at Girls' Latin School. She began to write as a young girl, and joined The Saturday Evening Quill Club, organized in 1925 by twenty Afro-American men and women who aspired to write. The club members, out of their own funds, published what W. E. B. DuBois described as "the most interesting and best of the booklets issued by young Negro writers."[2] Eugene Gordon, the president of the club, convinced the *Boston Post*, of whose editorial staff he was a member, to publish several of

West's stories. "An Unimportant Man" appeared in 1928 in the first issue of the club *Annual*, and was later reprinted in the *Columbia University Annual of Student Literature*. Another story, "Prologue to Life," appeared in the second issue of the Saturday Evening Quill's *Annual*, published in 1929. By the time it appeared, Dorothy West was in New York to receive the prize for yet another story, "The Typewriter." Only seventeen, she won a national competition sponsored by *Opportunity*, the literary organ of the National Urban League.

At that time, Dorothy West left Boston, both literally and psychologically, and found herself hailed as the young darling of the black writers and artists who made up the Harlem Renaissance. These young people who had gravitated to Harlem after World War I seemed to many—including themselves—to be a new breed: young, talented, sophisticated, and free. Alain Locke, the first black Rhodes scholar and distinguished professor of philosophy at Howard University, referred to them in a classic work as the New Negro[es].[3]

Older writers saw West as a charming, talented child, and her Bostonian accent sounded like a strange tongue. During this period, Countee Cullen was perhaps her closest male friend. In April 1931, he called her "a fascinating and lovable child. . . in spite of [her] terrible yearning towards grownupship and sophistication." Two years later, in August 1933, he offered her "his humble and ever deepening love." The following month, he invited her to come from the Vineyard to New York for dancing or the theater. He confessed in the next letter that they belonged together because "she seemed to understand him so thoroughly—more than most people."[4] There was clearly a bond of deep affection between them. And there were other relationships. Langston Hughes referred to her as "the Kid," and longed to see her smile once more,[5] while Harry T. Burleigh addressed her as "my Prodigal daughter," though his sentiments seemed to be more than purely paternal.[6]

Opportunity, restlessness, and curiosity took Dorothy West abroad, first to London for three months in 1929 as an extra in the cast of *Porgy*, and three years later, in 1932, to Russia as part of a group of writers including Langston Hughes, Henry Lee Moon, and Ted Poston.[7] She remembers scarcities and long queues for food, but also the charm and warmth of the White Russians. She would have continued on to China had she not learned of her father's death.

So Dorothy West returned to Boston, to her mother's home at 23 Worthington Street. One imagines that her mother planned to keep her only child in Boston, close to her. "Dorothy, you can't be sick, you are the family strength," Rachel West often told her. But the pull of New York was too strong. At first, because she needed funds after her father's death, she worked for two years in the Public Welfare Department (then called Home Relief). But many of the old group had disappeared. Zora had gone to Florida, Wallie to the West Coast. Moreover, she felt that new black writers were not appearing. With the depression, support for the arts, especially among blacks, had disappeared. Harlem was no longer fashionable.

Dorothy West initially decided to start a syndicated column featuring the writers she feared were disappearing from the scene. But a literary journal held a greater

appeal, possibly because of her experience in Boston with
The Saturday Evening Quill Club. She became the sole
editor and apparently only financial backer of *Challenge*,
which was "primarily an organ for the new voices...to
bring out the prose and poetry of newer Negroes...by
those who were the new Negroes now challenging them
to better our achievements. For we did not altogether live
up to our fine promise."[8] She managed to get contributions without payment from James Weldon Johnson,
Zora Neale Hurston, Claude McKay, Countee Cullen, and
Frank G. Yerby. She herself wrote under the pseudonym
Mary Christopher, which incorporated her father's
middle name.

The "old New Negroes" were generally enthusiastic
about the first issue of *Challenge*. Zora Hurston called her
"audacious and rejoiced that she had learned at last the
glorious lesson of living dangerously."[9] "Lang," however,
thought the issue was grand but refused to accept the
assertion that "all the old timers were dead." "A brave
little girl like you," he wrote, "ought to stir 'em to gallant
aid and assistance."[10]

Arna Bontemps, like Langston Hughes, welcomed
Dorothy West's endeavor but spoke more strongly about
the vitality of the old New Negroes:

> We're not washed up. Not by a jug full. It's a pretty pose, this
> attitude about "old before our time." I will not have it. . . . If the
> "younger writers" can take our crowns, here is their chance and
> here is our challenge.[11]

Carl Van Vechten, her old friend and patron of most of
the writers of the Renaissance, sent a check and ordered
several copies of the first issue. He wished her "567

penguin feathers and a blue owl."[12] Dorothy West received criticism, too. Her sharpest detractor was Wallace Thurman, who wrote from the New York hospital where he lay dying after too much Bohemian living, "Despite your belated knowledge of life you [are] as naive as ever.... *Challenge* lacks significance or personality—it is too pink tea and la de da...too high schoolish."[13] The idea was timely, he thought, but not in this form.

Nevertheless, Dorothy West published five issues of *Challenge* during that year. The poor quality of the material she received led her to transform the journal into a quarterly rather than a monthly. Louis Martin, Eslanda Robeson, and Arna Bontemps joined the first group of contributors. In January 1936, Harold Jackman, a public school teacher, became business manager; by June 1936, the price had increased from 15 cents to 25 cents an issue; and by Spring 1937 Jackman had become associate editor while Jimmie Daniels, a popular entertainer with a wide circle of influential white friends, replaced him as business manager. By the Fall 1937 issue the old *Challenge* had disappeared and a *New Challenge* had been born. Its structure was more complicated—Dorothy West and her friend Marian Minus were editors and Richard Wright, associate editor. Eugene Holmes, Margaret Walker (her first time in print), Alain Locke, Frank Marshall Davis, Sterling Brown, and Ralph Ellison were listed as contributing editors.

With this distinguished group of editors, the *New Challenge* voiced a different editoral policy:

> We want to see *New Challenge* as an organ of regional groups composed of writers opposed to fascism, war and general

reactionary policies.... While our emphasis is upon Negro writers and particular difficulties they must meet, we are not limiting our contributions to Negroes alone.... We hope that through our pages we may be able to point social directives and provide a basis for the clear recognition of and solution to the problems which face the contemporary writers.[14]

A storm was brewing. Dorothy West, like so many black writers and intellectuals of her day, was wooed by the Communists. Many of these blacks were seen at meetings addressed by Earl Browder and other Communists. West, herself, had a small meeting at her apartment involving Party members. Claude McKay, who missed the meeting but was friendly with several non-Communist liberals, inquired whether "the *Daily Worker* and that gang were behind her."[15]

This was a period of some tension between Communists and blacks. One of the most distinguished black Communists of the day, Richard Wright, had left Chicago for New York because of conflicts over Party policy and discipline. The Party sought vehicles for influencing black people; it may be that it saw *New Challenge* as an easy means for extending that influence.

But childlike as she may have seemed to her black mentors, Dorothy West had her own outlook and vision. She did not adopt the fellow-traveling posture sometimes found among writers of that day, whether or not they had traveled to the Soviet Union. Her trip may have been interpreted as a sign of her political inclination, thus accounting for the moves of the Left (which she called "the Chicago group") to control and redirect *Challenge*. But Dorothy West's views were securely rooted in the environment of her capitalist family. Isaac West was, after all, a businessman.

She began to resent the pressure exerted by the "Chicago group" to shape *New Challenge* in response to the Party line. They had not been part of her public, but had, she felt, moved to control the magazine because they saw the potential for influence she and others had established. But as Dorothy West had "borned" the *Challenge*, she could kill it. And so she did, after the issue which carried the editorial quoted above.

To support herself and continue her literary endeavors, Dorothy West briefly found employment with the Writers Project of the WPA under the direction of Roi Ottley, journalist and author of *New World A Coming*.[16] But funds for the project were cut off. That development, as well as pressures from home (the need to care for her mother and aunt, who were failing) brought her back first to Boston, and then to Martha's Vineyard. There she wrote *The Living Is Easy*—vividly reminded of her youth by her new proximity to her aging mother, Rachel—and there she still lives.

Even in its title, *The Living Is Easy* stands outside the more familiar descriptions of Afro-American life as harsh and painful if not pathological. *The Living Is Easy* is the story of Cleo Jericho Judson, as daughter, wife, mother, aunt, and friend, seen through the eyes of her only child, Judy. Cleo, born in the South and now living in Boston, is the wife of Bart Judson, twenty-three years her senior and proprietor of a successful business—Bartholomew Judson, Foreign and Domestic: Choice Fruits and Vegetables, Bananas a Specialty. He is a Southern-born, self-made man who is no match for his young, scheming wife, who frequently calls him "Mr. Nigger."

This is the story of a strained marriage, with each

partner seeking from the other what is not forthcoming. Cleo always wants more money than Bart can or will give her, and Bart always wants more affection and warmth than Cleo can or will give him. It is a story of a famiy where love, control, and weakness weave together in a web of dependency, despair, and power.

It is a story of a fragile black community in the North, where janitors and caterers were the leaders and blacks who could afford it hired Irish maids. In these circles pigmentation was very important. A dark complexion often made people, especially women, feel insecure and different. Status did not endure beyond one generation in this community, but Cleo believed that being alive and young made the living easy.

It is a story about life style—which parties and churches to attend and which to avoid. It is the story of black businessmen and black professionals attempting to survive without either a separate constituency on which to build or a real welcome from the larger society.

Northern blacks took pride in not living in a segregated society. They were, however, an insular group, a black village, a world apart in a white city. Whites controlled their destinies but hardly knew them; blacks were physically visible but socially invisible. On their part, blacks knew little beyond their psycho-social village boundaries and even less beyond their actual city limits.

Dorothy West, an exception to this insularity, chronicled the secret city. It was a vivid and proud world, not characterized by a search for African roots or survivals or Pentecostal churches. It was as American as apple pie— made of the best apples. She undersood the values of this world. There were places blacks wanted to live, for example—Brookline or hardly-discovered Roxbury rather than the South End. (Cambridge was acceptable, no doubt because of the smaller number of blacks living there). Blacks in this Boston understood the complexity of status within white society. They viewed Jews, Irish, and Italians according to ethnicity and class, not color—in contrast to the way they viewed Yankees. And Dorothy West knew the scandals or events that could upset the black village insularity—a gambling house run by a black woman, illegal abortions, the marriages of white (especially Irish) women to black men, business failures, unsuccessful professional practices, drinking, broken marriages—and marred the expectation of easy living in Boston.

West took pains both to inform and to disguise. The Binneys, the Harnetts, and the Judsons are all based on real people. For example, Simeon Binney was modeled on Monroe Trotter, Phi Beta Kappa graduate of Harvard and indefatigable editor of the *Boston Guardian*. He and George Forbes started the paper at the turn of the century to resist the infiltration of segregation into the Northern social system. The novel also introduces readers to such successful black businessmen as J. H. Lewis, whose tailoring establishment stood on the present site of Filene's department store. Lewis paid $10,000 a year in rent and employed more than fifty men and women.[17] Henry C. Turner's Boarding Stable and Garage catered to wealthy Bostonians; the building now houses Boston University's School of Engineering.

Last but not least, we meet, in the guise of Bart Judson, Dorothy West's father, Isaac Christopher West, "The Black Banana King." Isaac West used his contract with the United Fruit Company to build a thriving business, located

on Market Street across from Fanueil Hall, and won
special renown for his ability to ripen bananas. These men
were forced out of business by economic modernization
rather than race per se. It was difficult for black men to
compete with corporations which could wield considerable
capital and information about economic forces. However,
their existence demonstrates the potential of black
entrepreneurs who were able to extend beyond the needs
and resources of the black community.

The Living Is Easy is also about black women—
specifically about Cleo and the sisters she dominated and
ultimately destroyed as wives and as people. (The West
family home on Brookline Avenue at one time included
thirteen persons, all relatives of Rachel West, who was
one of twenty-two children.) Cleo is not reminiscent of the
familiar black women in American literature. She controls
Bart, but she is not really a matriarch. Others accept her
control as much from their weakness as from her strength,
and she does not control through love, as many black
matriarchs do. For her, any expression of love is weakness,
and the exercise of power seems to bring no happiness.
She wants money and the comforts of the good life for
herself. Judy is the tie that binds. She will keep Bart giving,
and her dark brown color, the permanent reminder of her
parents' bond, is a fact that Cleo must always acknowledge
to disbelievers. How could so fair a woman have so dark a
child?

Cleo does not have the warmth as a person or toward
her husband of a Mamma Younger in *Raisin in the Sun*,
or the quiet strength and courage of a Vyvy in *Jubilee*, nor
does she seek God to give her the power to cope and
control as does Sister Margaret in James Baldwin's *Amen*

Corner. As a strong, determined, controlling, beautiful woman of some means with an adoring husband, Cleo is new to black literature. She is reminiscent of Regina Giddons in Lillian Hellman's *Little Foxes* or Big Mamma in Tennessee Williams's *Cat on a Hot Tin Roof.*

It is time for *The Living Is Easy* to be read again, to introduce Dorothy West to a new generation of readers. There are, however, other reasons for reading this novel now. At this writing, Boston is a city in economic crisis and racial turmoil, a city which has lost its image of being the birthplace of freedom and a pioneer in educational excellence. The deplorable state of the school system— the stage on which the play of discrimination has been publically acted out—illustrates more than anything else the cost of racism to this city.

The small group of blacks about whom Dorothy West wrote has all but disappeared in mythology and in fact. Ironically, few of these people had children, and those who did sought other environments in which to rear them. The black community today, however, is far from invisible—its growing size and complexity result not only from a continuing stream of southern migrants like Bart and Cleo, but also from immigrants from Jamaica, Barbados, the Cape Verde Islands, and, most recently, Haiti. This community is conscious of itself, at least to the extent of breeching the wall of segregation and discrimination built around it. Protests have been made and some changes have occurred. The physical boundaries of the larger black community have extended far beyond the South End up the railroad line beyond Roxbury and into Dorchester and Mattapan. The movement by blacks into Brookline, Newton and the surrounding suburbs has been fueled by the expansion of economic opportunity—not for individual entrepreneurs like Lewis, Turner and West, but for organization men and women and professionals in law and medicine.[18]

The greatest progress has occurred, perhaps, in the fields of medicine and politics. Today, black doctors are affiliated with all the hospitals in the city, and teach on the faculties of the local medical schools. Black nurses, too, are commonplace. Except for an occasional political appointment, blacks held no offices in Cleo and Bart's Boston (although they had been politically active before the 1890s). Now blacks serve as members of the General Court (five in the House, one in the Senate), and a black chairs the school board. The first black United States Senator since Reconstruction owed some of his success to political support from the black community. On the other hand, there is only one, recently elected, black member of the Boston City Council, and only five of the eighteen judges in the Commonwealth of Massachusetts above the district level are black. This is a Boston neither Cleo nor Bart would have understood; it is likely that they would have felt alienated from and threatened by this new black community. Only Simeon Binney would have understood and fought for this change.

A group that does not know its history—all of it—is not only in danger of repeating its mistakes, but is vulnerable to the charge of never having achieved anything. Dorothy West's novel furnishes the reader of the present generation a glimpse of a black American past in contrast to the horrors of slavery or the blatant racism in the Chicago of Bigger Thomas. *The Living Is Easy*—if it really is easy—gives one reason to hope, or at least an understanding of another dimension of the black experience in this country. From her island retreat, Dorothy West has expanded our knowledge of black America.

NOTES

1. The same might be said of Margaret Walker, although she wrote *Jubilee* in the 1960s (Boston: Houghton Mifflin, 1966).

2. *Saturday Evening Quill* (1929). Back cover.

3. *The New Negro*, ed. Alain Locke (New York: Albert & Charles Boni, 1925).

4. Countee Cullen to Dorothy West (DW), 16 April 1931, 23 August 1933, 21 September, 1933. Special Collections, Mugar Library, Boston University. All letters are from this collection.

5. Langston Hughes to DW, 30 January 1934.

6. Harry T. Burleigh to DW, June 1933. Burleigh (1866–1949) was the first black to achieve national distinction as a composer, arranger, and concert singer.

7. Henry Lee Moon, for many years director of public relations for the NAACP, later edited the *Crisis*. Ted Poston wrote for several newspapers, including the *Amsterdam News* and the *New York Times*.

8. *Challenge* 1, no. 1 (March 1934): 39.

9. Zora Neale Hurston to DW, 24 March 1934.

10. Langston Hughes to DW, 22 February 1934.

11. Arna Bontemps to DW, n.d.

12. Carl Van Vechten to DW, 27 February 1937. Van Vechten (1880–1964) was a music critic who turned to fiction. The most famous or infamous of his novels was *Nigger Heaven* (New York: London, Knopf, 1926). Van Vechten was a personal patron of many of the aspiring writers, artists, and musicians of the Harlem Renaissance. According to Dorothy West, he enjoyed sending fanciful gifts such as penguin feathers and an owl.

13. Wallace Thurman to DW, 2 September 1934.

14. *New Challenge* 2, no. 2 (Fall 1937). There is some confusion in the chronology of the magazine. The first issue of *Challenge*, in March 1934, was vol. 1, no. 1. The last issue published under the name of *Challenge* was vol. 2, no. 1 (April 1937). In fact, six issues of *Challenge* were published. *New Challenge* began publishing as vol. 2, no. 2 (Fall 1937). Clearly, there was an attempt to maintain a semblance of continuity despite the change of name.

15. Claude McKay to DW, 10 June 1937.

16. For a description of what this project meant to writers of the day, see Ellen Tarry, "How the History Was Assembled: One Writer's Memories," in *The Negro in New York: An Informal Social History, 1626–1940,* ed. Roi Ottley and William J. Weatherby (New York: Praeger, 1967), pp. x–xii.

17. Dora Cole Lewis, unpublished manuscript (Afro-American Studies Department, Boston University).

18. John Daniels, *In Freedom's Birthplace: A Study of Boston's Negroes* (New York: Negro Universities Press, 1968), pp. 100, 102.

THE FEMINIST PRESS offers alternatives in education and in literature. Founded in 1970, this nonprofit, tax-exempt educational and publishing organization works to eliminate sexual stereotypes in books and schools and to provide literature with a broad vision of human potential. The publishing program includes reprints of important works by women, feminist biographies of women, and nonsexist children's books. Curricular materials, bibliographies, directories, and a quarterly journal provide information and support for students and teachers of women's studies. Inservice projects help to transform teaching methods and curricula. Through publications and projects, The Feminist Press contributes to the rediscovery of the history of women and the emergence of a more humane society.

Reprints from The Feminist Press

Brown Girl, Brownstones, a novel by Paule Marshall. Afterword by Mary Helen Washington. $6.95 paper.

Cassandra by Florence Nightingale. Introduction by Myra Stark. Epilogue by Cynthia Macdonald. $2.50 paper.

The Convert, a novel by Elizabeth Robins. Introduction by Jane Marcus. $5.95 paper.

Daughter of Earth, a novel by Agnes Smedley. Afterword by Paul Lauter. $10.00 cloth, $5.50 paper.

I Love Myself When I Am Laughing...And Then Again When I Am Looking Mean and Impressive by Zora Neale Hurston. Edited by Alice Walker. Introduction by Mary Helen Washington. $16.95 cloth, $7.95 paper.

Life in the Iron Mills by Rebecca Harding Davis. Biographical interpretation by Tillie Olsen. $4.50 paper.

The Living is Easy, a novel by Dorothy West. Afterword by Adelaide M. Cromwell. $6.95 paper.

The Maimie Papers. Edited by Ruth Rosen and Sue Davidson. Introduction by Ruth Rosen. $15.95 cloth, $6.95 paper.

Portraits of Chinese Women in Revolution by Agnes Smedley. Edited with an introduction by Jan MacKinnon and Steve MacKinnon. $4.50 paper.

Ripening: Selected Work, 1927–1980 by Meridel Le Sueur. Edited with an introduction by Elaine Hedges. $14.95 cloth, $7.95 paper.

The Silent Partner, a novel by Elizabeth Stuart Phelps. Afterword by Mari Jo Buhle and Florence Howe. $6.95 paper. (Available July 1982).

These Modern Women. Edited with an intoduction by Elaine Showalter. $4.95 paper.

Weeds, a novel by Edith Summers Kelley. Afterword by Charlotte Goodman. $6.95 paper.

The Woman and the Myth: Margaret Fuller's Life and Writings by Bell Gale Chevigny. $8.95 paper.

The Yellow Wallpaper by Charlotte Perkins Gilman. Afterword by Elaine Hedges. $2.25 paper.

Other Titles from The Feminist Press

Black Foremothers: Three Lives. Dorothy Sterling. $3.50 paper.

But Some of Us Are Brave: Black Women's Studies. Edited by Gloria T. Hull, Patricia Bell ·Scott, and Barbara Smith. $14.95 cloth, $8.95 paper.

Las Mujeres: Conversations from a Hispanic Community. Nan Elsasser, Kyle MacKenzie, and Yvonne Tixler y Vigil. $14.95 cloth, $5.95 paper.

Moving the Mountain: Women Working for Social Change. Ellen Cantarow with Susan Gushee O'Malley and Sharon Hartman Strom. $5.95 paper.

When ordering, please include $1.00 for postage and handling for one hardcover or two paperback books and 35¢ for each additional book. Order from: The Feminist Press, Box 334, Old Westbury, N.Y. 11568. Telephone (516) 997-7660.